MW00654165

Turkey–West Relations

This timely book fills an important gap in the literature of international relations, providing a thorough, up-to-date, empirically supported, and theoretically grounded analysis of how and why Turkish foreign policy has changed in recent years vis-à-vis the West. Presenting one of the first balancing studies that employs elite interviews as data, *Turkey–West Relations* develops a framework of intra-alliance opposition, classifying the tools of statecraft into three categories – boundary testing, boundary challenging, and boundary breaking. Six case studies are examined regarding Turkish foreign policy over the past nine years, exploring an array of topics including Turkey's foreign policy in relation to its immediate neighborhood and transatlantic actors, including the refugee crisis, defense procurement, energy policies, and more. Dursun-Özkanca demonstrates how international, regional, issue-specific, and domestic factors may serve to explain Turkey's increasing boundary-breaking behavior. This book is crucial for anyone who seeks to understand the recent growing rifts between Turkey and the United States, the EU, and NATO.

Oya Dursun-Özkanca is Professor of Political Science at Elizabethtown College. She served as LSEE Visiting Fellow at London School of Economics and has received grants from Georgetown University, European Commission, and various other sources. She has had articles featured in *Foreign Policy Analysis, Civil Wars*, and elsewhere.

Turkey–West Relations

The Politics of Intra-alliance Opposition

OYA DURSUN-ÖZKANCA
Elizabethtown College

CAMBRIDGE
UNIVERSITY PRESS

CAMBRIDGE
UNIVERSITY PRESS

University Printing House, Cambridge CB2 8BS, United Kingdom

One Liberty Plaza, 20th Floor, New York, NY 10006, USA

477 Williamstown Road, Port Melbourne, VIC 3207, Australia

314–321, 3rd Floor, Plot 3, Splendor Forum, Jasola District Centre, New Delhi – 110025, India

79 Anson Road, #06–04/06, Singapore 079906

Cambridge University Press is part of the University of Cambridge.

It furthers the University's mission by disseminating knowledge in the pursuit of education, learning, and research at the highest international levels of excellence.

www.cambridge.org
Information on this title: www.cambridge.org/9781108488624
DOI: 10.1017/9781316998960

© Oya Dursun-Özkanca 2019

This publication is in copyright. Subject to statutory exception and to the provisions of relevant collective licensing agreements, no reproduction of any part may take place without the written permission of Cambridge University Press.

First published 2019

Printed and bound in Great Britain by Clays Ltd, Elcograf S.p.A.

A *catalogue record for this publication is available from the British Library.*

Library of Congress Cataloging-in-Publication Data
NAMES: Dursun-Özkanca, Oya, author.
TITLE: Turkey-West relations : the politics of intra-alliance opposition / Oya Dursun-Özkanca, Professor of Political Science, College Professor of International Studies, Endowed Chair, Elizabethtown College.
DESCRIPTION: Cambridge, UK ; New York, NY : Cambridge University Press, 2019. | Includes bibliographical references and index.
IDENTIFIERS: LCCN 2019027236 (print) | LCCN 2019027237 (ebook) | ISBN 9781108488624 (hardback) | ISBN 9781316998960 (epub)
SUBJECTS: LCSH: Turkey – Foreign relations – 21st century. | North Atlantic Treaty Organization – Turkey. | European Union – Turkey. | Turkey – Foreign relations – Western countries. | Western countries – Foreign relations – Turkey.
CLASSIFICATION: LCC JZ1649 .D87 2019 (print) | LCC JZ1649 (ebook) | DDC 327.5610182/1–dc23
LC record available at https://lccn.loc.gov/2019027236
LC ebook record available at https://lccn.loc.gov/2019027237

ISBN 978-1-108-48862-4 Hardback
ISBN 978-1-108-72672-6 Paperback

Cambridge University Press has no responsibility for the persistence or accuracy of URLs for external or third-party internet websites referred to in this publication and does not guarantee that any content on such websites is, or will remain, accurate or appropriate.

For my mom, Dr. Gönül Oya Dursun (Köprülü), 1944–2017

Contents

List of Figures and Tables		*page* viii
Preface		ix
Acknowledgments		x
List of Abbreviations		xiii
	Introduction	1
1	Framework of Intra-alliance Opposition	22
2	Turkish Foreign Policy in the Western Balkans	38
3	The Turkish Veto over the EU–NATO Security Exchange	63
4	The EU–Turkey Deal on Refugees	83
5	Turkey's Energy Policies	98
6	Turkish Rapprochement with Russia in Security	113
7	Turkey's Foreign Policy on Syria and Iraq	126
	Conclusion: Turkey and the West – What Next?	147
Bibliography		174
Index		207

Figures and Tables

FIGURE

1 A framework of intra-alliance opposition *page* 31

TABLE

1 The intra-alliance opposition tools used by Turkey 149

Preface

Turkey's relations with the West are at an all-time low. Scarcely a day passes without a report or headline on the front page of leading newspapers questioning Turkey's reliability as a Western ally. The widening gulf between Turkey and the West and the increasing number and growing complexity of the issues over which the two sides differ make it imperative to understand the dynamics of the relationship between Turkey and the West, particularly the EU, NATO, and the United States. The developments in the aftermath of the failed coup attempt on July 15, 2016, the increasingly hostile rhetoric Turkish authorities use against the West, Turkey's rapprochement with Russia and Iran, the hostage diplomacy, the subsequent tariff wars in summer 2018, and the suspension of Turkey from the F-35 Joint Strike Fighter Program in March 2019 further illustrate the timeliness and value of the current analysis, as Turkey's future in the Western alliance increasingly becomes a topic of serious concern in Europe and the USA. Consequently, the puzzle this book seeks to explain is how and why does Turkey increasingly go its own way within the Western alliance and grow further apart from its traditional Western allies? Developing a framework of intra-alliance opposition, this book seeks to explain the trajectory of Turkish foreign policy behavior vis-à-vis the West and assesses the motives and dynamics behind the drastic shift in Turkish foreign policy behavior from 2010 to the first half of 2019.

Acknowledgments

I owe a profound debt to my mom, Dr. Gönül Oya Dursun (Köprülü), for all the love, care, and support she gave me and for serving as such an amazing role model, teaching me how to be strong yet compassionate. I wish to also thank my dad, Dr. Yunus Dursun, who, among many things, has always believed in me and taught me to never give up on my dreams. This book project is accomplished against all odds thanks to the resilience and the fighting spirit my parents have instilled in me.

The idea of this book originated when I was invited to be a Research Fellow at the London School of Economics (LSE) in the summer of 2013. At LSE, I continued adding to my research on Turkish foreign policy since 2003, especially to the interviews I conducted in Turkey and Cyprus in 2011. For my fellowship at LSE, I took my son Bora with me, who was a 2.5-month-old baby at the time, to conduct field research and interviews in the UK, Serbia, Bosnia and Herzegovina, and Turkey. I am grateful to my colleagues at the Research on South Eastern Europe (LSEE) at LSE, especially to James Ker-Lindsay, Vassilis Monastiriotis, and Spyros Economides, for their hospitality, inspiration, and supporting attitude when they first saw me enter Cowdray House with a stroller.

In 2015, I received a Sabbatical Research Grant from the Institute of Turkish Studies (ITS) at Georgetown University, which enabled me to take a year-long sabbatical leave in 2015–2016 to concentrate on my writing and research for an early iteration of this manuscript. Sinan Ciddi, the former executive director of the ITS, has been a supportive colleague.

Elizabethtown College has been a generous institution. I am grateful to the College for providing me with multiple grants to conduct fieldworks in Turkey, Cyprus, the United Kingdom, Bosnia and Herzegovina, and

Serbia. I also wrote a chapter of this book during my writer's retreat at the Bowers Writers House at Elizabethtown College, which provided me with a much-needed environment to hide in and focus on finishing the book, following the birth of my son Tolan in 2017.

Many people were willing to spend their valuable time reading and commenting on this manuscript. I owe a special thanks to Lisel Hintz, Norrin Ripsman, Wayne Selcher, Juliette Tolay, and the anonymous reviewers of the manuscript, who read this manuscript in its entirety. I am especially grateful to the guidance and support I received from Wayne Selcher, who read this manuscript multiple times and helped me edit it. Other colleagues who have been supportive throughout different sections of the manuscript and the manuscript writing process include William R. Ayres, David Brown, Zoltán Búzás, Birgül Demirtaş, Terri Givens, April Kelly-Woessner, Kyle Kopko, T. V. Paul, and Stefan Wolff. Each and every reader helped me make improvements to the arguments and the organization of this book. Having said that, all remaining problems are my full responsibility.

My participation at various conferences and workshops enabled me to exchange views with the leading experts in my field. Among those, especially helpful were the ones organized by the Stiftung Wissenschaft und Politik (German Institute for International and Security Affairs) in Berlin in December 2016 and the Belgrade Security Forum in October 2015. I would like to extend special thanks to all my interviewees, through whose insights I have acquired a better understanding of the topic at hand. They shared their precious time and perspective with me on different aspects of this research.

I would like to express my heartfelt gratitude to my editor, Robert Dreesen, for supporting me throughout this journey. Namaste! As the penultimate draft of the book was being completed, following his advice, I organized a mini-book manuscript conference in fall 2017, using a grant I received from Elizabethtown College. The participants of the mini-book manuscript conference – Lisel Hintz, Norrin Ripsman, Juliette Tolay, Wayne Selcher, and Dan Chen – were never short of criticism, but almost all of their advice was invaluable when I wrote the final draft. My students Kayla Gruber and Kenneth Wallace diligently took notes at the conference. I would like to also thank the whole production team at Cambridge University Press for all their meticulous support and professionalism.

Last, but certainly not the least, I thank my husband, Kemal Özkanca, for his endless love, understanding, and moral support during this protracted process, especially amidst first losing my mom and only eight months later my brother Can. I would not have survived this without the love and support of my family and friends.

Parts of Chapter 2 were incorporated from an article I wrote, "Turkey and the European Union: Strategic Partners or Competitors in the Western Balkans?" published by the *Journal of Regional Security* (volume 11, issue 1, February 27, 2016, pages 33–54 m UDK: 327 (4-672EU+497+560), https://scindeks-clanci.ceon.rs/data/pdf/2217-99 5x/2016/2217-995x1601033D.pdf). I published an earlier version of the analysis in Chapter 3 as "Turkish Soft Balancing Against the EU? An Analysis of the Prospects for Improved Transatlantic Security Relations," in *Foreign Policy Analysis* (volume 13, issue 4, October 1, 2017, pages 894–912, https://doi.org/10.1093/fpa/orw004). Parts of this article were reproduced here by permission of Oxford University Press.

Abbreviations

AKP	Justice and Development Party (*Adalet ve Kalkınma Partisi*)
BILGESAM	The Wise Men Center for Strategic Studies (*Bilge Adamlar Stratejik Araştırmalar Merkezi*)
CAATSA	Countering America's Adversaries Through Sanctions Act
CEF	Connecting Europe Facility
CFI	Connected Forces Initiative
CHP	The Republican People's Party (*Cumhuriyet Halk Partisi*)
CIA	Central Intelligence Agency
CPMIEC	China Precision Machinery Import and Export Corporation
CSDP	Common Security and Defence Policy
ECT	Energy Community Treaty
EDA	European Defence Agency
EEC	European Economic Community
ESDP	European Security and Defence Policy
EU	European Union
EUFOR-ALTHEA	European Union Force in Bosnia and Herzegovina
EULEX	European Union Rule of Law Mission in Kosovo
EUPM	European Union Police Mission
FDI	Foreign Direct Investment
FSA	Free Syrian Army
FTA	Free Trade Agreement
IEPG	Independent European Programme Group

IGO	Intergovernmental Organizations
ISAF	International Security Assistance Force
JCPOA	Joint Comprehensive Plan of Action
JSF	Joint Strike Fighter Program
KDP	Kurdistan Democratic Party
KFOR	Kosovo Force
MAP	Membership Action Plan
NAC	North Atlantic Council
NATO	North Atlantic Treaty Organization
NDAA	National Defense Authorization Act
NGO	Non-Governmental Organizations
ODA	Official Development Assistance
OECD	Organisation for Economic Co-Operation and Development
OES	Operation Euphrates Shield
OIC	Organization of the Islamic Conference
OOB	Operation Olive Branch
OSCE	Organization for Security and Cooperation in Europe
PfP	Partnership for Peace
PIC	Peace Implementation Council
PKK	The Kurdistan Workers' Party (*Partiya Karkeren Kurdistan*)
PSC	Political and Security Committee
PYD	The Democratic Union Party (*Partiya Yekitiya Demokrat*)
RCC	Regional Cooperation Council
SAM	Surface-to-Air Missile
SAP	Stabilisation and Association Process
SCO	Shanghai Cooperation Organization
SECI	Southeast European Cooperative Initiative
SEECP	South-East European Cooperation Process
SDF	Syrian Democratic Forces
SGC	Southern Gas Corridor
SNC	Syrian National Council
SU	Soviet Union
TEB	Turkish Economy Bank
TEPAV	Economic Policy Research Foundation of Turkey (*Türkiye Ekonomi Politikaları Araştırma Vakfı*)

TİKA	Turkish International Cooperation and Development Agency (*Türk İşbirliği ve Koordinasyon Ajansı Başkanlığı*)
TurkStat	Turkish Statistical Institute
USA	United States of America
WEAG	Western European Armaments Group
WEU	Western European Union
YPG	People's Protection Units (*Yekîneyên Parastina Gel*)

Introduction

Turkey's strategic geopolitical positioning as a bridge between Europe, the Middle East, the Balkans, the Mediterranean, the Black Sea, and South Caucasus – and its religious, cultural, and historical affiliations with countries in its immediate neighborhood – make it an indispensable actor in European and transatlantic security. In the early 1950s, Turkey was so eager to join the North Atlantic Treaty Organization (NATO) that it fought in the Korean War and incurred heavy casualties. Subsequently, it has traditionally been well embedded in Western security infrastructures. It has been a key and strategic NATO member since 1952 and a member of the Organization for Security and Cooperation in Europe (OSCE) since 1973. Despite a few periods of unease, it was considered a fairly reliable Western ally for over half a century. Even in the immediate aftermath of the Cold War, Turkey continued its alliance commitments. Turkey was among the first countries to condemn the September 11 terrorist attacks on the United States and to deploy troops to Afghanistan.

Those days are long gone. Turkey has been increasingly adopting a number of proactive, independent, and anti-Western foreign policies since 2010. Scarcely a day passes without a report or a headline on the front page of leading newspapers questioning Turkey's reliability as a Western ally. Turkey's relations with Russia, China, and Iran are improving significantly through a foreign policy doctrine, dubbed "earning more friends than enemies" (*Hürriyet Daily News* May 25, 2016). In addition to the rekindling of its relations with Russia and Iran, Turkey's relationship with the European Union (EU), NATO, and the USA especially came to a critical juncture in the aftermath of the failed coup attempt on July 15, 2016. The Turkish government frequently portrays the failed coup attempt as a conspiracy of Western (more particularly US) intervention in Turkish politics. Conspiratorial thinking concerning the motivations of the USA, the EU, and NATO seem to dominate the current Turkish public debate about the West, with seven out of ten Turks holding that the Central Intelligence Agency (CIA) was behind the coup attempt (Cook 2018).

Since the failed coup attempt, Turkey rarely sends Turkish military officers to NATO allies for training purposes. In May 2017, a top advisor to Turkish President Recep Tayyip Erdoğan threatened that Turkish rockets may target the US forces in northern Syria if their collaboration with the Kurdish fighters along the Turkish border continues (McLeary 2017). In response to a US commander in Syria's remarks to the *New York Times*, he said, "[T]hose who say, 'If you hit us, we'll hit back hard,' have never in their lives gotten an Ottoman slap" (quoted in Harvey 2018). Turkish Foreign Minister Çavuşoğlu blatantly criticized the United States for supporting the People's Protection Units (*Yekîneyên Parastina Gel*, YPG) in a *New York Times* op-ed by noting, "A NATO ally arming a terrorist organization that is attacking another NATO ally is a fundamental breach of everything that NATO stands for" (Çavuşoğlu 2018). In the summer of 2018, many Turkish TV programs were questioning whether Turkey should leave NATO. Exacerbating the situation, in the first quarter of 2019, Turkey was on its way to finalizing the purchase of S-400 missiles from the archenemy of the alliance, Russia, with the first delivery of the missiles scheduled for July 2019.

What had been completely inconceivable up until only a few years ago has indeed become perplexingly observable in Turkish foreign policy. Accordingly, the puzzle this book seeks to explain is: how did we get there, and why does Turkey increasingly go its own way within the Western alliance and grow further apart from its traditional Western allies? It seeks to assess the motives and dynamics behind the drastic shift in Turkish foreign policy behavior toward the West, particularly the EU, NATO, and the US, and explores the reasons behind Turkey's strategic estrangement, especially from 2010 to the first half of 2019. It further asks why states select the tools they use within an alliance. Using the existing theories of intra-alliance opposition such as soft balancing as a springboard, this book develops an analytical framework of the politics of intra-alliance opposition and provides a comprehensive and nuanced account of how and why Turkish foreign policy has changed within the transatlantic alliance. It ends with an exploration of three alternative futures for Turkey's relations with the West.

The international system is experiencing geopolitical and economic power shifts, requiring international relations (IR) scholars and practitioners to acquire a better understanding of the foreign policy motivations of regional powers. Regional powers like Turkey are not likely to give up their claim to a role in global governance and hence they seek to prove that they are pivotal in their regions by opposing their regional rivals (Paul 2016). In the words of a former member of the Turkish Parliament from the Justice and Development Party (*Adalet ve Kalkınma Partisi*, AKP), Turkish President "Erdoğan is not at peace with the way the world is governed" (Kınıklıoğlu 2014). Indicative of Turkey's global ambitions, Erdoğan is quoted as saying, "If you have a claim to become a big state, you need to reach every corner of the world" (quoted in World Bulletin March 8, 2013). Turkish policymakers regard Turkey as a "natural and ascending regional power in the Balkans, Caucasus, and the Middle East" (Davutoğlu 2001) and see a "relative decline" of the West in the post–Cold War international system (Davutoğlu, quoted in Park 2015, p. 596). Ahmet Davutoğlu, the architect of Turkish foreign policy in the 2000s and the former prime minister of Turkey, frequently called for both "strategic pragmatism," based on prioritizing Turkey's national interests, and "the revival of the conventional balance of power politics," strategically linking political and economic processes of negotiation and competition with the actors in the West (Davutoğlu 1994, p. 125).

The surge in interest in Turkey is palpable in both policymaking and academic circles. Increasingly, the study of Turkish foreign policy must confront the question of the nature of the relationship between Turkey and the West. Against the background of heightened urgency for better transatlantic security dialogue, Turkey's increased self-confidence in its foreign policy, and its turbulent relations with the EU, NATO, and the United States, the need for scholarly analyses of Turkish foreign policy has become more evident. The harsh measures taken by the Turkish government against dissidents in the aftermath of the failed coup attempt on July 15, 2016, increasingly hostile rhetoric Turkish authorities use against the West, Turkey's rapprochement with Russia and Iran, the hostage crisis, the subsequent tariff wars in summer 2018, and the suspension of Turkey from the F-35 Joint Strike Fighter (JSF) Program in March 2019 further illustrate the timeliness and value of the current analysis, as Turkey's future in the Western alliance increasingly becomes a topic of serious concern in Europe and the United States. The findings of this research have wide-ranging and significant policy implications for the transatlantic alliance and Middle Eastern and European security and contribute to the theoretical debate in IR circles about intra-alliance conflict/opposition.

This chapter places Turkey's relations with the West in a historical perspective. Subsequently, it discusses the main research questions explored throughout the manuscript and then explains the research methodology used in addressing these questions. It concludes by discussing the outline of the book.

A TRANSITIONING TURKEY IN A CHANGING ALLIANCE: A HISTORICAL PERSPECTIVE

Turkey is frequently characterized as a country in transition, both in its domestic politics and in its foreign policy (Albright et al. 2012, Lesser 2017, Cook 2018, Rubin 2018). The collapse of the Soviet Union (SU) and the end of the Cold War "removed the main rationale behind the US–Turkish security partnership and reduced Ankara's dependence on Washington" (Larrabee 2011, p. 2). Many policy-makers interviewed acknowledge that Turkey wants to shape developments in its neighborhood more proactively. Turkish leaders and society resent as a national humiliation the past decades of Western paternalism aimed at domestic transformation. The Turkish government has been using an increasingly belligerent language toward the West and adopting a confrontational posture and actions against the EU, NATO, and the United States, especially since the failed coup attempt. Consequently, many observers draw attention to Turkey's strategic estrangement from the West and question whether its positions on key issues are in fact inimical to Western goals (Lesser 2017, Cook 2018, Rubin 2018). Nevertheless, Turkey's relations with the West have not always been this tumultuous.

Turkey–EU Relations

Turkey has been aspiring to become a part of the European integration process for more than half a century. It applied for associate membership in the European Economic Community (EEC) in 1959 and signed the Ankara Agreement with the EEC in 1963, aiming to bring Turkey into the Customs Union. Turkey applied for full EEC membership in 1987 and signed the Customs Union Agreement in 1995. The Customs Union Agreement came into force in January 1996, providing further trade integration with the EU without full membership. In 1992, Turkey became an Associate Member of the Western European Union (WEU), an organization that has over time become the military wing of the EU.

Turkey did not become an official candidate for the EU until the Helsinki Summit in December 1999. On October 3, 2005, accession negotiations with the EU were opened. Turkey's EU accession negotiations have reached a stalemate over the past few years. In the EU accession negotiations process, sixteen chapters (4 – Free Movement of Capital; 6 – Company Law; 7 – Intellectual Property Law; 10 – Information Society and Media; 12 – Food Safety, Veterinary and Phytosanitary Policy; 16 – Taxation; 17 – Economic and Monetary Policy; 18 – Statistics; 20 – Enterprise and Industrial Policy; 21 – Trans-European Networks; 22 – Regional Policy; 25 – Science and Research; 27 – Environment; 28 – Consumer and Health Protection; 32 – Financial Control; 33 – Financial and Budgetary Provisions) have been opened to negotiations, and only one of them (Chapter 25 – Science and Research) has been provisionally closed since 2005 (Turkish Ministry of Foreign Affairs 2019a).

Despite its strong aspiration to become a full member, Turkey has had a bumpy relationship with the EU. It has always been considered an outsider, as many in the EU questioned Turkey's credentials as a European country. Especially since 2007, the reform process experienced a significant stalemate. Besides its faltering track record on human rights and rule of law, one of the main reasons behind the stalemate in its accession negotiations process has been its failure to ratify and implement the 2004 Ankara Protocol (the Additional Protocol) and extend the Customs Union Agreement to the Republic of Cyprus.[1] Turkey declares that unless the Republic of Cyprus opens the ports and airports in the north, allows direct trade with the north, and removes its economic isolation of the "Turkish Republic of Northern Cyprus," Turkish airports and ports would remain inaccessible to vessels and planes from Cyprus.[2] Because all EU member states are potential veto players on the issue of Turkish accession, Turkey finds the implementation of the Additional Protocol to be a risky move. This, in turn, caused the European Council to veto opening up of eight key accession negotiation chapters (1 – Free Movement of Goods; 3 – Right of Establishment and Freedom to Provide

---

[1] Turkey signed the Protocol in July 2005 but underlined that the signature of the Protocol does not mean the diplomatic recognition of the Republic of Cyprus.
[2] Interview with a European Union official in Nicosia, July 20, 2011; Interview with a Member of Turkish Parliament from AKP, Ankara, July 13, 2011; Interview with a Turkish diplomat in Ankara, July 18, 2011; Interview with an International NGO official, Istanbul, July 11, 2011; Interview with a former Minister of the Republic of Cyprus, in Nicosia, July 20, 2011; Interview with a Greek Cypriot diplomat, Nicosia, July 21, 2011.

Services; 9 – Financial Services; 11 – Agriculture and Rural Development; 13 – Fisheries; 14 Transport Policy; 29 – Customs Union; 30 – External Relations) since December 2006. The European Council further declared that no chapter would be closed until Turkey applies the Additional Protocol to the Ankara Agreement to the Republic of Cyprus. In 2007, five chapters (one of which intersects with the eight chapters blocked by the EU) were blocked by a French veto (Barysch 2010).[3] The Republic of Cyprus also unilaterally vetoes six chapters.

The political difficulties Turkey encountered in its EU accession negotiations process confirmed the existence of European prejudice against Turkey in the minds of Turkish policymakers. Turkish authorities have frequently criticized the discriminatory political treatment of Turkey by the EU and expressed their frustration that the political obstacles "undermine the credibility of the EU" (Davutoğlu 2010, pp. 14–15). Since its EU accession was considered an open-ended rather than an automatic or guaranteed process, Turkey had approached its EU accession negotiations with skepticism (Uğur 2010). Amidst a rise in anti-Turkish rhetoric in Germany and France, whose leaders called for a privileged partnership with Turkey in 2009, the AKP government "lost interest in Europe, beginning instead to focus on consolidating its power" (Cornell et al. 2012, p. 21). As Nathalie Tocci (2010, p. 6) argues, due to EU "placing the bar [for Turkish accession] too high," Turkey was "pushed away" from its European dream. Turks predominantly feel that the EU treats Turkey differently, leading to increasing anti-European sentiments (Cornell et al. 2012). Years of frustration with the EU accession process have caused Euroskepticism among Turkish security elites as well as the public (Yılmaz 2011). The Gezi Park protests in 2013 led to the adoption of an accusatory and hostile rhetoric against the EU, through which the Turkish government hoped to boost its domestic electoral support.

The EU–Turkey deal on refugees, i.e. the EU–Turkey Joint Action Plan, activated on November 29, 2015, and the EU–Turkey Statement, announced on March 18, 2016, brought a limited momentum to Turkey–EU relations. Turkish policymakers frequently voice their cynicism about the renewed recognition of Turkey's significance by the European leaders following the refugee crisis (Bozkır 2016). However, the domestic developments in the aftermath of the failed coup attempt on July 15, 2016, have drastically changed the nature of Turkey–EU

---

[3] In February 2013, France declared the removal of its blockage of Chapter 22. As such, in 2019, technically seventeen chapters were off limits in Turkey–EU accession negotiations.

relations. The Turkey–EU relationship has taken a sharp turn for the worse. Turkish authorities regularly expressed their frustration with the lack of solidarity from the EU in response to the coup attempt. Bozkır (2016), the former Turkish minister of EU Affairs, characterized Turkey's disappointment as "a broken heart story," adding that Europe's reaction to the failed coup broke the resilience of Turkey "to continue this relationship."

On November 24, 2016, the European Parliament overwhelmingly voted to advise the EU to initiate a temporary freeze on the ongoing accession negotiations with Turkey and committed to reviewing its position once the state of emergency in Turkey was lifted (European Parliament 2019). In response, Turkish leaders have threatened to end the EU–Turkey refugee deal. Following the failed coup attempt in Turkey, there are serious concerns about the reintroduction of the death penalty. EU leaders consistently note that the reinstatement of the death penalty would be a "deal-breaker" for the EU accession process (Mogherini 2016).

To make things more complicated, the referendum campaign in 2017 for the proposed constitutional amendments started a feud or a war of words between Turkey and some members of the EU, such as the Netherlands, Denmark, and Germany. While the Dutch government banned public speeches by Turkish officials, Germany allowed local officials to ban such visits, and Denmark asked Turkish officials to delay their visits on the referendum campaign among the Turkish citizens living in Europe. Turkish officials have responded with rhetoric, posturing, and diplomatic arm wrestling. In the fallout of the crisis, Deputy Prime Minister Numan Kurtulmuş asserted that the "biggest damage" would be to Europe and not to Turkey (quoted in Peterson and Miller Llana 2017). Following the diplomatic clashes with the Netherlands, Denmark, and Germany, Erdoğan renewed his threats in March 2017 that he would allow the Syrian refugees back into Europe.

During his victory speech in the aftermath of the constitutional referendum in April 2017, Erdoğan reiterated the threat that he might call for a popular referendum on Turkey's EU candidacy and reinstate the death penalty. With the approval of the proposed constitutional changes in the April 2017 referendum, for all practical purposes the EU–Turkey accession negotiations came to an end due to the consolidation of presidential power under Turkey's new political system. Many EU leaders called for the suspension of Turkey's accession talks. The EU's Enlargement Commissioner Johannes Hahn indicated that "the current situation [of

Turkey's EU accession process] is not sustainable" and noted that he would seek a mandate from EU foreign ministers to explore new arrangements to replace the accession process (Beesley 2017). On March 13, 2017, EU High Representative for Foreign Affairs and Security Policy Mogherini and Commissioner Hahn concurred with a report published by the Venice Commission, an advisory body to the Council of Europe on constitutional law, that the transition from a parliamentary to a presidential system would further weaken the democratic checks and balances in Turkey, erode judicial independence and oversight of the executive, and give the new president too much power over the legislative branch (Council of Europe 2017). Mogherini and Hahn further announced that the fact that the referendum was held while Turkey was still under the emergency law (declared due to the failed coup on July 15, 2016) made it even more problematic (European Commission 2017c).

In July 2017, the European Parliament called on the EU to formally suspend the accession negotiations with Turkey without delay in case of the implementation of the constitutional reform package. On June 26, 2018, the European Council acknowledged that "Turkey has been moving further away from the European Union" and declared that "Turkey's accession negotiations have therefore effectively come to a standstill and no further chapters can be considered for opening or closing and no further work towards the modernization of the EU-Turkey Customs Union is foreseen" (European Council 2018). On March 13, 2019, the European Parliament voted to recommend the European Commission and the Council of the EU to formally suspend the accession negotiations with Turkey (European Parliament 2019). The Turkish Ministry of Foreign Affairs dismissed the European Parliament's 2019 vote as "one-sided" and "baseless" (*Deutsche Welle* March 13, 2019).

Turkey has been disillusioned with the EU over the lack of progress in its EU accession negotiations, the visa liberalization talks, the Customs Union Agreement modernization talks, and the EU's reaction to both the government's post-coup purges of academics, bureaucrats, military officers, and Kurdish politicians and the outcome of the constitutional change referendum. Furthermore, with Brexit, Turkey is expected to lose one of the most fervent supporters of its EU membership. All in all, Turkey's EU candidacy is now over in all but name.

Despite these fundamental problems, Turkey and the EU still exchange ideas on important issue areas, such as counterterrorism, bilateral trade, and diplomatic relations. To illustrate, following a four-year break, the 54th Turkey–EU Association Council Meeting was held on March 15,

2019. The two sides confirmed the strategic importance of Turkey for the EU on important issues, such as migration, counterterrorism, energy, transport, the economy, and trade (European Council 2019). Following this historical overview of Turkey's relations with the EU is a synopsis of the history of its relations with NATO and the United States.

Turkey–USA–NATO Relations

Turkey's official diplomatic relations with the United States go all the way back to 1927. The relationship first gained momentum through the Economic and Technical Cooperation Agreement in July 1947, which implemented the Truman Doctrine (US Department of State 2017). Turkey participated in the Korean War with three brigades between 1950 and 1953. Five years after the Truman Doctrine, Turkey joined NATO, and it has played a significant role against Soviet expansionism throughout the Cold War. During this time period, Turkish and US interests in the Middle East generally converged (Altunışık 2013). However, challenging the "nostalgically imagined" nature of Turkey–USA relations during the Cold War, Burwell (2008, p. 4) notes:

That relationship was based primarily on narrow geopolitical considerations, specifically, Turkey's value as a strategically located piece of real estate that offered an opportunity for the United States and its allies to position themselves close to Russia's southern flank. The US–Turkish discussion was often about the use of airbases or stationing of military forces, while the relationship was largely managed by the Turkish defense forces and the US Department of Defense.

Former Turkish Ambassador to the United States Faruk Loğoğlu (2008, p. 31) reminds us that, during the Cuban Missile Crisis, "the Turks were never consulted about the deal" that dismantled the US missiles on Turkish soil and that in 1964, in response to Turkey's threats to intervene in Cyprus to help Turkish Cypriots, US President Johnson sent the infamous Johnson Letter, warning the Turkish prime minister that "if the Soviet Union attacked Turkey to protect the Greek Cypriots, the United States and NATO allies might not – contrary to their obligations under the NATO Treaty – come to Turkey's defense." The then Turkish Prime Minister İsmet İnönü made it public that the cancellation of the planned landing was due to opposition from the United States.

This marked a low point in Turkey's relations with the USA and NATO. Subsequently, Turkish leaders reevaluated the country's foreign

policy and determined that Turkey's pro-Western alignment caused isolation in a rapidly changing international system (Bölükbaşı 1988, Sakkas
and Zhukova 2013). Turkey accordingly developed a close relationship
with the SU, in order to force the USA to reconsider its stance on the
Cyprus issue and to win Soviet support for its position on Cyprus. By the
end of the 1960s, Turkey became a top recipient of Soviet economic
assistance among the Third World countries (Bölükbaşı 1988). This, in
turn, led to suspicions about Turkey's loyalties.

In the summer of 1974, Turkey militarily intervened in Cyprus. While
the then US Secretary of State Henry Kissinger, President Ford, and the US
military were reluctant to antagonize Turkey, the US Congress imposed an
arms embargo on Turkey. This, according to many accounts, contributed
to the "loss of mutual confidence" between Turkey and the United States
(Loğoğlu 2008, p. 31). The Carter Administration determined that the
embargo took a serious toll on Turkey's defense posture and had serious
ramifications for NATO's viability. As such, the administration successfully lobbied for the US Congress to overturn it in the summer of 1978
(Zierler 2014).

During the 1980s, relations between the USA and Turkey gradually
improved. The two signed the Defense and Economic Cooperation
Agreement on March 29, 1980, which restored the level of activity that
the USA had prior to the arms embargo (US General Accounting Office
1982). The military coup in September 1980 helped with the recovery of
bilateral relations (Çağaptay 2015). The two countries continued their
cooperation to contain communism. The policies of Prime Minister
Turgut Özal further contributed to the creation of a stronger strategic
partnership. Accordingly, from 1987 to 1992, the USA provided historically unprecedented amounts of military assistance to Turkey (Zanotti
2011).

Following the end of the Cold War, Turkey's strategic importance
for the USA and NATO diminished somewhat, at least initially. The
Gulf War presented the first challenge to USA–Turkey relations in the
1990s (Kramer 2000, Larrabee and Lesser 2003, Hale 2013, Altunışık
2013). Turkey was concerned about the US policy of promoting
Kurdish control of northern Iraq, causing anti-American sentiments
and mistrust toward the USA (Altunışık 2013). Nevertheless, Turkey
was the first country to support the imposition of UN economic
sanctions against Iraq.

The September 11 terrorist attacks on the United States underscored
the significance of Turkey in combating terrorism. With the Greater

Middle East Project, the George W. Bush Administration started to promote Turkey as a model Islamic democracy. As a part of the war on terror, Turkey was ambivalent toward supporting a possible US intervention in Iraq. The Memorandum of Understanding that was signed for the intervention in Iraq failed to receive approval from the Turkish Parliament in March 2003, which caused significant mistrust on the part of the US authorities toward Turkey, since then Turkish Prime Minister Erdoğan promised that the motion would pass in the Turkish Parliament.[4]

In July 2003, what is now commonly referred to as the "sack incident" or "hood event" took place, when US forces apprehended a group of Turkish Special Forces members in northern Iraq. This represented an all-time low in Turkey–USA relations and caused anger in Turkish public opinion (Güney 2008). Since then, despite efforts on the part of the Obama Administration to form a "model partnership" with Turkey, bilateral relations continued to have their ups and downs, after going through a brief honeymoon period as President Obama chose Turkey as the first Muslim nation he visited. Nevertheless, in 2010, Turkish–Israeli tensions in the aftermath of the Mavi Marmara incident and the Turkish–Brazilian initiative to broker the Iranian nuclear swap deal without consultation with or involvement of the USA caused further tensions in Turkey–USA relations (Pieper 2017).

The tensions in Turkey–Israel relations following then Prime Minister Erdoğan's outburst in January 2009 at Davos over Israel's attack on Gaza raised serious concerns in US policymaking circles. Due to Turkey's veto, in October 2009, Israel was disinvited to join the NATO military exercises in Turkey. The flotilla incident with Israel was the final blow to the Turkish–Israeli partnership. As a part of a multinational humanitarian aid convoy for the Gaza Strip, the Mavi Marmara flotilla, which was carrying a Turkish flag, tried breaking Israel's blockade of the Gaza Strip. The Israeli Defense Forces' raid in international waters caused the death of eight Turkish citizens and one Turkish-American citizen in May 2010. Following the incident, Turkey withdrew its ambassador to Israel and asked for a UN Security Council resolution condemning the attack (Lynch 2010). The lack of US support for the Turkish request caused further tensions in USA–Turkey relations.

Much to the surprise and the distaste of the United States and the United Kingdom, Brazil and Turkey negotiated a deal with Iran in May 2010 to send some of its low-enriched uranium abroad in exchange

---

[4] Personal communication with a US Army War College faculty member, January 10, 2017.

for access to fuel for a medical reactor (MacFarquhar 2010). The USA and
the other permanent members of the United Nations Security Council
(UNSC) did not accept the deal. The UNSC voted a new set of sanctions
against Iran. The USA and the EU member states perceived the Turkish
objection against the new UNSC sanctions against Iran as alarming. There
were reports about President Obama warning then Prime Minister
Erdoğan that, if Turkey did not change its policy on Iran, Turkey would
risk not obtaining weapons to be used in counterterrorism operations
against PKK (Dombey 2010).

Nevertheless, as a highlight of the bilateral relations in the aftermath of
these two crises, Turkey accepted the deployment of a NATO missile
shield in Malatya in September 2011 (Altunışık 2013). The Arab Spring
and Turkey's popularity in the Arab world mainly due to its anti-Israeli
stance initially emphasized the importance of Turkey during this transformation in the Middle East. Turkey and the USA shared similar interests
in promoting further democratization in the region. Hence, during the
initial days of the Arab Spring, Turkey emerged as a winner and was
presented as a role model for the Arab countries.

This initial optimism came to an end as Turkey had to deal with
security challenges in Syria and the ousting of Morsi from power in
Egypt, leading to the failure of its "zero problems with neighbors" foreign
policy (Martin 2015). Ankara started to "take sides ever more clearly,"
generating concerns about its intentions in Iran, Israel, Sudan, and relations with NATO (Cornell et al. 2012, p. 36). Turkey opposed the Obama
Administration's efforts to impose additional UN sanctions on Iran and
helped Iran evade those sanctions (Cook 2018). The Syrian quagmire and
the different priorities of the two allies in response to the Syrian civil war
deepened the rift between the USA and Turkey. Turkey expected a quick
fall of the Assad regime from power and sponsored the Syrian National
Council (SNC) and the Free Syrian Army (FSA). Turkish authorities were
very vocal about their disappointment in the lack of response from the
West to the Syrian civil war, especially to their calls to establish
a "humanitarian corridor" through a no-fly zone in northern Syria (Park
2015, p. 584).

Under the Trump Administration as well, Turkey–USA relations have
been tense over the US support for the Syrian Kurds in the fight against the
Islamic State (IS) terrorist organization, as the two countries find themselves supporting different actors in the Middle East. The extradition of
Fethullah Gülen, a Muslim cleric who lives in self-exile in Pennsylvania
and is the alleged mastermind behind the failed coup, proved to be a major

factor causing bilateral tensions. Volkan Bozkır (2016), a former Turkish minister of EU Affairs, identifies the extradition of Gülen as "the main issue" in Turkey–USA relations. In the aftermath of the failed coup, Turkish authorities have accused Gülen of being a mastermind behind the coup attempt and asked for the US to extradite Gülen to Turkey. Nevertheless, the US authorities emphasize the lack of any direct evidence implicating Gülen's direct involvement with the failed coup attempt (Jeffrey 2016).

In May 2017, following his visit to the White House, members of Erdoğan's security detail physically attacked peaceful protesters in Washington DC, causing arrest warrants (Bump 2017). In October 2017, the USA and Turkey suspended issuing bilateral nonimmigrant visas to each other's citizens. Many attract attention to the existence of a hostage diplomacy, as the Turkish government is increasingly arresting or detaining the nationals of the United States, Germany, Greece, and the Netherlands, in an attempt to seek an exchange of the people allegedly linked to the failed coup attempt who are located in these countries (Cupolo 2018, Erdemir and Edelman 2018). Erdoğan himself publicly tied the release of Andrew Brunson, an American pastor detained in Turkey for charges of terrorism, to the extradition of Fethullah Gülen. He was quoted as saying: "'Give us the pastor back,' they [the US authorities] say. You have one pastor as well. Give him to us ... Then we will try him [Brunson] and give him to you" (quoted in Cupolo 2018). Brunson was released in October 2018, after two years of detention (Cunningham 2018). Nevertheless, the hostage diplomacy seems to continue with the continued imprisonment of Serkan Gölge, a Turkish-American NASA scientist, the local staff from the US Mission in Turkey, as well as some Europeans (Jones 2019).

All these developments in the country's relations with the West at the elite level are translated to the public level. As indicated by an interviewee, there is a widespread "perception [in Turkey] that either the US didn't support the [Turkish] government sufficiently or the US or the elements of US such as the CIA were behind the coup attempt."[5] According to a 2018 public opinion poll, Turkish society is united in terms of distrust toward the West. About 87 percent of the respondents hold that "European states want to disintegrate Turkey as they have disintegrated the Ottoman Empire," and 54 percent believe that the USA is Turkey's biggest security threat (Ünlühisarcıklı 2018). According to a November 2016 survey, 79 percent of Turks believed the USA was behind the 2016 coup attempt

[5] Phone Interview with a Turkish-American academic, October 21, 2016.

(Zanotti and Thomas 2017). This indicates that wide sectors of the Turkish people and the elites see the USA in particular and the West in general as threats to Turkey's security.

This historical overview by no means intends to imply that there were no problems in Turkey's relations with the West prior to 2010. On the contrary, it indicates that Turkey's relations with the West have always been somewhat strained and fraught with tensions. Turkey has long been identified as a difficult partner. While it is natural to observe occasional divergence of opinion between partners, the frequency and the intensity of such disagreements have increased sharply over time, creating major trust issues between allies. Turkey's relations with the West are at an all-time low. The widening gulf between Turkey and the West and the increasing number and the growing complexity of the issues over which the two sides differ make it imperative to understand how we got here. In order to explain the trajectory of Turkish foreign policy behavior vis-à-vis the West, this book develops a framework of intra-alliance opposition.

METHODOLOGY

The main research questions this book addresses are: What are the motivations of Turkish foreign policy vis-à-vis the EU, the USA, and NATO? How did we arrive at this point? What does the future hold for Turkey's relations with the West? It presents the author's original analysis that draws on extensive fieldwork and more than 200 semi-structured elite interviews conducted with government officials, diplomats, academics, intergovernmental (IGO) and non-governmental organization (NGO) officials, and journalists in Turkey, Serbia, Bosnia and Herzegovina, Cyprus, the United Kingdom, Germany, and the United States from 2011 to 2017.

The fieldwork was made possible through multiple grants and fellowships, such as faculty research grants received from Elizabethtown College in 2011, 2013, and 2017, a Research on South Eastern Europe (LSEE) Visiting Fellowship at London School of Economics (LSE) in 2013, and a Sabbatical Research Grant received from the Institute of Turkish Studies at Georgetown University during the 2015–2016 academic year. The semi-structured elite interviews included open-ended questions revolving around Turkish foreign policy priorities vis-à-vis the EU, the USA, and NATO, the state of Turkey–EU and Turkey–USA–NATO relations, the impact of the Cyprus problem on Turkey–EU and EU–NATO relations, the EU–Turkey refugee deal, the energy security aspect of Turkey–West

relations, Turkish foreign policy in the Middle East, and the implications
of the revival in Turkey–Russia relations for Turkey's relations with the
West. This research deals with a recent case and a state of emergency that
was declared in the aftermath of the failed coup and extended seven times
until its expiration on July 18, 2018. The state of emergency mandated the
president to preside over the cabinet that can pass decrees without the
scrutiny of the parliament or the possibility of appeal to the constitutional
court. It effectively allowed the government to restrict rights and freedoms. Human Rights Watch (2017) indicates that many decrees passed
involved dismissal from public service without an investigation, confisca-
tion of property, police custody of up to a month, and ill treatment of the
detainees. In order to protect the identities of the interviewees, sources are
anonymized in a fashion similar to comparable studies in the literature.[6]
As "interviewers need to gain the trust of their respondents in order to
collect high quality data," the author assured that any information they
provided would be treated anonymously and confidentially (Harvey
2011, p. 433).

The book examines a sample of empirical and policy-relevant case
studies in Turkey's contemporary relations with the West under the
AKP government, from the start of the Arab Spring in 2010 up until
the local elections during the first half of 2019: 1) Turkey's pragmatic
foreign policy in the Western Balkans; 2) the Turkish veto over the EU–
NATO security exchange; 3) the EU–Turkey deal on the refugee crisis;
4) Turkey's energy policies; 5) Turkish rapprochement with Russia in
security and defense; and 6) Turkish foreign policy on Syria and Iraq.
These cases are by no means exhaustive but nevertheless were chosen
due to their significance in creating substantial divergences between
Turkey and its transatlantic allies during the tenure of the AKP government in Turkey. The cases examined in the book help us identify
a trajectory of Turkish foreign policy behavior vis-à-vis the West, as it
shows the progression of Turkey's motivations within the Western
alliance over time.

When examining these case studies, a process-tracing methodology is
adopted in order to determine whether there is a causal chain between an
independent variable and the outcome of the dependent variables (Checkel
2008, George and Bennett 2005). It is important to acknowledge that there
may be discrepancies between the rhetoric and actions of the elites that were
interviewed. In order to achieve an accuracy of analysis about motives, and

[6] See Hufnagel (2013) and Harvey (2011) for examples.

in line with the norms in the literature, this book utilizes the triangulation process, offering a cross-reference between primary sources, such as semi-structured interviews, and documentary sources (Lustick 1996, George and Bennett 2005, Checkel 2008).

Hitherto, the works focusing on the challenges facing NATO and the liberal international order have focused on challenges posed by the end of the Cold War, intrastate conflict, and violent nonstate actors. This work presents a novel perspective, which concentrates on the impact of existing members' changing foreign policy prerogatives and regional interests and the strain it bears upon the Western alliance. As explained in detail in the subsequent chapter, in an attempt to develop a comprehensive framework of intra-alliance opposition, the book offers three categories of intra-alliance opposition behavior: boundary testing, boundary challenging, and boundary breaking. These three categories are helpful in demonstrating the different levels of intensity of the tools of statecraft mainly identified by the soft balancing literature. This book consequently divides the tools identified in the soft balancing literature into these three categories in order to differentiate between the motivations behind the use of each tool. Another important methodological contribution of the book is that it represents one of the first balancing studies using elite interviews as data. Finally, it integrates the concept of veto players as well as domestic factors into the literature on alliances and balancing.

OUTLINE OF THE BOOK

Chapter 1 identifies the gaps in the existing literature and formulates a framework of intra-alliance opposition. The extant literature on soft balancing is theoretically vague (Brooks and Wohlforth 2005) and lacks rigor in terms of the definition of the tools of statecraft a second-tier power utilizes within an alliance. There is conceptual overlap between different tools that are identified by the IR literature in general, and the soft balancing literature in particular, which leads to theoretical confusion, as they may also be used for different ends, i.e. bargaining, issue linkages, retaliation, and tit-for-tat strategies. Accordingly, Chapter 1 offers a clear delineation of the interactive processes of intra-alliance opposition and attempts to unpack the factors in explaining the motivations of opposition from secondary powers within an alliance.

Chapter 2 explores Turkish foreign policy in the Western Balkans, as the region carries geostrategic importance for the EU, NATO, and

Turkey. Against the background of deteriorating relations between the EU and Turkey and EU's multiple crises, including the enlargement fatigue, the Eurozone crisis, the refugee crisis, anti-EU populism, and the Brexit crisis, Turkey has been attempting to use its soft power to consolidate its influence in the Western Balkans and fill a power vacuum left by the EU in the region. It makes a point that Turkey pursues pragmatic Neo-Ottomanism. Turkey engages in active diplomacy through bilateral, tri-lateral, and multilateral initiatives and in economic statecraft through visa liberalization and free trade agreements with the countries in the region as a part of its pragmatic Neo-Ottomanism in the Western Balkans. The underlying rationale is to establish itself as an economic and political power in the region before these countries become EU members. As long as Turkey's accession to the EU remains deadlocked and the Turkish political elites feel alienated from the West, Turkey is tempted to split with the EU to pursue an increasingly independent foreign policy or play a spoiler role in the Western Balkans. Therefore, the Turkish foreign policy behavior in the region is classified as going from boundary testing to boundary challenging, as Turkey increasingly competes against the EU for regional influence.

Chapter 3 analyzes the role Turkey plays in the development, or the lack thereof, of transatlantic security relations between the EU and NATO. While the changing security environment necessitates an enhanced dialogue between the EU and NATO, Turkey, along with Cyprus, is increasingly criticized for obstructing the coordination between the two organizations. This chapter makes the argument that through its NATO membership, Turkey constitutes a veto player in the inter-institutional relations between the EU and NATO and engages in boundary testing using active diplomacy, entangling diplomacy, and issue-linkage bargaining. It further makes a case that Turkey engages in boundary challenging through strategic noncoo-peration and inter-institutional balancing against the EU. Through its veto power in NATO, Turkey seeks to strengthen its negotiating position vis-à-vis the EU and to constrain the EU's alternatives without directly engaging in military confrontation. The veto gives Turkey a voice against the EU and helps Turkey pursue long-term interests, such as increasing its leverage against the EU in its accession negotiations, resolving the Cyprus problem to its advantage, and getting fully integrated into the European Defence Agency (EDA). The chapter concludes that as long as the uncertainties around Turkey's EU accession and EDA associate membership remain and the Cyprus conflict remains unresolved, Turkey will continue to chal-lenge its boundaries against the EU. The Turkish foreign policy behavior may be classified as going from boundary testing to boundary challenging on this particular issue.

Chapter 4 delves into an analysis of the Turkey–EU deal on the refugee crisis. It makes the argument that Turkey uses the urgency of the refugee crisis and its position as a major transit country for refugees en route to Europe fleeing from civil wars and instability in the Middle East and North Africa as leverage to acquire visa liberalization with the EU and to bring momentum to its accession negotiation talks. Through the EU–Turkey refugee deal, by using active diplomacy and issue-linkage bargaining, Turkey was also able to secure the EU's commitment to modernization of the Customs Union Agreement and provision of financial support for the welfare and protection of Syrian refugees in Turkey (European Commission 2015b). After the signing of the deal and following a number of frustrations Turkey had with the EU in terms of the implementation of the deal (due to Turkey's difficulties in implementing the legal changes that are required by the EU, such as changes in Turkey's anti-terrorism laws and the degraded situation in human rights and the rule of law) among other reasons, Turkey started to engage in boundary challenging against the EU through the use of blackmail power and compellent threats. As Marc Pierini, former EU ambassador and Head of Delegation to Turkey, notes, through the deal Turkey sees a "historic opportunity to play hardball with a weakened Europe and attempt to weaken it further" (Pierini 2016a).

Chapter 5 focuses on Turkey's energy policies in the context of the country's relations with the West. Using the cases of Turkey's rejection of full membership status in the Energy Community Treaty (ECT), the reinstating of the Turkish Stream pipeline project (or commonly referred to as TurkStream) with Russia, and Turkey's refusal to implement the renewed sanctions for Iran, the chapter illustrates that Turkey engages in informed strategic noncooperation with the EU based on the lessons the country drew from its experience signing the Customs Union Agreement without full EU membership. The chapter further argues that Turkey–Russia rapprochement in energy constitutes collaborative balancing against the EU in the energy security sector and makes the argument that Turkey engages in boundary challenging against the EU on energy. In order to strengthen its hand in the negotiations against the EU, Turkey has been signaling to the EU that it can undertake alternative projects, such as the Russia-proposed Turkish Stream project, which competes against a project that is of strategic importance for the EU, i.e. the Southern Gas Corridor (SGC) project. Since the EU is interested in diversifying its energy supply and increasing its energy security as a way to decrease its dependency on Russia, the revival of Turkey–Russia relations since summer 2016, and the Turkish Stream pipeline project is a good evidence for Turkey's aspirations to leverage its influence vis-à-vis the EU. The chapter concludes with an examination of both the case of Halkbank's evasion of Iran sanctions from 2010 to 2015 and the Turkish government's announcement against the implementation of renewed sanctions against Iran. It argues that Turkey engaged in boundary breaking against the West, mainly against the United States through its evasion of Iran sanctions.

Chapter 6 analyzes Turkey's rapprochement with Russia, particularly in the security and defense sectors. Ever since 2016, Turkey repeatedly threatened to find alternative allies and join the Shanghai Cooperation Organization (SCO). Illustrating that the SCO is being portrayed as an alternative to the EU, Erdoğan refers to the undesirability of EU membership during many of his remarks on Turkey's potential SCO membership. This may be labeled as a compellent threat or as an attempt to increase the leverage or maneuvering space for Turkey vis-à-vis the EU or even NATO (as the SCO increasingly acquires a security/defense dimension). Furthermore, in the beginning of 2019, Turkey was on its way to purchasing a missile defense system from Russia, much to the dismay of the USA and other NATO allies. The potential purchase of an S-400 missile defense system from Russia comes at the expense of NATO's interoperability principle, while also risking Russian intelligence infiltration in NATO's defense network systems. Chapter 6 makes the argument that Turkey signals its resolve to engage in cooperative balancing with Russia on security and defense, utilizes costly signaling, threatens to join an alternative alliance, uses blackmail power, and makes compellent threats, which indicate a major switch from boundary-challenging to boundary-breaking behavior against the Western alliance.

Chapter 7 provides an analysis of the implications of Turkish foreign policy on Syria and Iraq for Turkey–USA/NATO relations. It makes a case that Turkey's foreign policy significantly diverges from that of the USA on both the role of the Syrian Kurds in the fight against the IS and its involvement in the military operations to liberate Raqqa and Mosul and also the Operations Euphrates Shield (OES) and Olive Branch (OOB) that Turkey conducted in northern Syria. It presents evidence for Turkish boundary-challenging behavior against the USA and NATO in the Middle East in the context of Turkey's long-lasting reluctance to join the fight against the IS, lax control of its border with Syria, and boundary-breaking behavior against these two actors through the denial of the İncirlik Air Base to US warplanes in the fight against the terrorist organization up until July 2015, the Russian air support to Turkey's OES and OOB, involvement in Astana peace talks, and the Russia–Turkey–Iran trilateral agreement reached in May 2017 on the establishment of de-escalation zones in Syria. It concludes that Turkey utilizes costly signaling, territorial denial, compellent threats, and cooperative balancing with Russia against the USA and other NATO allies and that Turkish foreign policy starts showing tendencies for boundary breaking against the West.

The conclusion chapter reflects on the findings of this research and places them in a larger context of foreign policy behavior within alliances. It explores the theoretical implications of the findings regarding Turkey's foreign policy behavior within the Western alliance. It argues that Turkey has initially been experimenting with different foreign policy tools, in an attempt to increase the space of what is acceptable in interactions with the transatlantic community. The chapter continues to argue that, from 2010 to 2019, the intensity of Turkey's intra-alliance opposition has increased, as Turkish foreign policy behavior went progressively from boundary testing to boundary challenging to boundary breaking. The case studies indicate that the intensity of the tools the country used has increased from entangling diplomacy and strategic noncooperation to costly signaling, territorial/asset denial, compellent threats, blackmail, and collaborative balancing with Russia.

Through these foreign policy tools, Turkey has initially been seeking to maintain a more equitable relationship with the West, accomplish the resolution of the Cyprus problem in line with its key interests, and consolidate its power and sphere of influence in the Middle East and the Western Balkans, while seeking to become a member of the EU. As the prospects of its EU membership became dim, and its relationship with the USA and other NATO allies deteriorated due to irreconcilable national interests with regard to the Middle East and a crisis of trust, Turkey seems to increasingly adopt an aggressive and confrontational foreign policy vis-à-vis the West. The goal is to signal that the country has other options beyond the Western alliance. To illustrate, US foreign policy in the Middle East is observed with a growing concern by the Turkish policymakers as posing a serious threat to Turkey's sovereignty. Having said that, the United States is still perceived as a major source of public goods in both the economic and security areas that cannot simply be replaced quickly. Additionally, Turkey recognizes that the USA cannot easily retaliate to boundary-breaking behavior because Turkey does not challenge the USA's power position with military means directly.

The conclusion chapter identifies three major factors behind the Turkish foreign policy behavior vis-à-vis the West. It ends with a discussion of three alternative future scenarios in Turkey's relations with the West and argues that Turkish hard balancing against the West is on the horizon. It concludes by making recommendations for engaging Turkey in a mutually beneficial way.

I

Framework of Intra-alliance Opposition

While Turkey has been traditionally deeply entrenched in the Western alliance, the country lately has had a significant deterioration of its relationship with the West. As one study notes, "Grounding the multifaceted change in Turkish foreign policy on a sound theoretical basis remains a challenge for scholars of international relations" (Hatipoğlu and Palmer 2016, p. 231). The purpose of this chapter is to address this gap and situate the Turkey–West relations into a framework of intra-alliance opposition.

Although there are a number of works in the literature that examine Turkey's relations with the West, problems of Turkey's EU accession and Turkey–EU relations, and Turkey–USA–NATO relations, such works either lack a theoretical framework (Oran 2010, Hale 2013, Kirişci 2018) and are outdated in light of the most recent developments in Turkish foreign policy (Robins 2003) or uniformly adopt Europeanization and/or Constructivism theories and examine the harmonization of Turkish foreign policy with the West (Öniş 2003, Aydın and Açıkmeşe 2007, Özcan 2008, Öniş 2008, Öniş and Yılmaz 2009, Terzi 2010, Demirtaş 2015, Nas and Özer 2016, Hintz 2016, 2018). Most of what has been written in the literature comes in the form of newspaper articles, op-eds, or journal articles. None of the existing books in the literature offer a systematic and theoretical examination of Turkey's relations with the West, taking into account the most recent developments in the domestic and foreign policy of Turkey. Therefore, this book fills in a very important gap in the literature and provides a thorough, up-to-date, empirically supported, and theoretically grounded analysis of Turkey's relations with the West.

The increased activism in Turkish foreign policy is generally attributed to different causes, such as Turkey's Europeanization process and geopolitical transformations in its neighborhood (Kirişci 2009). Europeanization is understood as the emergence of new rules, norms, practices, and structures of meaning to which member states and candidate states are exposed and which they have to incorporate into their domestic structures (Börzel 2002, Schimmelfennig and Sedelmeier 2005, Börzel and Risse 2007). The Europeanization thesis as applied to Turkish foreign policy made the argument that Turkish foreign policy is starting to be increasingly conducted in line with that of the EU, not only substantially but also stylistically.

The application of the Europeanization thesis to Turkish foreign policy comes in the form of analyses of Turkish foreign policy in the Middle East or the Balkans (Özcan 2008, Terzi 2010, Demirtaş 2015). Demirtaş (2015), for instance, concludes that Turkey pursues Westernized foreign policy tools, such as the promotion of Turkish-language education, and cultural diplomacy, in the Western Balkans. Terzi (2010) observes a shift in Turkish foreign policy approach from hard to soft power as a result of the country's EU accession process. Especially the period between 2002 and 2005 is characterized as the "golden age of Europeanization in Turkey" (Öniş 2008, p. 40). Nevertheless, such works face the challenge of accounting for the change in Turkish foreign policy orientation away from Europeanization, especially in the face of the standstill in EU–Turkey accession talks and a drastic change in the course of Turkey–EU relations. While the Europeanization theory sheds some light into developments in Turkish foreign policy in the beginning of 2000s, it no longer holds a significant explanatory power for Turkish foreign policy vis-à-vis the West in the last decade, as Turkey increasingly distances itself from the EU.

Another theory frequently used by the scholars of Turkish foreign policy is Constructivism. The main argument is that the different national preferences with regard to the West may be attributed to the conceptions of national identity. As Menon and Welsh (2011, p. 88) note, "Member states in part define themselves and their place in world politics as a function of their role in particular organizations"; they add, "Member states' particular identities can also limit what they can do as part of an organization; thereby, hampering organizational effectiveness."

Constructivists mainly highlight the issue of identity in foreign policy and often emphasize soft power. Nevertheless, a major shortcoming of such studies is the failure to fully measure or appreciate the impact of soft power (Miskimmom et al. 2013). Constructivist studies of Turkish foreign policy generally emphasize the importance of democratic tradition, free market economy, shared history rhetoric, public diplomacy and mediation, and the overall use of soft power by Turkey to become a key player in regional and global politics (Öniş and Yılmaz 2009, Kaya 2013, Yeşiltaş and Balcı 2013, Danforth 2014).

In the Turkish context, works that embrace Constructivism also explore the relationship between Islam and Islamism and Turkish foreign policy. Göl (2013), for instance, analyzes Turkey's engagement with modernity during its transition from the Ottoman Empire into a modern nation-state and makes the argument that Turkey's promise as a regional and global player is related to its historical legacies. While her contribution provides a helpful historical overview of Turkish foreign policy-making mechanisms and the relationship among Islam, modernity, and foreign policy, it does not focus on contemporary Turkish foreign policy. Hintz (2016, 2018), on the other hand, focuses on contemporary Turkish foreign policy from the perspective of Constructivism and argues that the debates over national identity spill over into foreign policy. She develops a theory of inside-out identity contestation and examines the conditions under which interaction among groups with competing proposals for identity spill over into foreign policy, using an original methodology, applying intertextual analysis to a variety of sources ranging from Turkish governmental archives and news media to novels, films, and TV series (Hintz 2018). She concludes that Turkey's internal discursive struggles result in varied international outcomes and that the AKP takes "Ottoman Islamism" outside through the use of Turkish foreign policy (Hintz 2018). While such studies are revealing works and provide some valuable insight, they are limited in that they focus only on a narrow aspect or a limited time period of the relationship. Changes in Turkey's attitudes toward the West and Russia under the tenure of the AKP government may not be solely explained as a factor of national identity contestation.

This book provides an intra-alliance opposition/conflict perspective to the study of Turkey–West relations. Alliances are more than aggregation of military power: they prescribe behavioral roles and constrain activity (Wallander 2000). There are costs that are associated with maintaining such institutions, but costs are typically lower than those associated with creating new institutions. Nevertheless, changed circumstances, such as shifts in the distribution of power, changes in national policies, and incomplete information are likely to change the original cost–benefit calculations of the allies, changing the value they place on the alliance (Papayoanou 1997, Wallander 2000).

THE LITERATURE ON ALLIANCES

In the IR literature, there are two main theories that focus on alliances: neoliberalism and neorealism. Neoliberalism holds that institutions promote stability through inducements, such as increasing returns to their members, and path dependence (McCalla 1996, Wallander 2000, Pierson 2000, Lieberman 2002). This theory emphasizes structure over agency. Ikenberry (1998), for instance, maintains that there is "institutional stickiness" as the institutions sunk their roots more deeply into the political and economic systems of states, causing member states to develop vested interest in maintaining the institutions. Institutionalism, however, suffers from a major shortcoming: the theoretical assumption of institutional stability leads to the overlooking of the crucial role of intra-alliance conflict/opposition in shaping institutional development and undermining institutional performance and collective action (Thelen 1999, Capoccia and Kelemen 2007, Menon and Welsh 2011). There are a number of ways alliances end, such as through abrogation or premature termination due to the violation of their terms, fulfillment of their goals, exogenous loss of independence, or renegotiation and replacement with different obligations (Leeds and Savun 2007, Kim 2016).

The second IR theory, neorealism, has a number of different sub-theories dealing with intra-alliance opposition/conflict. The External Threat hypothesis suggests a link between alliances and the presence of threats. It argues that states engage in alliances in order to check threats from enemies (Kupchan 1988). The rationale is that in the face of rising threats, alliance cohesion increases (Snyder 1991, 1997). The absence of a common threat renders distributional conflict between member states more likely and reduces intra-alliance cohesion (Holsti et al. 1973, Grieco 1988, Walt 1997, Menon and Welsh 2011).

Russian power and ambitions are on the rise, especially in Turkey's immediate neighborhood. If the External Threat hypothesis were correct, we would have seen more coherence and cohesion within NATO. However, Turkey seems to increasingly challenge the unity within NATO, threatens to join alternative alliances such as the Shanghai Cooperation Organization, and engages in military collaboration with the alliance's archenemy Russia.

There is another neorealist hypothesis, the Alliance Security Dilemma, which argues that the interests of allies are never entirely congruent and that alliance cohesion is a function of coercive potential of the alliance leader vis-à-vis the weaker partners of the alliance. From the very beginnings of institutional creation, members' competing preferences collide, creating two major challenges: "a collective search for an optimal solution to the problem at hand and a need to satisfy the distributive demands of all participants" (Menon and Welsh 2011, p. 85). In asymmetric alliances, the stronger side is after gaining autonomy in exchange for providing security to the weaker ally. In return, the weaker ally receives enhanced security for providing its stronger ally with greater autonomy (Morrow 1991).

The Alliance Security Dilemma hypothesis is based on the assumption that weaker partners of the alliance face a central dilemma in determining their degree of commitment to the alliance leader's policies: If they choose to support the dominant member, they face "entrapment" in its good decisions as well as in its follies. The tension between the allies is based on the fear of "abandonment" (the "constant worry of being deserted") and the fear of "entrapment," which are inversely related. Snyder (1997, p. 181) posits that the fear of entrapment is due to the possibility of being dragged into a war or a conflict over the interests of an ally. In abandonment, the ally "may realign with the opponent, or may merely de-align, abrogating the alliance contract, may fail to make good on its explicit commitments, or may fail to provide support in contingencies where support is expected" (Snyder 1984, p. 466).

In an attempt to mitigate the fear of abandonment, a partner endorses a strategy, which highlights its commitment to its ally. Eventually, the ally's security improves, and it is less tempted to defect. In turn, however, the partner's chances of becoming entrapped by its ally increases. If a particular state fears entrapment, it may withhold its support or commitment to its ally. Nevertheless, this has the risk of devaluing the alliance and causing the ally to defect. None of these fears identified by the Alliance Security Dilemma hypothesis seem to motivate Turkish foreign policy behavior within the transatlantic alliance. Turkish foreign policy behavior indicates neither a fear of entrapment nor a fear of abandonment, as Turkey has increasingly challenged the policies of the United States and the European allies and seems to have already engaged in a number of provocative behaviors that transcend into the realm of boundary breaking.

Another neorealist theory that focuses on intra-alliance opposition/conflict is soft balancing. Realism's balance of power theory distinguishes between two types of balancing behavior: hard and soft balancing.[1]

---

[1] Soft balancing theory originates from attempts to explain why US power remains under-balanced in the post–Cold War era despite the predictions of the balance of power theory (Levy 2004).

Balancing is defined as "behavior designed to create a better range of outcomes for a state vis-à-vis another state or coalition of states by *adding* to the power assets at its disposal, in an attempt to offset or diminish the advantages enjoyed by that other state or coalition" (Art 2005, pp. 183–184, italics in original). Balance of power theory was modified by Walt (1987), when he shifted the emphasis away from balancing against power to balancing against threats, which, he argued, is more common in regional subsystems. The extent of threat is produced by the presence of four factors: aggregate power, geographic proximity, offensive power, and aggressive intentions (Mearsheimer 2001).

While hard balancing is exercised through strategies to build and update military capabilities (internal balancing) as well as through the creation and maintenance of formal alliances and counteralliances (external balancing), soft balancing strategies involve diplomacy, international institutions, and economic statecraft (Joffe 2002, Khong 2004, Paul et al. 2004, Paul 2005, Pape 2005, He and Feng 2008, Whitaker 2010, Saltzman 2012a). Soft balancing theorists postulate that despite the absence of hard balancing in the contemporary international system, there is ample evidence of soft balancing (Paul 2004). Soft balancing puts perceptions at the center of balance of power analysis (Fortmann et al. 2004, p. 366, Friedman and Long 2015). It is caused by two international systemic variables: power disparity or perceived threats to an actor's pre-eminence in the neighborhood and economic interdependence (Paul 2004, He and Feng 2008, Whitaker 2010). In case of high power disparity and economic dependence between the target state and potential balancers, states are less likely to prefer hard balancing, as the cost of breaking with the target state is too high (Paul 2004, He and Feng 2008). Hard balancing is also not feasible when democratic partners have a disagreement (Kelley 2005).

Therefore, soft balancing occurs in power asymmetries (He and Feng 2008) and is considered a category of intra-alliance opposition that accepts the existing balance of power while seeking to obtain better outcomes or increased influence within it (Oswald 2006, Walt 2009, Whitaker 2010, Catalinac 2010). Through soft balancing, states are able to "delay, frustrate, and undermine" the policies of the stronger actors (Pape 2005, p. 7) and protect their interests in the long run by increasing their bargaining position against stronger actors, limiting the exercise of power by a more powerful actor, and inducing a more equitable partnership without direct confrontation of the stronger state's power (Brooks and Wohlforth 2005, Kelley 2005, Pape 2005, Oswald 2006, He and Feng

2008, Whitaker 2010, Cantir and Kennedy 2015). Soft balancing may occur in the form of both cooperative and unilateral efforts (Schaefer and Poffenbarger 2014). Paul (2005, p. 47) lists three conditions under which soft balancing occurs:

1) the hegemon's power position and military behavior are of growing concern but do not yet pose a serious challenge to the sovereignty of second-tier powers, 2) the dominant state is a major source of public goods in both the economic and security areas that cannot simply be replaced, and 3) the dominant state cannot easily retaliate either because the balancing efforts of others are not overt or because they do not directly challenge its power position with military means.

Soft balancing is criticized for failing to consider alternative explanations of state behavior other than a mere systemic need, such as posturing for domestic aims, or concerns with regard to economic interests or regional security (Brooks and Wohlforth 2005). Lieber and Alexander (2005) make the argument that the soft balancing theory is flawed and non-falsifiable and that soft balancing is simply mistaken for diplomatic frictions or bargaining. On its distinction from intra-alliance bargaining, Art (2005, p. 184) notes that while both aim at achieving better outcomes vis-à-vis the unipole, soft balancing is a future-oriented strategy or "an attempt to augment assets so as to produce better outcomes the next time." Kupchan (2011) argues that in soft balancing, the intentions to constrain the unipole is important.

While it certainly contributes to our understanding of intra-alliance conflict/opposition, the extant literature on soft balancing lacks clarity in terms of the definition of the tools of statecraft a second-tier power utilizes within an alliance. There is conceptual overlap between different tools it identifies, which may lead to confusion, as such tools may be used not merely for soft balancing but also for bargaining, issue linkages, retaliation, and tit-for-tat strategies. Accordingly, a clear delineation of the interactive processes of bargaining, soft balancing, and hard balancing is needed (Friedman and Long 2015).

Soft balancing may turn into hard balancing "if and when security competition becomes intense and the powerful state becomes threatening" (Paul 2004, p. 3). The outcome of intra-alliance bargaining is determined by a combination of international and domestic factors (Putnam 1988, Kim 2016). Walt (1997) anecdotally argues that besides changes in perceptions of threat, alliances may collapse as a result of declining credibility and changes in domestic politics. Another study notes that an increase in the capabilities of the minor partners in asymmetric alliances potentially destabilizes such alliances (Chung 2016). Chung (2016, p. 236) concludes that "whether increased capabilities of minor powers can lead to alliance termination is conditional upon their economic dependence on major powers because, under economic dependence, ending the alliance can jeopardize economic benefits from the alliance relationship which may provide the very sources for the increased capabilities of those minor powers."

Both neorealism and neoliberal institutionalism fail to recognize the conditions under which there will be cooperation and discord within an alliance (Papayoanou 1997, Menon and Welsh 2011). In order to understand the motivations of intra-alliance opposition from the perspective of secondary powers, it is also important to examine the influence of domestic factors (Capie 2004). This is where neoclassical realism may prove to make a useful contribution to the literature. Neoclassical realism retains the significance of the international system that the structural realists emphasize while adding a new emphasis on intervening variables at the state and individual levels (Ripsman et al. 2016). It seeks to explain the anomalies in state behavior that cannot be explained by solely relying on international systemic variables.

To illustrate, intra-alliance opposition and conflict becomes more likely if the members of the alliance do not place a high value on the alliance or if the domestic public opinion would dictate more unilateral-type preferences (Papayoanou 1997). The calculated utility for intra-alliance cooperation, the stakes in a particular situation, the existence of domestic opposition against the alliance, and the expected duration of power of a leader all have an impact on the bargaining power of the leader within an alliance and have consequences on intra-alliance conflict (Papayoanou 1997, Kim 2016). Allies regularly engage in cost–benefit calculations and decide to engage in intra-alliance opposition, when the expected benefits of opposition are greater than the expected costs (Papayoanou 1997). For instance, Kim (2016, p. 119) notes that when a neutralist leader (defined as a leader who does not have a high utility for intra-alliance cooperation) is expected to stay in power for a long time, "an ally is more strongly compelled to deal with said leader because a stalemate is more costly to the ally than to the leader."

As maintained by diversionary theory, "Political elites often embark on adventurous foreign policies or even resort to war in order to distract popular attention away from internal social and economic problems and consolidate their own domestic political support" (Levy 1989, p. 259). Diversionary politics "often leads to myopic foreign policies, with leaders pursuing more popular, confrontational policies in the short run, at the expense of longer-term national interests" (Horowitz and Tyburski 2012, p. 165). Leaders that are authoritarian or that show authoritarian tendencies are more likely to engage in such behavior (Miller 1999, Horowitz and Tyburski 2012). The suppressed political opposition and press freedoms "insulate authoritarian leaders from effective internal criticism of diversionary policies" (Miller 1999, Horowitz and Tyburski 2012, p. 165).

As illustrated in the literature review, the literature on alliances is underdeveloped in terms of a theory that can identify different degrees of intra-alliance opposition/conflict. Therefore, this book integrates the tools of statecraft identified in the IR literature into the literature on alliances to have a more accurate understanding of the degrees of intra-alliance opposition. The next section offers a framework of intra-alliance opposition and delineates when certain tools of statecraft are used within an alliance and to what purpose.

A FRAMEWORK OF INTRA-ALLIANCE OPPOSITION

Intra-alliance opposition is defined here as the instances where there is conflict between the members of an alliance or between one member of the alliance and the alliance itself. Members of an alliance may have different policy preferences. There is also uncertainty with regards to the perception of such preferences. The intra-alliance opposition has significant implications for the effectiveness of the response of the alliance to the pressing issues that the alliance faces. Therefore, it is important to understand the motivations behind the intra-alliance opposition behavior.

In order to develop a framework of intra-alliance opposition, it is imperative to classify tools of statecraft based on their intensity. This helps better delineate the nature of intra-alliance opposition behavior and understand the implications of such behavior for the future of the alliance member's relations with the alliance. This research elucidates degrees of intra-alliance opposition and identifies which tools are used in which stage of intra-alliance conflict/opposition. Using the Turkish foreign policy as a case study, the analysis here contributes to the empirical and conceptual development of the scholarly literature on intra-alliance opposition by distilling different tools that are at the disposal of the secondary powers within alliances into three categories and by delineating the motivations for such states to engage in different stages of opposition within an alliance. This section offers a definition of the tools of statecraft identified by the extant literature and classifies them into three different categories of intra-

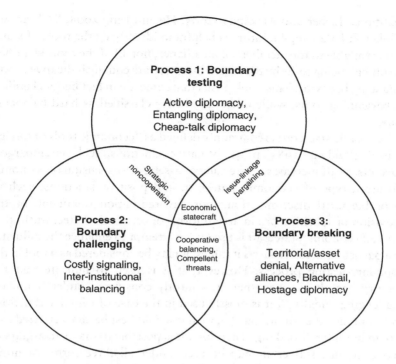

FIGURE 1 A framework of intra-alliance opposition

alliance opposition behavior: boundary testing, boundary challenging, and boundary breaking (see Figure 1).

Tools of Statecraft Used within Alliances

There are different tools and strategies of statecraft used within an alliance, which are identified mainly by the IR literature. Such tools or strategies of statecraft include economic statecraft (Baldwin 1985, Pape 2005), cheap-talk diplomacy (Trager 2010, Ramsay 2011), territorial denial, entangling diplomacy, signaling of resolve to participate in a balancing coalition (Pape 2005), formal alliances, informal alignments, voting and veto power in international institutions, institutional binding (Ikenberry 2001), strategic noncooperation (Art 2005, He 2008, He and Feng 2008, Ferguson 2012, Saltzman 2012a, Flemes and Wehner 2015, He 2015, p. 212), compellent threats (Sechser and Fuhrmann 2013), provision of aid to rivals, and cooperative balancing and countervailing coalitions (Lieber and Alexander 2005, He and Feng 2008, Walt 2009). While soft balancing literature is helpful in identifying the tools of statecraft available to the members of an alliance, not all of the tools identified as soft balancing tools by the extant literature are equally indicative of soft balancing behavior. This book posits that some are in fact better classified as bargaining tools, while others are better classified as hard balancing tools.

Economic statecraft is commonly defined as "economic tools of foreign policy" (Baldwin 1985, p. 4). Negative sanctions, such as embargos, boycotts, tariff increases, or freezing of assets, or suspension of economic aid are a type of economic statecraft, and positive sanctions, such as favorable tariff discrimination, most-favored-nation treatment, or the provision of subsidies or aid are all forms of economic statecraft. In that sense, if economic statecraft is used in an attempt to enhance the influence of a particular actor vis-à-vis its allies, it may be considered as a tool in the boundary-testing process. However, if it is used to indicate that the country has alternatives, then it is mostly considered under boundary challenging. Finally, if it is mostly used in the case of negative sanctions and to punish the counterpart(s), then it would best be characterized as a tool in boundary breaking. Therefore, it is possible to make an argument that economic statecraft may be used under all three forms of intra-alliance opposition behavior.

Active diplomacy, as the name connotes, is a high volume of diplomatic exchanges and interactions between the country and other countries. It generally entails increased levels of political, economic, and cultural ties between countries. It is best considered under the realm of boundary testing, as the country tries to assess what the limits of its power and influence are vis-à-vis the other members of the alliance through increased interactions with third parties that hold strategic importance for the members of the alliance.

Through cheap-talk diplomacy, states may send costless signals and inform other states about their intentions (Schelling 1960, Kurizaki 2007, Trager 2010, Ramsay 2011). Through cheap talk, "information is conveyed by threats because states understand the dangers of altering other states' perceptions of their intentions, and yet choose to threaten anyway when they are sufficiently resolved" (Trager 2010, p. 347). Therefore, it is best categorized under boundary testing.

Issue-linkage bargaining is yet another tool of statecraft used in boundary testing. In issue-linkage bargaining, by simultaneously discussing two or more issues for joint settlement the country aims to increase the probability of reaching a negotiated agreement and seeks to motivate its counterpart to remain committed to the agreement (Morgan 1990, Poast 2013). If the stakes on the future of the alliance are higher, issue-linkage bargaining may best be considered under boundary breaking.

Entangling diplomacy refers to the use of the rules and procedures of international institutions to influence the counterpart's foreign policy (Paul 2005). It is slightly lower in intensity when compared to institutional binding, leveling strategy, or inter-institutional balancing (Ikenberry 2001, Pape 2005, Kelley 2005, He and Feng 2008, Saltzman 2012b), which occurs when states seek to restructure the asymmetrical situation either by constraining the alternatives of stronger states or by increasing the options available to them (Kelley 2005). Inter-institutional balancing occurs when a state uses one institution to challenge the relevance of another institution (He 2015).

Entangling diplomacy is best classified under boundary testing, and inter-institutional balancing is best placed under boundary challenging, since the main goal is to undermine the power and constrain the influence of the threatening actor without direct military confrontation (He and Feng 2008).[2] A key concept to be mentioned here is veto players – "a certain number of individual or collective actors [that] have to agree to the proposed change" in order to change policies (Tsebelis 2002, p. 2). Veto players are rational actors that seek to maximize self-interest and would only adopt a new policy if it makes them better off than the status quo (Tsebelis 2002, p. 20).

Strategic noncooperation occurs when a weaker state seeks to increase future leverage vis-à-vis a stronger state by rejecting cooperation that is deemed to be inequitable to avoid being stuck in an asymmetric bargaining relationship (Kelley 2005). Costly signaling, which is the opposite of cheap talk, is the signaling of resolve to maintain a more equitable relationship with the alliance as a whole or with its members (Fearon 1994, 1995, Slantchev 2005). It indicates that the country is willing to incur real costs in order to signal its determination to level the relationship with its allies. Only in cases where there are real costs attached to the messages can sincere senders be distinguished from those that are simply bluffing (Fearon 1995). Both strategic noncooperation and costly signaling are

---

[2] Inclusive institutional balancing occurs when a state includes the target state within a multilateral institution to constrain the target state's behavior, and exclusive institutional balancing occurs when a state excludes a target state from an institution and relies on the cohesion of the institution to put pressure on the target state (He 2015).

best classified as statecraft tools under boundary challenging. However, it is important to acknowledge that sometimes, depending on the motivations of the actors, strategic noncooperation may also be used for boundary testing, in order to determine the value that the allies assign to the issue where there is strategic noncooperation.

Another tool of statecraft under boundary challenging is cooperative balancing. Cooperative balancing is defined as "the conscious coordination of diplomatic action in order to obtain outcomes contrary to US preferences, outcomes that could not be gained if the balancers did not give each other some degree of mutual support" (Walt 2009, p. 104). It is nevertheless important to note that cooperative balancing may also be classified as a tool of boundary breaking, especially if the cooperation between the actors is on military and defense issues.

Compellent threats revolve around the concept of military coercion to change the status quo. Typically, the goal is to frighten the counterpart into relinquishing a valuable possession or altering its behavior (Schelling 1960, Sechser 2011, Sechser and Fuhrmann 2013). They are normally used in disputed territories, payment of reparations, or reversal of unfavorable policies (Sechser and Fuhrmann 2013). They are best categorized as a tool of statecraft used in boundary breaking. However, if the threats are not reasonably credible, it is better to categorize them under boundary challenging.

Territorial denial is when a weaker state denies access to its territories, when it would benefit superior states to have access to the territory of third parties for staging ground forces or providing transit for air and naval forces (Pape 2005). In the words of Pape (2005, p. 36), "Denying access to this territory can reduce the superior state's prospects for victory, such as by increasing the logistical problems for the superior state or compelling it to fight with air or sea power alone, constraints that effectively reduce the overall force that a stronger state can bring to bear against a weaker one." Similarly, asset denial is when a state denies the stronger state access to its assets, such as military weapons or the use of military technology, in an attempt to change the behavior of its counterpart.

Countervailing or alternative alliances are ones that a country may develop with the rival countries of its existing alliance in an attempt to match the benefits of the current alliance. This tool of statecraft most certainly falls under boundary breaking. Hostage diplomacy, another tool of statecraft that may best be classified under boundary breaking, occurs when a country detains or arrests the citizens of another country in an attempt to extract concessions to their demands, which typically involve requests for the release of its citizens held by its counterpart(s). Hostage diplomacy is not something that is typically used between allies, as such countries have more peaceful mechanisms for resolving such demands. Finally, blackmail is another tool of statecraft identified by the balancing literature. As noted by Jesse et al. (2012, p. 13), blackmail constitutes another "strategy of resistance . . . states can try to gain concessions" from their target through the threats of "undesirable consequences." Walt (2006) notes that blackmailing can be an effective strategy and only work in specific circumstances, especially if the counterpart cannot easily protect itself against a credible threat. Territorial/asset denial, alternative alliances, hostage diplomacy, and blackmail are considered to be tools used in boundary breaking. Following this discussion of the tools of statecraft used within alliances, the next section offers a framework of intra-alliance opposition.

Processes of Intra-alliance Opposition

The framework of intra-alliance opposition presents the conditions under which countries use the tools and strategies they do when engaging in interactions within an alliance. In the first process of intra-alliance opposition, boundary testing, the parties engage in bargaining. Testing and exploring boundaries is an important venture in alliances in order for alliance members to understand which lines are not to be crossed. These boundaries present a set of behavioral patterns that are reinforced by experience and interactions in the past. Throughout this process, actors engage in self-limiting and rely on existing patterns of behavior. Boundary testing is part of an attempt to know and understand what the limits are when navigating relations with the other members of the alliance. The goal in this initial process of boundary testing is for the country to understand what the acceptable norms and expectations are for interacting with its counterparts within the alliance. Boundary testing typically includes active diplomacy, entangling diplomacy, cheap-talk diplomacy, and economic statecraft. Testing the boundaries is a constructive process, as long as the relationship is perceived to be a reciprocal one. As long as the Turkish behavior is to compel accession to the EU, to seek further integration with the EU, or to obtain more benefits from its alliance with the West, we can determine that this behavior is in line with boundary testing or bargaining.

In the second process, boundary challenging, the challenging party seeks independence from within the alliance. Boundary challenging,

which typically falls under the realm of soft balancing, involves inter-
institutional balancing, cooperative balancing, strategic noncooperation,
and costly signaling. Pape (2005, p. 36, fn. 59) argues, "Soft balancing
differs from everyday international diplomacy, which often seeks to
resolve disputes through compromise rather than through changes in the
balance of power or the use of policies that limit a strong state's military
power." Art (2005, pp. 183–184) further notes that soft balancing is a
"future-oriented strategy," through which actors attempt "to augment
assets so as to produce better outcomes the next time," whereas bargaining "is the attempt to produce favorable outcomes with current assets." In
that sense, in boundary challenging, the goal is to produce better outcomes the next time around. Nevertheless, the key thing to emphasize here
is that even though the allies pursue independent foreign policies that
diverge from that of the alliance, they actively work to signal their willingness to remain within the alliance and fulfill commitments to their
allies.

Finally, the third process of intra-alliance opposition is boundary
breaking, which typically signals a growing dissatisfaction with membership in the alliance and an increasing willingness to transition into hard
balancing. In boundary breaking, the opposing party seeks independence
from without and increasingly engages in foreign policy behaviors that
undermine the integrity of the alliance. This third form of intra-alliance
opposition typically witnesses threats of military balancing on the part of
the opposing party against the member(s) of the alliance or the alliance
itself. Boundary breaking includes compellent threats, territorial and asset
denial, alternative alliances, hostage diplomacy, and blackmail. It signals
the breaking up of the relations between the member and the alliance
itself. It is accompanied by significant trust issues between the opposing
party and the alliance and a resistance to comply with the alliance commitments. The opposing party increasingly explores alternative alliances
that may potentially undermine its existing alliance obligations and make
alternative commitments outside of the alliance. In that sense, boundary
breaking may be regarded as a transitional process that signifies a move
from intra-alliance opposition to opposition to the alliance from the
outside.

CONCLUSION

This book argues that some of the tools identified in the literature are only
used initially in the boundary-testing process, while others are used in

boundary challenging and boundary breaking. As illustrated by the overlapping Venn diagram in Figure 1, this book further holds that the three categories of intra-alliance opposition behavior identified here are not mutually exclusive and that there are continuum and convergence between them. It is important to underline that boundary testing does not inevitably lead to boundary challenging, and boundary challenging does not automatically lead to boundary breaking. At any time, the parties may revert back to a lower-intensity intra-alliance opposition behavior, provided that there is no irreparable damage to intra-alliance dynamics. The final outcome, as illustrated in this book, depends on a variety of conditions, such as the issues at stake, the irreconcilability of the positions of the parties on such issues, and the perceived value of the existing relationship for each party.

Turkey is aggrieved. It feels like its voice is not heard by its Western allies, and that it is not accepted as an equal by them. It is not co-opted into the EU's defense initiatives, and it saw its interests being ignored or opposed by the United States and other NATO allies in the Middle East. There is therefore a dynamic of pushback. Consequently, the subsequent chapters seek to identify which intra-alliance opposition/conflict behaviors Turkey engaged in during the time frame of this study and to what end.

2

Turkish Foreign Policy in the Western Balkans

The Western Balkans[1] are situated on alternative energy routes and have regularly experienced great power competition for centuries. The region has been important for Turkish foreign policy due to implications of regional stability for Turkey's security, successive migration waves from the region, and the region's position as a bridge between Turkey and Europe (Eroğlu 2005). Accordingly, since the 1990s, establishing peace and maintaining stability in this region have been among the top priorities for the foreign policy of Turkey. Turkey's "geopolitical position in the Balkans was imposing on Turkey the role of a regional power" (Kut 1999, p. 41). Turkey's religious, cultural, and historical affiliations with countries in the region have proven to be a key comparative advantage of the country in the region and a strategic asset for transatlantic security infrastructures.[2] Turkey has been among the biggest contributors to the peacekeeping operations in the region, and its historical affiliation with those countries has proven to be a valuable asset during these missions. Turkey has also played an active role in the establishment of regional initiatives such as the Southeast European Cooperative Initiative (SECI), the Stability Pact, the South-East European Cooperation Process (SEECP), and the NATO-led South East Europe Initiative. Turkey is a member of the Peace Implementation Council (PIC) Steering Board, representing the Organization of the Islamic Conference (OIC).

---

[1] Turkish policymakers prefer using the term "Western Balkans," rather than "Southeast Europe," in an attempt to emphasize the country's historical ties with the region.
[2] Email exchange with a NATO official, October 27, 2015.

Despite all that, in the 1990s Turkish policymakers exercised restraint in influencing the region due to their sensitivities to "the allegations that Turkey intends to create a neo-Ottomanic zone of influence in the Balkans" (Kut 1999, p. 43). Nevertheless, much of this has changed, as Turkish foreign policy has gained further momentum through frequent high-level visits between Turkey and Balkan countries since 2009, and sought to assert a sphere of influence by consolidating Turkey's political, diplomatic, cultural, and economic influence in the region (Bechev 2012, Rašidagić 2013). In his best-selling book *Strategic Depth*, the future Turkish Foreign Minister and Prime Minister Ahmet Davutoğlu (2001) characterized Turkey as a natural and ascending regional power in the Balkans and other neighboring territories. Since 2009, Turkey has approached the region with a "better structured vision, greater pro-activeness, [and] significant exercise of its soft power capabilities" and is increasingly involved in the "regional balance of power" (Mitrović 2014, p. 60).

TURKEY AND THE WESTERN BALKANS

Despite a few descriptive and outdated articles on Turkish foreign policy in the Balkans, there is no theoretically informed and up-to-date analysis of Turkish foreign policy in the Western Balkans in the literature, analyzing it from the perspective of Turkey–West relations (Athanassopoulou 1994, Sayarı 2000, Rüma 2011, Demirtaş 2015, Dursun-Özkanca 2016, Vračić 2016). Most of what has been written comes in the form of journal articles, newspaper articles, and op-eds (Strauss 2009, Judah 2010, Kohen 2010, Cain 2010, Sokollu 2013, Kütük 2015, Büyük 2016, Gotev 2016, Muhasilović 2016, Young 2016). In order to fill this gap in the literature, this chapter explores the motivations behind Turkish foreign policy in the Western Balkans. It investigates whether Turkey's pragmatic and proactive foreign policy in the Western Balkans can best be explained by changing international and regional dynamics, such as a regional power vacuum created by the lack of EU's commitment to the region, by the crisis in the EU–Turkey accession process, or by party preferences of the AKP and Neo-Ottomanist ideology.

Turkey's Increased Soft Power in the Western Balkans

Turkey has been increasingly attempting to use the legacy of the Ottoman Empire that ruled over the region for over 500 years for bolstering its soft power.[3] As a Turkish diplomat emphasizes, the Western Balkans is a "natural hinterland"[4] for Turkish influence, as the country considers itself a Balkan state (Danopoulos 1997). In the words of a NATO official, "Turkey's interest in the region stems from its past connections and legacies."[5] There is a significant human-to-human linkage between Turkey and the Balkans.[6] One-fifth of the Turkish population is estimated to have Balkan origins (Eroğlu 2005). Additionally, more than one million Turks live in Balkan countries, constituting a bridge between these countries and Turkey (Voskopoulos 2013, Türbedar 2011).

Turkey's economic growth and cultural attractiveness contribute to its activist foreign policy in the region (Bechev 2012, Linden and İrepoğlu 2013, Mitrović Bošković et al. 2015). Through increased personal contacts and positive image conveyed by the soap operas, Turkey's overall image is bolstered "even among the traditionally suspicious or outright hostile non-Muslim audiences in the region" (Rašidagić 2013, p. 184). Turkish TV series, movies, and broadcasting channels have become popular throughout the Balkans and elsewhere (Kütük 2015, Hintz 2016). In 2013, eighteen Turkish soap operas were broadcasted across the Western Balkans (The Economic Policy Research Foundation of Turkey [*Türkiye Ekonomi Politikaları Araştırma Vakfı*, TEPAV] 2015). These series help create curiosity about the Turkish lifestyle, portray Turkey as a modern society, and generate tourism potential for Turkey.[7] An increasing number of people from the Balkans visit Turkey, learn Turkish, and aspire to the Turkish lifestyle.

Turkish Airlines is a significant soft power tool that contributes to Turkey's attraction (Selçuk 2012).[8] Many interviewees from the Balkans highlight the similarities in "culture, traditions, the way of life, and

---

[3] The Balkans, beginning in the sixth century, became a land of settlement for the various Turkish tribes (İnalcık 1993). The history of the Ottoman existence in the Balkans goes all the way back to the thirteenth century. In its foundation stage, the Ottoman Empire started as a Balkan state. Many Turkish populations have been moved to the newly conquered lands in the Balkans, starting in 1354 (Karpat 1996). The Balkans region was under Ottoman rule for about five centuries, which left a deep imprint on the culture, political institutions, and social life of the region (Todorova 1996). In the words of a leading late Turkish historian, "Ottoman heritage could easily be observed not only in the languages but also in the style of the attire, the folk music, the culinary taste, and in the traditions and the modes of human behavior in the Balkans" (İnalcık 1993, p. 23).

[4] Interview with a Turkish diplomat in Sarajevo, May 9, 2013.

[5] Email exchange with a NATO official, October 27, 2015.

[6] Email exchange with an LSE academic, October 18, 2015.

[7] Exchange with a Turkish scholar, Berlin, December 15, 2016.

[8] Email exchange with a NATO official, October 27, 2015.

cuisine" and welcome the cultural influence of Turkey in the region.[9] Others emphasize that Turkey's influence in the region is preferable to that of Saudi Arabia, Qatar, or Iran, due to its "more moderate form of Islam,"[10] helps balance "Salafi influences among Muslim populations in the region" (Bugajski and Conley 2011, p. 23), and acts as a shield against religious extremism (Muhasilović 2016).

The Turkish International Cooperation and Development Agency (*Türk İşbirliği ve Koordinasyon Ajansı Başkanlığı*, TİKA) similarly contributes to the soft power of Turkey (Aydın-Düzgit and Keyman 2014)[11] by running a complementary policy of increasing cooperation with Muslim organizations in the Balkans and restoring Ottoman monuments, libraries, and mosques. Turkey allocates a considerable amount of Official Development Assistance (ODA) to the countries in the region. According to a Turkish Development Assistance Report, Turkey provided approximately 134 million USD to the Balkans and Eastern Europe, helped modernize and renovate classrooms and educational institutions in many Western Balkan countries, such as Kosovo, Bosnia, Serbia, and Macedonia, and provided vocational training to a variety of people in different sectors (TİKA 2017).

The Yunus Emre Institute founded in 2007 works toward the promotion of Turkish language, culture, literature, history, and arts around the world. There are twelve Yunus Emre Cultural Centers in six Balkan countries, contributing to an increase in the number of Turkish speakers in the region (Ekinci 2014). Moreover, there are about 100 educational institutions in the region that serve as "volunteer consulates for both sides" and educate the young people and the future elites of the region (Yenigün 2011, p. 544).

For emerging powers, soft power is key to realizing their aspirations, as hard power is "less relevant, since [they] do not expect to fight their way to leadership" (Mares 2016, p. 249). Soft power is generally "*directed to the underrepresented that the emerging power claims to represent*, not to the leading great powers" (Mares 2016, p. 249, italics in original). With its predominantly Muslim population, Turkey has a considerable soft-power potential, especially among the Muslim populations in the region.[12]

---

[9] Interviews with two Serbian academics and a high-level Kosovo government official, Belgrade, October 1, 2015; Email exchange with an LSE academic, October 18, 2015.

[10] Interview with a Serbian academic, Belgrade, October 1, 2015.

[11] Email exchange with a NATO official, October 27, 2015.

[12] Email exchange with an LSE academic, October 18, 2015; Email exchange with a NATO official, October 27, 2015.

Turkish foreign policy seems to be mainly directed to the Muslim populations in the Western Balkans, as Turkey regularly seeks to present itself as the main representative of Muslim interests in the region. For instance, the Turkish Office of Religious Affairs (*Diyanet*) "offers religious education, theological guidance, direct financial assistance and even mediates in disputes between regional governments and local Muslim communities," as is the case in Montenegro and Serbia (Büyük 2016). Similarly, Davutoğlu, in *Strategic Depth* (2001, p. 291), recommends that Turkey maintain a special relationship with the Muslim communities in the region in order to establish a sphere of influence in the Balkans (Davutoğlu 2001, p. 317). Through attempts at increasing its soft power, Turkey seems to engage in boundary testing, in order to determine how the country may contribute to the stability, security, and the economic development of the region, goals that are shared by both the EU and NATO. It is therefore reasonable to conclude that Turkey initially engaged in boundary testing to determine what the acceptable norms and expectations were in establishing the parameters of its foreign policy in the Western Balkans region. By framing the increased momentum of Turkish soft power in the region as an attempt to contribute to the European and transatlantic institutions' goals, Turkish authorities signaled that they accept the vision of the EU and NATO in the region and sought to reaffirm their commitment to that vision by finding a niche in the transatlantic attempts to stabilize and contribute to the economic development of the region.

Turkey's Active Diplomacy in the Region

As acknowledged by multiple interviewees, the Turkish presence has become significantly noticeable throughout the region.[13] Given its deeply rooted ties with the region, it is less costly for Turkey to capitalize on its power and leverage in the Western Balkans, when compared to any other of its immediate neighborhoods. Active diplomacy through bilateral, trilateral, and multilateral regional diplomatic initiatives and attaining leadership positions in regional institutions is perceived to enhance Turkey's soft power with other countries, especially the ones with significant Muslim populations, and thereby provides support for its demand

---

[13] Interview with a former minister in Bosnia and Herzegovina, Belgrade, October 1, 2015; Email exchange with a NATO official, October 27, 2015; Email exchange with a LSE academic, October 18, 2015.

that other great powers recognize its emergence as a regional power. As noted by an Austrian diplomat, the Balkans region is "a good area for Turkey to have success stories in its foreign policy."[14] Ever since 2009, Turkey has been seeking to take an active role in the multilateral regional institutions and increase the number of its bilateral and trilateral diplomatic initiatives with other countries in the Balkans.

Through high-level visits between Turkey and the other countries in the Balkans, Turkey seeks to more independently assert its influence beyond the Euro-Atlantic frameworks. In many of his writings and public speeches, the former Turkish Prime Minister Davutoğlu highlighted the significance of strengthening regional ownership of cooperation initiatives and frequently called to "reinvent the underlying dynamics of [the Ottoman] period" (Davutoğlu 2009, p. 17). In a 2009 speech, Davutoğlu (2009, pp. 16–17) proclaimed:

Balkan history is not only a history of conflicts: on the contrary, between the 16th and the 19th centuries, Balkan history was a success story. We can reinvent and reestablish this success by creating a new political ownership, a new multicultural coexistence and a new economic zone . . . As the Republic of Turkey, we would like to construct a new Balkan region based on political dialogue, economic interdependence, cooperation and integration, as well as cultural harmony and tolerance. These were the Ottoman Balkans, and hopefully we will reestablish the spirit of these Balkans.

Turkey's use of active diplomacy can be interpreted as both boundary testing and boundary challenging. Turkish authorities increasingly claimed ownership of the region at the expense of the transatlantic allies. They sought to establish the country as a mediator in the region, without much consultation with the transatlantic partners.[15]

Turkish activism resulted in a number of positive outcomes. One of the most successful outcomes has been the improvement of bilateral relations with Serbia in the past decade. In October 2009, then Turkish President Abdullah Gül visited Belgrade – the first official visit by a Turkish head of state since 1986. In March 2010, following several meetings between Turkish and Serbian officials, the Serbian parliament passed a resolution apologizing for failing to prevent the Srebrenica massacre of 1995. In 2009, Turkey and Serbia signed a free trade agreement, resulting in a significant increase in their bilateral trade volume. The trade volume of 568 million

[14] Interview with an Austrian diplomat, Belgrade, September 29, 2015.
[15] Email exchange with a NATO official, October 27, 2015.

USD in 2011 increased to 596 million USD in 2012[16] and to 844 million USD in 2015 (Young 2016). In 2016, Turkey and Serbia targeted to have 1.11 billion USD of bilateral trade (Young 2016). According to the 2017 foreign trade statistics, Turkey–Serbia trade volume has increased further, reaching 907 million USD in 2016, albeit falling short of the targeted figure (Turkish Statistical Institute [TurkStat] 2017).

Furthermore, the fact that Turkey was left out of the Butmir negotiations led by the United States and the EU, despite its requests to be a part of it, and the unsuccessful outcome of the Butmir process in addressing the constitutional reform question in Bosnia and Herzegovina encouraged Turkey to pursue its own high-level diplomacy among the parties (Türkeş et al. 2012). Turkey initiated two trilateral consultation mechanisms, one with Bosnia and Serbia and another with Bosnia and Croatia, without any coordination with the EU or NATO. There have been three trilateral summits at the presidential level between Turkey, Bosnia, and Serbia from 2010 to 2013. The first trilateral summit was hosted by then Turkish President Abdullah Gül in Istanbul on April 24, 2010, during which the presidents of the three countries signed the Istanbul Declaration on Peace and Stability in the Balkans, guaranteeing the territorial integrity and sovereignty of Bosnia. As a Serbian diplomat observes, "The Istanbul Declaration signed in April 2010 was perceived by Berlin like a finger in the eye: a green light from Belgrade to Turkey's entry in the Balkans" (Spasojević 2014). The trilateral consultation mechanism with Bosnia and Serbia helped secure the appointment of a Bosnian ambassador to Belgrade. Turkey also successfully lobbied NATO to offer Bosnia and Herzegovina a Membership Action Plan (MAP) in April 2010. However, Turkey failed to broker a new government in Sarajevo after the October 2010 parliamentary elections.

The second summit was hosted by then Serbian President Boris Tadić on April 26, 2011, and the third one took place in May 2013, where the three presidents signed an agreement on economic cooperation and started exploring the possibility of establishing a trilateral board for trade. The first trilateral meeting of the economy and trade ministers of the three countries took place in April 2013. The cordial relationship continued after the change of government in Serbia, despite a few hiccups.[17] These trilateral and bilateral agreements raised eyebrows in

---

[16] Interview with a Turkish diplomat, Belgrade, May 7, 2013.
[17] The inflammatory rhetoric of then Turkish Prime Minister Erdoğan, announcing that "Kosovo is Turkey, and Turkey is Kosovo," caused the cancellation of the fourth

the transatlantic community, as Turkey did not share the information about these initiatives with the transatlantic and European allies before undertaking them, illustrating the boundary-challenging aspect of Turkish foreign policy in the region.

Turkish ODA is another solid demonstration of the diplomatic activism toward the region. While Turkey does not normally make it to the top ten donors of ODA in Albania and Serbia, it is listed as the fourth-largest donor of ODA to Bosnia and Herzegovina, donating 32.9 million USD (following the EU institutions, the USA, and Germany); as the fifth-largest contributor in Macedonia, donating 13.8 million USD (following the EU institutions, Germany, the USA, and Switzerland); as the third-largest ODA donor to Montenegro, donating 9.6 million USD (following the EU institutions and Germany); and as the seventh-largest ODA contributor in Kosovo, donating 16.5 million USD (following the EU institutions, the USA, Switzerland, Germany, OSCE, and Sweden) (Organisation for Economic Co-operation and Development [OECD] 2016). In the last five years, Turkey's ODA assistance to Bosnia and Herzegovina and Macedonia has more or less doubled, from 17.9 million USD in 2011 to 32.9 million USD in 2014, and from 6.8 million USD in 2011 to 13.8 million in 2014 (OECD 2016). The Turkish ODA to Montenegro has seen the most dramatic increase, with aid nearly tripling between 2011 and 2014 (OECD 2016).

The diplomatic activism of Turkey led to "questions as to Turkey's 'true intentions' in the Balkan countries" (Türbedar 2011, p. 140).[18] A Serbian NGO official interviewee gave the examples of Turkey's attempts to mediate between Sarajevo and Belgrade, and between Sarajevo and Banja Luka, and emphasized that Turkey's independent and active diplomacy in the region is not welcome.[19] A number of analysts argue that Turkey is "on a mission to establish 'hegemonic control' over the Balkans" (Stojanović 2011). Various pundits and scholars label this foreign policy behavior as an evidence of Neo-Ottomanism (Taşpınar 2008, Tanasković 2013, Kiper 2013, Arin 2014, Ünver 2014a).[20]

---

trilateral presidential-level meeting, scheduled to take place in December 2013 in Belgrade.

[18] Email exchange with a NATO official, October 27, 2015.

[19] Exchange with a Serbian NGO official, Berlin, Germany, December 15, 2016.

[20] The AKP leadership is criticized for neglecting "the disastrous policy of Ottoman expansion into the area of the Middle East and the Balkans" and adopting "a nostalgic notion of the Ottomans as the benign 'master-nation' in the region" (Murinson 2012, p. 7). Many scholars argue that the emergence of a Neo-Ottomanist discourse is a result of "the West's

Tanasković, one of the most prominent scholars of Neo-Ottomanism, defines the concept as "an ideological amalgam of Islamism, Turkism, and Ottoman imperialism" (Tanasković 2010, p. 19).

Other analysts disagree with the argument that Turkish foreign policy in the region is motivated by Ottoman nostalgia (Taşpınar 2008, Eralp 2010, Somun 2011, Türbedar 2011). A former ambassador of Bosnia and Herzegovina to Turkey notes that Turkey pursues a "very pragmatic and realistic endeavor to secure the ground under its own feet by establishing a peaceful environment around its borders and creating opportunities for its economy to progress" (Somun 2011, pp. 37–38). Others argue that Turkey's desire to gain Balkan countries' support for its EU membership bid is a main factor in its activist foreign policy (Eralp 2010, Türbedar 2011). Such scholars maintain that Turkish foreign policy in the region is aimed at making the country "indispensable to the EU in the region and thus enhancing its attractiveness as a prospective EU member" (Linden and İrepoğlu 2013, p. 236) and call for the EU to better appreciate Turkey's regional initiatives.[21]

Turkey's Emphasis on Regional Ownership and Economic Statecraft

As the prospects for its EU accession become dim, Turkey is more tempted to switch from boundary-testing to boundary-challenging policies within the transatlantic alliance. As the Turkish authorities increasingly recognize that Turkey does not stand much of a chance in terms of an eventual membership into the EU, and as its rift with NATO over the acquisition of S-400 missile defense system continues, they are more motivated to pursue higher-intensity tools of statecraft that seek to challenge the policies of the EU and NATO in the region. This arguably leads to more boundary-challenging behavior.

As Demirtaş (2015, p. 133) indicates, "Turkey's regional activism [in the Balkans] should be understood within the framework of the power vacuum existing in the Balkans, mainly because the US and the EU did not pay great attention to solving the regional problems since they had different priorities in recent years." Indicative of the increasing

---

inefficient policies" during the Balkan civil wars and of the rise of a pro-Islamist bourgeoisie in Turkey with economic liberalization in the 1990s (Eroğlu 2005, p. 15, Yavuz 2001).

[21] Exchange with a Turkish scholar, Berlin, December 16, 2016.

attempts of Turkey's independence-from-within approach, Turkey places a heavy emphasis on regional ownership and seeks to acquire a leading role in the regional diplomatic initiatives that fall outside of the initiatives of the EU and NATO. As these initiatives are taken amidst a growing power vacuum in the region due to the EU's enlargement fatigue and the basic challenges to the EU's key concepts by nationalistic populism in Europe, they increasingly risk putting the country in political competition with the EU. To illustrate, Turkey is an active member and one of the largest contributors to the budget of the Regional Cooperation Council (RCC), a "regionally owned and led framework" that "focuses on promotion and enhancement of regional cooperation" in the Balkans (RCC 2017). Turkey chaired the South East European Cooperation Process (SEECP) in 2009–2010. The slogan of the Turkish Chairmanship of the SEECP, "From Shared History to Common Future," is telling about Turkey's attitude toward the Balkans.

Effectively illustrating Turkey's interest in creating further autonomous regional institutions, in 2015 Turkey advocated for establishing a Secretariat for the SEECP Parliamentary Assembly (SEECP PA) in Istanbul and pledged to underwrite all associated costs of such establishment for the first five years (TimeTurk.com 2015). Turkey sees SEECP PA as a unique opportunity to reflect "the genuine voice of the Balkan people" (TimeTurk.com 2015). It may be inferred that the EU or NATO-led initiatives are not regarded as reflecting the genuine voice of the people in the region. A leaked US diplomatic cable underlines that Turkey's proactive foreign policy "brings with it great frictions" with the USA and the Europeans (Wikileaks 2010).

Another important tool Turkey uses in its pragmatic and activist foreign policy in the Western Balkans is economic statecraft. Pape (2005, p. 37) notes:

One way of balancing effectively, at least in the long run, would be to shift relative economic power in favor of the weaker side. The most obvious way of doing this is through regional trading blocs that increase trade and economic growth for members while directing trade away from nonmembers.

One of the novel developments in Turkish foreign policy toward the Western Balkans, enabling Turkey to increasingly position itself more independently vis-à-vis the transatlantic allies, is a new emphasis on economic statecraft and Turkish economic interests in the region. Illustrating this point, at every occasion of a high-level diplomatic visit by Turkish government officials to the region, a group of Turkish businesspeople is also brought along to establish economic ties between Turkey and the rest of the region. In the words of a prominent Turkish scholar, Turkey has transformed itself into a "trading state" in which the national interest is no longer considered to mean national security alone (Kirişçi 2009, p. 33). Attributing a pragmatic Neo-Ottomanist tone to this new foreign policy approach of Turkey, a high-level Turkish diplomat interviewee notes that Turkish businesses are the "new Janissaries" in the Balkans.[22]

Through economic statecraft, Turkey has managed to gradually transform its increasing cultural power in the Western Balkans into economic power. While the Western Balkan countries are waiting in line for EU membership, Turkey allows for privileged access to goods from the region. Turkey established a visa-free travel regime and signed free trade agreements with all Balkan countries (with the exception of Croatia, after the country's accession to the EU). Turkish policymakers are cognizant of the fact that Turkey's geographical proximity to the Balkans reduces transportation costs and provides good incentives for increasing the trade volume and boosting the economic side of the relationship. Every year about 151,000 Turkish trucks pass through the Balkans.[23] The similarities in consumption habits between the people in Turkey and the Balkans make the region a very profitable market for Turkish companies. Accordingly, Turkish companies flourish in finance, construction, medical, and insurance sectors and increasingly win the bidding offers for privatization of state-owned enterprises in the Balkans (Dursun-Özkanca 2010).

As Rašidagić (2013, p. 184) notes, with Turkey's "growing economic might" comes a "growing self-awareness of [its] importance and political and economic clout" in the region. At the June 2010 summit of the SEECP in Istanbul, then Turkish Foreign Minister Davutoğlu expressed Turkey's eagerness to make the region "a hub for infrastructure, transportation, and energy projects as well as financial transaction" (Davutoğlu 2010). In April 2012, then Turkish Deputy Prime Minister Babacan said, "The Balkans should be a single economic zone in which borders and visas were lifted, more free trade agreements were made, customs duties and quotas were removed" (Anadolu Agency April 6, 2012). In order to improve trade with the Balkans, the Turkish government formed a Balkan Countries Working Group under the Under-Secretariat for

[22] Interview with a high-level Turkish diplomat, Belgrade, May 8, 2013.
[23] Interview with a Turkish diplomat, Belgrade, May 7, 2013.

Foreign Trade (Türbedar 2011, p. 142) and adopted a regional cooperation and competition strategy to facilitate an active economic presence in
the region (Ekinci 2014).

All these initiatives seem to have paid off for Turkey. The trade volume
between Turkey and the Balkans, which was around 2.9 billion USD in
2000, increased to 16.2 billion USD in 2016 (TurkStat 2017). In 2016, the
Balkan countries accounted for 6.7 percent of Turkey's total exports and
3.4 percent of its total imports (TurkStat 2017). Among all Western
Balkan countries, the country with which Turkey has the largest export
volume is Serbia (582 million USD), followed by the Former Yugoslav
Republic of Macedonia (378 million USD), Bosnia (309 million USD),
Albania (305 million USD), and Kosovo (261 million USD) (TurkStat
2017). However, it is important to note that the Balkan countries have
a trade deficit vis-à-vis Turkey: i.e. Turkey exports more when compared
to the imports from the region. Turkish imports from Bosnia and Serbia
are the largest among the Western Balkan countries, each approximately
288 million USD, followed by imports from the Former Yugoslav
Republic of Macedonia (83 million USD), Albania (21 million USD),
and Kosovo (8.5 million USD) (TurkStat 2017).

The cumulative value of Turkish foreign direct investments (FDI) in the
Balkans in 2009 was around 4.6 billion USD (Türbedar 2011, p. 142).
Turkish FDI toward the region is especially directed toward Croatia
(164 million USD), Romania (133 million USD), and Bosnia
(126 million USD), "accounting for 60% of total FDI inflows to the
Balkans" (Çakır 2014, p. 83). Turkey had the fifth-largest FDI stocks in
Albania in 2011 and the third-largest FDI stocks in Kosovo in 2013 (Çakır
2014).[24]

Turkish financial corporations are similarly increasing their presence in
the Balkan markets. The Turkish Economy Bank (TEB) has already
opened branches in Kosovo. Other major Turkish banks, including
İşbank, Ziraat Bank, and Halkbank, made new acquisitions in the
Balkans. As one analyst notes, "these banks have become the most

---

[24] A number of interviewees noted that the unfair business practices by Turkish companies
in the Balkans cause further alienation from the Balkan people (Interviews with a Kosovar
scholar and a Kosovar NGO official, Belgrade, October 1, 2015). One interviewee noted
that there is an overwhelming feeling among Kosovars that they "are selling everything to
the Turks," due to "favoritism" on the part of the elites toward Turkey, referring to the
increasing number of tenders that go to the Turkish companies (Interview with a Kosovar
scholar, Belgrade, October 1, 2015).

important source of information for both the sector specific developments and the business cultures of these economies" (TEPAV 2015).

The investment integration between Turkey and the Western Balkans is stronger than trade integration (TEPAV 2015). Turkish businesses find the Balkans market very appealing for business opportunities, especially given that the countries in the region are en route to EU admission. This situation provides an added incentive for the Turkish companies to invest in the region, as the labor costs are "almost half of those in Turkey and the price of industrial land is as low as [5 percent] of the Industrial Zones in the Marmara region" (TEPAV 2015). The engagement of the Turkish private sector is low in Serbia and Montenegro, medium in Bosnia and Herzegovina and in Kosovo, and high in Albania and in Macedonia (TEPAV 2015). Turkish companies see the Balkans "as a first step towards going regional and then global" (TEPAV 2015).

Through its "omnipresent economic cooperation with Balkan countries," Turkey increases its chances of becoming a regional hegemon (Brljavać 2011, p. 524). As a high-level Turkish diplomat acknowledges, "Turkey wants to consolidate its economic power in the region, before the countries in the region become EU members."[25] Another interviewee agrees: "Turkey wants to infiltrate the economies of Western Balkans since Western Balkans will become EU members before Turkey ... in order to sell Turkish products to the EU markets."[26] The rationale is that if Western Balkan countries get into the EU before Turkey does, Turkey will find it difficult to compete with the EU member states and to engage in deeper economic ties with the Balkan countries.

Competition between Turkey and the EU in the Region?

The EU is arguably still the most important actor in the region. It seeks to stabilize the region through its Stabilisation and Association Process (SAP), ensuring a swift transition of the countries to market economies, with the end goal of eventual EU membership.[27] Euro-Atlantic integration and the enlargement of NATO and the EU are still seen as major pathways

---

[25] Interview with a high-level Turkish diplomat, Belgrade, May 8, 2013.
[26] Interview with a Kosovar scholar, Belgrade, October 1, 2015.
[27] The Instrument for Pre-Accession (IPA) Funding adopted by the EU in 2006 comprises of 11.5 billion EUR and is intended for assistance for transition and institution-building, regional integration and development, human resources, and rural development. IPA II covers the period between 2014 and 2020 and has a budget of 12 billion EUR. Different than IPA I, it includes regional cooperation initiatives.

to maintaining stability and peace and establishing democracy in the Western Balkans. The region has a rising significance for the EU, due to concerns about radicalization, organized crime and drugs trafficking, and immigration.[28] The EU and NATO continue to maintain civilian and military missions and have a high trade and investment volume in the Western Balkans.

Many scholars underline the interconnectedness of the EU and the Western Balkans (Bislimi 2011). In 2014, in an attempt to re-energize the relations between the EU and the Western Balkans, German Chancellor Angela Merkel organized the Berlin process, emphasizing that the future of the Balkans remains within the EU. At the Vienna Summit in August 2015, and later at the Paris Summit in July 2016, the European perspective of the region and the resolution of open bilateral issues impacting the European integration process were put on the table. The European Commission published a Communiqué in February 2018, outlining a "credible enlargement perspective for and enhanced EU engagement with the Western Balkans" (European Commission 2018a). However, a Slovenian diplomat elaborates on Turkey's appeal when compared to the mainly abstract or on-paper initiatives that the EU takes on and notes that Turkey engages in energy and infrastructure projects that have concrete results for the people in the region.[29]

Many experts draw attention to the weakening of the EU's conditionality leverage in the Western Balkans because of enlargement fatigue. This poses a serious credibility problem for the EU (Vejvoda 2016). Due to the fact that there are no realistic prospects for the entry of Western Balkan countries into the EU in the short term, "there is a power vacuum in the Western Balkans to be filled."[30] Even then Turkish Foreign Minister Davutoğlu (2008, p. 88) acknowledged that there is a geopolitical "strategic vacuum" in the Balkans. The power vacuum stems not only from the enlargement fatigue and the decreased credibility of the EU in the Western Balkans but also from the multiple crises the EU faces, such as economic, refugee/migration, anti-EU populism, and Brexit crises (Alic 2010, Stojanović 2011, Yohannes 2011, Türbedar 2012, Bechev 2012, Linden and İrepoğlu 2013, Dursun-Özkanca 2016).

---

[28] Exchange with a German diplomat, Berlin, December 16, 2016.
[29] Exchange with a Slovenian official, Berlin, Germany, December 16, 2016.
[30] Exchange with a US academic, Berlin, December 15, 2016.

As noted by many, the EU's impact in the region is in decline, as the Union has fewer resources, is reluctant to engage in the Western Balkans, and has less leverage in the region.[31] One interviewee attracts attention to the low bar that the EU has for defining political stability in the region and notes it does not sufficiently emphasize the respect for the rule of law and human rights.[32] Many acknowledge the need for the EU to be more proactive in the region.[33]

Against the background of a regional power vacuum, Turkey is willing to step in to fill the void created by the EU.[34] As indicated by many interviewees, Turkey seeks to acquire more power and leverage in regional and global politics "to be perceived as an equal partner" by its European counterparts.[35] A number of experts draw attention to the fact that Turkey has been "sidelined by the EU."[36] Turkish officials regularly urge European diplomats to treat Turkey as a "partner, who can make significant contributions for peace and stability in the Western Balkans" (Türbedar 2011, p. 154). As one interviewee notes, while the EU is not used to seeing Turkey as an active player in this region, it "needs to adjust to this new reality."[37]

In the words of an interviewee, given how "long and arduous" its EU candidacy has been, "it is only realistic that Turkey seeks to change the regional balance of power to its advantage."[38] Boundary challenging emerges as a major strategy to assert a more equal partnership with the EU. Through its active foreign policy in the Western Balkans, Turkey seeks to constitute a "replacement community" in order to serve Turkish interests better, given the waning of its EU prospects (Linden and İrepoğlu 2013, p. 237).

Many observers emphasize the potential rivalry between Turkey and the EU in the Balkans (Linden and İrepoğlu 2013, Stojanović 2011, Yohannes 2011, Brljavać 2011, Alic 2010). They note that some European allies perceive the motivations behind Turkish foreign policy as competitive and react with unease (Brljavać 2011, Somun 2011, Türbedar 2012). One expert concludes, "The EU is suspicious of what

[31] Exchange with an Italian economist and a Kosovar NGO official, Berlin, December 16, 2016.
[32] Exchange with a Montenegrin NGO official, Berlin, December 16, 2016.
[33] Exchange with a Slovenian diplomat and a German diplomat, Berlin, December 16, 2016.
[34] Exchange with a US academic, Berlin, December 16, 2016; Interview with a Croatian government official, Belgrade, September 29, 2015.
[35] Interview with a US diplomat, Belgrade, October 2, 2015.
[36] Interview with an OSCE official, Belgrade, October 1, 2015.
[37] Interview with a Norwegian NGO official, Belgrade, September 29, 2015.
[38] Interview with a Croatian government official, Belgrade, October 1, 2015.

Turkey is doing in the Western Balkans."[39] Another analyst concurs that the EU and the United States "are increasingly wary of Turkey's growing clout, particularly in places like Bosnia, Serbia, and Albania, which like Turkey itself are stuck in the limbo of a snail-paced EU membership process" (Stojanović 2011). In the words of a former ambassador of Bosnia and Herzegovina to Turkey, Europe is "nervous" about the recent Turkish activism in the region (Somun 2011, p. 41). Warning about the dangers of Turkey's economic and foreign-policy dynamism in the Balkans, an analyst is quoted as noting that Europe "may miss the boat" (Misha Glenny, quoted in Stojanović 2011). On the topic, a British academic maintains:

Economic aspects are indeed the most important points of contention, as for both the EU and Turkey economy represents their biggest strength in the region. Turkey has still an indirect advantage from the fact that the business culture in the region is not very accustomed to the rather inflexible rule based system of the EU. Moreover, Turkey ... doesn't really condition cooperation on political reforms. Politically as well, Turkey can present itself as an alternative to the overtly liberal EU, where conservative values (which are still very important in some countries in the Balkans) do not have any real influence.[40]

The pro-Muslim tone in Turkey's Western Balkans foreign policy causes many in Europe to see Turkey's more active policy approach "as an attempt by Turkey to establish a 'Muslim arc' on Greece's northern border and as part of a larger strategic plan by Turkey to reassert its former hegemonic role in the Balkans" (Larrabee and Lesser 2003, p. 95). In the words of an Austrian diplomat, there is a "rising paranoia about Islam" in Europe, which causes "skepticism about the political impact of Turkey in the Balkans, due to the increased role of political Islam in the country."[41] Turkish activism in the Balkans creates "fear that Islam's influence will rise in the region."[42] As a leaked US diplomatic cable noted, Europeans are "furious with Turkey's presenting itself as the 'Islamic' voice or conscience" in the region (Wikileaks 2010). All in all, the Turkish foreign policy behavior in the Western Balkans seem to increasingly test the limits of the partnership with the EU.

　　When compared to the EU, Turkey has a greater degree of flexibility at its disposal to adjust its foreign policy and can react more quickly to new

---

[39] Exchange with a Serbian NGO official, Berlin, December 15, 2016.
[40] Email exchange with an LSE academic, October 18, 2015.
[41] Interview with an Austrian diplomat, Belgrade, September 29, 2015.
[42] Interview with a Kosovar NGO official, Belgrade, October 1, 2015.

developments in the Western Balkans, as it lacks the complex decision-making procedures of the EU. Many Turkish authorities interviewed hold the opinion that it is important for Turkey to increase its economic presence in the region, since it presents a win-win situation for Turkey as well as the other Balkan countries in the region. This is regarded as cheap-talk diplomacy, as it is relatively costless for Turkish authorities to indicate their intentions about the region to their European counterparts. Turkish foreign policy offers benefits that are both "tangible (investment) and intangible (cultural and political models) that Europe may not match" (Linden and İrepoğlu 2013, pp. 237–238). One expert notes that the differences between the interests of Turkey and the EU lead to perceptions of Turkey as an "adversary to the EU" in the region.[43]

Having said all this, there are substantial obstacles preventing Turkey from converting its cultural and economic soft power into increased political and diplomatic leverage in the region. It is important to acknowledge that Turkey is logistically at a disadvantage when compared to the EU. As one Serbian NGO official puts it, "Turkish foreign policymakers' eyes are bigger than their stomachs."[44] As a number of interviewees highlight, while Turkey may be considered a competitor to the EU in Western Balkans economically, it may not be so politically.[45] This further illustrates the cheap-talk diplomacy aspect of intra-alliance opposition behavior. Turkey does not have nearly as many tools at its disposal as the EU has.[46] As a leaked US diplomatic cable warns:

Despite their success and relative power, the Turks really can't compete on equal terms with either the US or regional "leaders" (EU in the Balkans, Russia in the Caucasus/Black Sea, Saudis, Egyptians and even Iranians in the ME). With Rolls Royce ambitions but Rover resources, to cut themselves in on the action the Turks have to "cheat" by finding an underdog ... [Such] an approach provides a relatively low cost and popular tool to demonstrate influence, power, and the "we're back" slogan.

Additionally, there are significant negative sentiments against the growing Turkish influence in the region. Turkish officials frequently ignore that the Ottoman historical legacy has not always been perceived

---

[43] Exchange with a Slovakian NGO official, Berlin, December 15, 2016.
[44] Interview with a Serbian NGO official, Belgrade, May 6, 2013.
[45] Interview with an Austrian diplomat, Belgrade, September 29, 2015; Email exchange with a NATO official, October 27, 2015.
[46] Interview with a Bosnian policymaker, Belgrade, October 1, 2015; Exchange with a Serbian NGO official, Berlin, December 15, 2016; Exchange with a German journalist, Berlin, December 15, 2016.

to be a positive one, especially among the non-Muslim populations in the region (Türbedar 2011, Dursun-Özkanca 2016, Vračć 2016, Serwer 2017).[47] Many note that Turkey is mainly seen as a biased third party, favoring the Muslim populations in the Balkans, which in turn undermines the country's aspirations to emerge as a regional peacemaker (Vračć 2016, Büyük 2016). To illustrate, a June 2012 survey by the Wise Men Center for Strategic Studies (*Bilge Adamlar Stratejik Araştırmalar Merkezi*, Bilgesam) think tank in eight Western Balkan countries indicated a difference between Muslim and non-Muslim perceptions of Turkey, with the non-Muslim populations less sympathetic toward Turkey and the Turks (Turkish Review 2012). While welcoming Turkish FDI and contractors, many Croats and Serbs "have been nervous about Turkish cultural inroads, as parts of the region lived for centuries under Ottoman domination" (Serwer 2017).

It is also important to note that EU accession remains a priority for the countries of the Western Balkans. The potential EU accession of Balkan countries prevents Turkey's relationship with the region from reaching its full potential (Bilgesam 2014). An OSCE official interviewee notes that the Balkan people "want to distance themselves from Turkey" since they think that it will come at the expense of their countries' Western dreams.[48] In the foreseeable future, Balkan policymakers will try to avoid creating the impression that by moving closer to Turkey they are surrendering their EU membership aspirations.

A number of interviewees add that the Turkish foreign policy activism in the region might be in vain once the Western Balkan countries become integrated into the EU. They cite the example of all programming initiatives Turkey undertook with Croatia coming to an end following Croatia's EU membership.[49] In a similar vein, an NGO official cautions, "Regional cooperation cannot be a substitute for EU integration."[50] Another NGO official adds, "Western Balkans can't integrate with Turkey or Russia, as their social and economic structures are deeply integrated with the EU."[51] Therefore, the Turkish authorities must be cognizant of limitations to Turkey's political leverage in the region vis-à-vis the

---

[47] Email exchange with a NATO official, October 27, 2015.
[48] Interview with an OSCE official, Serbia, October 1, 2015.
[49] Interviews with a Turkish NGO official, Belgrade, September 29, 2015, and with a Kosovar scholar, Belgrade, October 1, 2015.
[50] Interview with a German NGO official, Belgrade, September 29, 2015.
[51] Exchange with a German NGO official, Berlin, December 16, 2016.

EU's conditionality leverage, even though it is commonly characterized as decreasing.

Turkish policymaker and diplomat interviewees regularly emphasize that the diplomatic activism of Turkey in the region is not intended to be in competition with or at the expense of the Euro-Atlantic frameworks and is concordant with the EU and NATO policies in the region. They present the evidence that Turkey supports both the Membership Action Plan (MAP) and the EU membership of these countries. Many underline that Turkey can successfully serve as a model for regional states (Oğuzlu 2007, Batalla-Adam 2012). As Demirtaş, a prominent Turkish scholar on the Balkans, puts it, "The fact that Turkey has been among the most Europeanized among other south-eastern European states contributed to its promotion of *primus inter pares* ... [and] Ankara tried to use its European credentials as a means of legitimizing its own policies [in the region]" (Demirtaş 2015, p. 137).

Many Turkish diplomats interviewed note that Turkey would be a great asset for the Western Balkans countries in their accession process, as it has developed a wealth of experience during its own EU accession negotiations process.[52] They note that one of the important sources of Turkish soft power is Turkey's EU accession prospects and its NATO membership, and they maintain that Turkey's Western orientation helps to increase the desirability of Turkey's foreign policy activism in the region in the eyes of the Balkan countries.[53]

Despite its recent alienation from the Euro-Atlantic frameworks, Turkey still continues to collaborate with the EU and NATO in the Western Balkans. No boundary breaking is observed on this issue yet. Turkey does not act like a spoiler when it comes to NATO and the EU's policies toward the countries in the Western Balkans region. In the words of a NATO official, Turkey is "a strong promoter of NATO's enlargement in the Western Balkans," "closely aligned with NATO's and EU's policies" in terms of its support for enlargement processes, and hence plays "a constructive role in the region."[54] The country also contributes about 350 military personnel to NATO's Kosovo Force (KFOR) in Kosovo and is the second-largest contributor to the

---

[52] However, on this issue, Balkan elites frequently complain that they receive no advice or mentorship from their Turkish counterparts about the EU accession process (Exchange with a Bosnian NGO Official, Berlin, December 15, 2016).

[53] Interview with a Member of Turkish Parliament from AKP, Ankara, July 13, 2011.

[54] Email exchange with a NATO official, October 27, 2015.

European Union Rule of Law Mission in Kosovo (EULEX) among non-EU member states (with eighty-one personnel) and the second-largest contributor to European Union Force in Bosnia and Herzegovina-Operation ALTHEA (EUFOR-ALTHEA) (with 300 military personnel) (Turkish Ministry of Foreign Affairs 2019b). As noted in Chapter 3, Turkey still hopes to enhance its cooperation with the Common Security and Defence Policy (CSDP) and sign an Associate Membership Agreement with the EDA.

Nevertheless, the positive sentiments toward the EU among the Turkish elites are dwindling. It is realistic to expect Turkey to adopt an increasingly competitive or even hostile foreign policy toward the Euro-Atlantic institutions in the region, due to its stalled EU accession negotiations and rising frictions in its relationship with NATO. As explored in Chapter 4, despite some incremental momentum in EU–Turkey relations achieved through the EU–Turkey Joint Action Plan on the Refugee Crisis, if Turkey's accession to the EU remains deadlocked, Ankara might be tempted to split with the EU in order to further enhance its independent role in the region. As one expert cautions, "When circumstances change, roles may do so as well," emphasizing the EU's skepticism toward Turkey's intentions in the region.[55] To illustrate, in April 2017, the European People's Party adopted a resolution raising concerns about the increasing influence of Turkey in the Western Balkans on a political and financial level. Croatian Prime Minister Andrej Plenković warns, "If [the EU] is hesitant or slow to bring the [Western Balkans] more rapidly closer to us, others will not hesitate and drift them away from the EU" (quoted in Michalopoulos 2017). Similarly, Hungarian Prime Minister Viktor Orbán cautions against growing Turkish influence in the context of declining EU influence in the region (Michalopoulos 2017).

Against the background of increasing nationalism in the region, there is growing skepticism about the motivations of Turkey's proactive foreign policy in the Balkans. Many analysts emphasize the need to avoid using colonialist language in Turkish foreign policy, noting that there is a "nostalgia for Neo-Ottomanism" among the Turkish policymakers.[56] Even among the Muslim populations, there is skepticism about Turkey's motivations.[57] As a Bosnian NGO official alerted, "Bosnian people love Turkey, but they trust the US."[58]

---

[55] Exchange with a Slovakian NGO official, Berlin, December 15, 2016.
[56] Exchange with a Turkish scholar, Berlin, December 16, 2016.
[57] Email exchange with a NATO official, October 27, 2015.
[58] Interview with a Bosnian NGO official, Washington DC, October 10, 2012.

One Turkish diplomat acknowledges that "Turkey has an image pro-blem in Bosnia, and it needs to work on changing the perception that it only supports one entity."[59] A Serbian academic concurs that this image problem is due to the fact that "Turkey feels compelled to play a big brother role for the Bosnian Muslims."[60] A Bosnian think tank similarly recommends that Turkish foreign policymakers actively work toward developing an improved image in the entirety of Bosnia and Herzegovina, "even if that means formalizing existing relations" and refraining from being perceived as pro-Bosniak (Populari 2014, p. 50).

As one study concludes, even though Turkey has raised its diplomatic, cultural, and economic profile in the Western Balkans, the pattern is that "religious and ethnic 'kin' groups receive particular attention and bene-fits" (Mitrović Bošković et al. 2015, p. 111). Some note that it might be more appropriate to argue that Turkey enjoys greater soft power in the predominantly Muslim parts of the Balkans, such as the northern part of Serbia.[61] Others draw attention to the downside of the Turkish soap operas and note that they may create an adverse impact due to the fact that "many portray a traditional culture," while the people of the region aspire for modernization instead.[62] Similarly, Turkish investments are primarily directed toward Muslim areas in the region. To illustrate, out of the twenty-five branches of the Turkish Ziraat Bank in Bosnia and Herzegovina, only one is located in Republika Srpska.[63] TİKA is also perceived to improve conditions in Muslim societies in Bosnia, Kosovo, and Western Macedonia.[64]

Overall, the trade volume between Turkey and the countries in the region has yet to reach its full potential, despite the amplified rhetoric (Mitrović Bošković et al. 2015). Turkey is not listed among the top three trading partners of many countries in the region (Özkan 2012). Therefore, there is an unmet potential in terms of Turkey's greater economic influ-ence in the region. Nevertheless, as indicated by an interviewee, against this reality "the perception is completely different. When you ask people who they think invests more in the Western Balkans, Turkey comes up in the top three."[65]

[59] Interview with a Turkish diplomat, Sarajevo, May 9, 2013.
[60] Exchange with Serbian academic #1, Atlanta, Georgia, March 19, 2016.
[61] Exchange with Serbian academic #2, Atlanta, Georgia, March 19, 2016.
[62] Exchange with Serbian academic #1, Atlanta, Georgia, March 19, 2016.
[63] Exchange with a Bosnian NGO official, Berlin, December 15, 2016.
[64] Exchange with a Bosnian NGO official, Berlin, December 15, 2016.
[65] Exchange with a Bosnian NGO official, Berlin, December 15, 2016.

There is also the problem of "careless public rhetoric" on the part of the Turkish authorities, which damages bilateral relations.[66] This similarly illustrates the use of cheap-talk diplomacy. Moreover, indicating the top-down formulation of Turkish foreign policy in the region and a lack of a "consultative process," one international NGO official notes, "Turkish diplomats are usually the last ones to learn about the Turkish foreign policy in Western Balkans."[67] There seems to be a consensus among the interviewees that there is a need to be careful in communicating messages, as careless rhetoric has the potential to "fuel conflicts among different communities" in religiously heterogeneous societies.[68] A Bilgesam report (2014, p. 63) similarly warns that Turkish politicians should pay more attention to the rhetoric they adopt, as it has more negative than positive implications for Turkish foreign policy in the region. A high-level Kosovar policymaker adds, "Animosity towards Turks is a function of Communist legacy and the need to distinguish itself from the Ottoman past."[69]

Turkey's increasingly illiberal and majoritarian democracy presents a problematic role model for the Western Balkan countries, where there are plenty of ethnic divisions and gridlock. The negative trends in Turkish domestic politics, such as the deterioration of human rights, erosion of civil liberties and freedoms, the suppression and intimidation of the opposition, the growing tensions with the Kurdish minority, and an "electoral authoritarianism of a more markedly Islamic character" seem to backfire against Turkey's attempts to present itself as a country that wants further democratization, multiculturalism, and reform in the region (Özbudun 2014, p. 155, Dursun-Özkanca 2016, Vrăǎć 2016). As cautioned by an expert, "Turkey's soft power capability is decreasing amidst instability and decline in the economy."[70]

Erdoğan traditionally receives strong levels of support from the Balkans. Nevertheless, in the aftermath of the Gezi Park protests,[71] he lost some of that support in the Balkan public opinion (Sokollu 2013).

---

[66] Exchange with a Bosnian NGO official, Berlin, December 15, 2016.
[67] Interview with a Norwegian NGO official, Belgrade, September 29, 2015.
[68] Exchange with a Bosnian NGO official, Berlin, December 15, 2016.
[69] Interview with a high-level Kosovar politician, Belgrade, October 1, 2015.
[70] Interview with a Turkish NGO official, Belgrade, September 29, 2015.
[71] At the end of May 2013, Turkey experienced significant volatility during the Gezi Park protests, when a group of environmentalists initially protested against the plans to destroy Gezi Park in Istanbul's Taksim Square. The protests then spread throughout Turkey, with activists protesting the lack of pluralistic democracy, lack of freedom of speech, media, and assembly in the country, and interference in the citizens' private lives. The Gezi Park protests further polarized Turkish society (Özbudun 2014).

One interviewee states, "Many people would like to distance themselves from Turkey to acquire a more Western identity, especially with growing conservative and authoritarian tendencies in Turkey."[72] Yet, a number of Balkan Turkish NGOs still moved on with organizing rallies in Kosovo, Macedonia, Albania, and Bulgaria to indicate their support of Erdoğan (*Anadolu Agency* June 14, 2013).

During the attempted coup d'état in July 2016, many Balkan elites, including elites from Serbia, supported Erdoğan. In the words of an analyst, "Most of the Western Balkan officials somehow felt threatened that something similar could happen to them."[73] Immediately following the coup attempt, the government blamed the Gülenist factions in the military for attempting the coup. The tensions between the Turkish government and the Gülen movement had significant implications for the Western Balkans. While there was once a "significant pressure from the Turkish officials to open up Gülenist schools in the region, following the coup attempt, the Turkish diplomats are asking the Balkan countries to close these schools immediately."[74] On this topic, one expert indicates that the recent tensions between the Turkish government and the Gülen movement cause "a certain degree of conflict export from Turkey to Bosnia, Macedonia, and Kosovo ... [especially] in Turkish-led schools and some Islamic communities."[75] Others note that Turkey follows "a risky and polarizing foreign policy towards the Balkans" by favoring certain political elites in the Balkans (Büyük 2016). Some even argue that the increased authoritarian tendencies of Erdoğan and the strained relations with the United States cause Turkey to begin "a more Islamist push, especially with Bosnian Muslims and President Bakir Izetbegovic" (Serwer 2017).

CONCLUSION

Against the background of multiple crises in the EU, Turkey has been trying to fill a void in the region. Turkey increasingly pursues a more independent and active foreign policy in the Western Balkans and capitalizes on its rising cultural and economic presence to maximize its political power in the region in order to test and challenge the boundaries of its

[72] Interview with a Kosovar NGO official, October 1, 2015.
[73] Exchange with a Serbian NGO official, Berlin, December 15, 2016.
[74] Exchange with a Serbian NGO official, Berlin, December 15, 2016.
[75] Email correspondence with a German journalist based in Serbia, January 3, 2017.

partnership with the EU. Turkey pursues *Realpolitik*, a pragmatic and interests-based, rather than ideological, foreign policy in the region, and uses pragmatic Neo-Ottomanism through active diplomacy and economic statecraft to counter the influence of the EU in the region before the countries in the region become EU members. In the words of a British academic, "Turkey is in a similar position to Russia, as further penetration of EU rules in the Western Balkans means less market accessibility for Turkish companies."[76] Affirming the pragmatic nature of its foreign policy, a Bosnian policymaker interviewee notes that the Turkish foreign policy in the region is "all about economic interests, rather than emotions or ideology."[77] Similarly, another observer of Turkish politics notes, the AKP "instrumentally uses tradition" and is a "pragmatic Islamicist" party.[78] In the words of a scholar, "While the EU has brought together Turkey and the Balkans, the faltering influence of the Union now adds to Turkish confidence and prestige, bolstering a go-it-alone approach" (Bechev 2012, p. 138).

Changes in Turkish foreign policy are an attempt to respond to both deteriorating relations with the EU, due to serious setbacks in its EU accession negotiations process, and the decreasing leverage and presence of the EU in the region. Turkey's increased ambitions and activism in the region increasingly run the risk of putting the country in a strategic competition with the EU. Through boundary testing and challenging, Turkey seeks to hedge EU interests and power in the Western Balkans. It has furthered economic, diplomatic, cultural, and military ties with countries in the Western Balkans and elsewhere in its immediate neighborhood. Referring to the characterization of Turkey as a "Rover" in a leaked US diplomatic cable, a Balkans expert notes, "Rover is not a bad car, mainly because it is apparently quite affordable and accessible to all" (Šoštarić 2011).

Having said that, Turkey is increasingly apprehensive about its marginalization in the Euro-Atlantic security infrastructures. Turkish authorities interviewed strongly believe that the change in the region will come neither exclusively from the EU nor from NATO. They indicate that the human linkage, cultural interactions, and trade relations between Turkey and the Western Balkans are very important. With this comparative advantage, they maintain that Turkey has a remarkable potential to emerge as a regional power.

---

[76] Email exchange with an LSE academic, October 18, 2015.
[77] Interview with a Bosnian policymaker, Belgrade, October 1, 2015.
[78] Interview with an American academic, Washington DC, September 30, 2016.

This, in turn, raises the question of "whether Turkey would use the Western Balkans as a spoiler like Russia does."[79] Similarly, the Turkey–Russia rapprochement contributes to the concerns that Turkey increasingly pursues a spoiler role (Makovsky 2015). To illustrate, some Bosniak leaders in Montenegro "are taking Erdoğan's hint, viewing Moscow in a more positive light and connecting with the Chechen leadership" (Serwer 2017). This may have important implications for Bosnian Muslim elites in Bosnia (Serwer 2017). If Turkey increasingly plays a spoiler role, it would be possible to conclude that its Western Balkans foreign policy is in line with the process of boundary breaking with the West. However, thus far, Turkish foreign policy in the region employs boundary testing, through the use of active diplomacy and cheap-talk diplomacy, and goes as far as boundary challenging, through the use of economic statecraft and regional ownership, emphasizing the need for establishing more organic institutions for regional collaboration.

[79] Exchange with a Slovakian NGO official, Berlin, December 15, 2016.

3

The Turkish Veto over the EU–NATO
Security Exchange

Turkey is a member of NATO and not the EU, and the Republic of Cyprus[1] is a member of the EU and not NATO. Since the admission of the Republic of Cyprus into the EU in 2004, the EU–NATO official coordination efforts have been blocked by double vetoes from Turkey and Cyprus, making it impossible for the transatlantic partners to formally discuss issues that are central to both organizations (Müftüler-Baç 2008, European Commission 2009, Koops 2011, Dursun-Özkanca 2017). While the Republic of Turkey "refuses to allow Cyprus to participate in European Security and Defence Policy (ESDP) [and its successor CSDP][2] missions involving NATO intelligence and resources" and threatens to veto the Partnership for Peace (PfP) application of Cyprus with NATO, the Republic of Cyprus "refuses to allow Turkey to engage in the overall development of ESDP [and CSDP] to an extent commensurate with Turkey's military weight and strategic importance to Europe and transatlantic alliance" and vetoes the association of Turkey with the EDA (*Official Journal of the EU* 2010, E/75).

THE TURKISH VETO

Even though the EU and NATO conduct operations side by side, as in the cases of Afghanistan, the coast of Somalia, and more recently in the

---

[1] This book adopts the standard international usage of "Cyprus" a la Ker-Lindsay (2007) to mean the Republic of Cyprus.
[2] The ESDP has been renamed the CSDP following the ratification of the Lisbon Treaty in 2009.

Mediterranean Sea and at the Turkish-Syrian border,[3] the Turkish and Cypriot vetoes "prevent a deepening inter-organisational integration at the strategic level" (Koops 2011, p. 352). To illustrate, in 2007 NATO was unable to conclude an agreement with the EU police mission in Afghanistan to allow for the use of NATO capabilities, due to objections from Turkey.[4] As concisely summarized by a European Commission representative, "Whenever the EU talks about CSDP operations, Cyprus asks Turkish representatives to leave the room; and whenever NATO talks about NATO–EU relations, Turkey asks the Cypriot representatives to leave the room."[5] This situation causes annoyance to Euro-Atlantic allies and imposes real costs for the transatlantic community at a time when Western strategic interests in Ukraine, Iraq, Libya, and Syria require an enhanced dialogue and partnership between the EU and NATO, which share twenty-two members in common.[6]

In an attempt to go around the vetoes by Cyprus and Turkey, the EU and NATO have devised creative methods, including regular staff-to-staff contacts,[7] informal reciprocal briefings on operational issues of common interest and cross-invitation of the EU High Representative to the North Atlantic Council and the NATO Secretary General to the Political and Security Committee (European Council 2009, p. 2). Due to their informal status, the staff-level meetings lack the authority to formally take decisions on issues concerning EU–NATO collaboration (Duke 2008). Consequently, these institutions run the risk of duplicating each other's capabilities, as each seeks to improve its own effectiveness and capabilities in security affairs without well-functioning coordination.

---

[3] While NATO has been conducting the International Security Assistance Force (ISAF) in Afghanistan since August 2003, the EU has been conducting a police mission (EUPOL) since 2007. Similarly, since September 2008, NATO and EU naval forces have been deployed side by side, off the coast of Somalia, conducting anti-piracy operations. More recently, following the request of Turkey, Germany, and Greece in February 2016, NATO commenced its intelligence, surveillance, and reconnaissance activities in the Aegean Sea and at the Turkish-Syrian border and started to cooperate with the EU's Frontex border management agency to stem illegal trafficking and illegal migration in the Aegean Sea.

[4] The problem was practically addressed when the United States offered a solution, through which the EU mission would directly contact the NATO commander in Afghanistan when it needed NATO capabilities.

[5] Interview with an NGO official, Istanbul, July 11, 2011. Turkey has been opposing NATO's sharing of sensitive intelligence information with non-NATO EU members that did not sign a bilateral agreement with NATO on protecting classified information.

[6] This number will decrease to twenty-one following the United Kingdom's withdrawal from the EU.

[7] Interview with a Turkish diplomat, Ankara, July 18, 2011.

At NATO's Warsaw Summit in July 2016, the EU and NATO signed a Joint Declaration to improve the coordination between the two organizations in countering hybrid threats, enhancing resilience, defense capacity-building, cyber defense, maritime security, and exercises (NATO 2018). On December 6, 2016, the two organizations adopted forty-two actions in seven areas of cooperation identified in the Joint Declaration, including countering hybrid threats, operational cooperation concerning maritime issues, cyber security and defense, defense capabilities, defense industry and research, parallel and coordinated exercises, and defense and security capacity-building (European External Action Service 2016). There has been an increasing degree of coordination between the EU and NATO, especially at the staff level on practical issues such as hybrid operations and military exercises in the aftermath of the Warsaw Summit in 2016.[8]

Nevertheless, as the leaders of both organizations regularly acknowledge, this strategic partnership's full potential is yet to be realized (NATO 2010a, Rasmussen 2013, Tusk 2016, NATO 2017), and there is an urgent need for improvement of inter-organizational coordination, especially in "planning, procurement, and operations"[9] (NATO 2010b) and with regards to the "Berlin-Plus arrangements" (*Official Journal of the EU* 2010, E/69). Hence, it is important not to be overly optimistic about the future of EU–NATO cooperation,[10] as it has still not reached the strategic level in the aftermath of the Warsaw Summit.[11] As a US diplomat maintains, the "Berlin-Plus arrangements are not usable anywhere other than Bosnia right now."[12] As the European Council President Donald Tusk acknowledged following the signature of the EU–NATO Joint Declaration in Warsaw in July 2016, "Sometimes it seems as if the EU and NATO are on two different planets" (Tusk 2016).

The past decades witnessed the increasing ambitions of both NATO and the EU in security and defense. Both organizations have been expanding the scope of their activities in an attempt to respond to the changing security needs. Accordingly, besides lack of coordination and communication, another major concern is that these two organizations are increasingly duplicating each other's capabilities by "fishing from the same pool

---

[8] Exchange with a NATO official, Berlin, December 16, 2016.
[9] Interview with a top-level NATO official, Belgrade, October 2, 2015.
[10] Interview with a German NGO official, Belgrade, October 2, 2015.
[11] Interview with a NATO official, Berlin, December 16, 2016.
[12] Interview with a US diplomat, Belgrade, October 2, 2015.

of resources in terms of personnel and capabilities," creating a serious risk for amplified inter-institutional competition (Solana 2008). NATO's relationship with the EU has turned into a "frozen conflict," and only two out of the eight CSDP operations have been conducted within the Berlin-Plus arrangements (Martin 2015, p. 142). This creates a need to "ensure that countries are not developing duplicative capabilities."[13]

Despite the pertinence of this topic for theoretical and policy purposes, the motivations behind the Turkish veto have not received due attention in the academic literature. While there have been a number of academic works focusing on the pre-2003 impasse in the EU–NATO security relationship due to a diplomatic row between Turkey and Greece (Tocci and Houben 2001, Bağcı 2001, Missiroli 2002, Bilgin 2003, Çayhan 2003, Tsakonas 2008, Eralp 2009), there is a relative paucity of academic works that focus on the post-2003 impasse (see Keohane 2006, Ker-Lindsay 2007, Hofmann 2009, and Dursun-Özkanca 2017, for exceptions). Moreover, none of the existing scholarly works seek to embed Turkey's motivations into a conceptual framework. This chapter seeks to fill this important gap in the literature.

Turkey's Veto as Strategic Noncooperation

One of the main reasons behind Turkey's veto over NATO–EU security coordination is the country's exclusion from EU defense infrastructures, specifically the EDA. Using a phrase from the memoirs of US Secretary of State Dean Acheson (1969), the shared sentiment among the Turkish security elites interviewed for this research is that while Turkey was "present at the creation" when the foundations of European security infrastructures were laid, it is currently left absent in the finale of European defense cooperation despite original assurances from the EU. Turkey was historically well integrated into the European defense frameworks up until the early 2000s (Bağcı 2001, Dursun-Özkanca 2008). For instance, since its inception in 1976, Turkey was a founding member of the Independent European Programme Group (IEPG), a thirteen-member forum composed of the defense ministers of the European members of NATO to promote European cooperation on armaments and on research and development in defense technologies. In response to a decline in US military spending toward the end of the 1980s, the European members of NATO decided to take a more active role in military affairs and authored

[13] Interview with a US diplomat, Belgrade, October 2, 2015.

the IEPG Action Plan, which aimed to improve the "competitiveness of the European defense equipment industry" and develop a "European armaments market" (Walker and Gummett 1989, p. 430).

On December 4, 1992, the defense ministers of the IEPG nations agreed to transfer IEPG functions to the Western European Armaments Group (WEAG) in WEU, with the acknowledgment that all IEPG members should be entitled to fully participate in the activities of WEU, and with the same rights and responsibilities, in any future armaments cooperation forum (WEU 2014). While Turkey was a full member of the WEAG, it acquired associate member status in the WEU in 1992, due to its non-EU member status. As an associate member, Turkey enjoyed the same rights as the EU member states, including the right to present proposals and fully participate in the meetings of the General Affairs Council in operations in which it took part.

In November 1994, an informal group of experts of the EU and WEU was formed to study the options for a European Armaments Policy. However, the group declared that conditions did not exist for the creation of a European Armaments Agency. One of the unresolved issues was the relationship with Norway and Turkey. In order to alleviate the concerns of these NATO allies regarding the possibility of exclusion from the evolving European security frameworks, then US Secretary of State Madeleine Albright (1998) urged the alliance to follow the "3Ds": no duplication of capabilities, no diminution of NATO (or, as it was more commonly referred to as, no decoupling of forces between NATO and the EU), and no discrimination against the non-EU European members of NATO. At its Washington Summit in April 1999, the alliance confirmed the significance of the 3Ds, and emphasized "the utmost importance to ensuring the fullest possible involvement of non-EU European Allies in EU-led crisis response operations" (NATO 1999, paragraph 9d).

Following these assurances, Norway and Turkey gave permission for the transfer of WEU missions to the ESDP in 1999. In the subsequent summits, the European Council continued to promise non-EU European Members that they would not be excluded from any future inter-European collaboration on defense matters and that EU's ESDP capabilities would not be used against Turkey.[14] Similarly, during NATO's Prague Summit

[14] During the European Council Summit in Nice in December 2000, the EU member states elaborated on the proposals for asset borrowing from NATO and the participation of non-EU NATO members in the different phases of crisis management operations. Annex VI of the Presidency Conclusions states that the EU "wishes to receive contributions from

in November 2002, NATO announced its commitment to the EU–NATO relationship and emphasized "the need to find solutions satisfactory to all Allies on the issue of participation by non-EU European Allies, in order to achieve a genuine strategic partnership" (NATO 2002, paragraph 11). At the Copenhagen Summit of the EU on December 12–13, 2002, Turkey was promised that the EU operations would only be open to EU states that are either NATO allies or partners (European Council 2002b, p. 171). This seemed to ease the Turkish concerns, since this clause would exclude the participation of Cyprus in EU operations once it becomes a member of the EU. Moreover, at the same summit, December 2004 was designated as a date for starting the accession negotiations with Turkey. The designation of a specific date for starting the accession negotiations helped further alleviate the original Turkish concerns. Turkey therefore removed its veto over the signature of an EU–NATO agreement.

On December 16, 2002, NATO and the EU announced a Joint Declaration on ESDP, which initiated the Berlin-Plus Agreement. In that document, the EU ensured "the fullest possible involvement of non-EU European members of NATO within ESDP, implementing the relevant Nice Agreements" (NATO 2002b). The Berlin-Plus Agreement, which became effective in March 2003, aimed at reducing the likelihood of duplication between the two organizations and increasing coordination

the non-EU European NATO members and other countries which are candidates for accession to the EU, in particular those which have the determination and capability to commit considerable resources to participate in the Petersberg tasks" and "to consult such countries on a regular basis when there is no crisis and to associate them to the greatest possible extent in EU-led military operations in times of crisis" (European Council 2000, Annex VI). Formal relations between the two institutions were initiated through an exchange of letters between the NATO Secretary General and the EU Presidency in January 2001. Under UK and US leadership, through support from Spain and the Netherlands, the "Istanbul letters" were prepared to enable Turkey to send representatives to the Political and Security Committee of the EU, both "periodically" and "in the event of a crisis" (Martin 2015, p. 70). This initiative also proposed an improved role for the Committee of Contributors and "reassurance that Turkey would be involved in operations that either used NATO assets or were in the vicinity of Turkey" (Martin 2015, p. 70). Later on, the Istanbul letters were revised and introduced under the name the Ankara Document, which gave the guarantee that the ESDP missions would not be used against Turkey. At the European Council's Brussels Summit in October 2002, the EU gave assurances that "under no circumstances, nor in any crisis, will ESDP be used against an ally" in Annex II of the Presidency Conclusions, a document commonly referred to as the Nice Implementation Document or the Ankara Agreement (European Council 2002a, pp. 136–137). Building on the outcome of the Nice Summit, in October 2002, the European Council (2002a, p. 137) reiterated that the EU would have "permanent and continuing consultations with the non-EU European allies, covering a full range of security, defence, and crisis management issues."

among them. It was agreed that any formal political exchange between the two organizations is to take place through meetings between the Political and Security Committee (PSC) and the North Atlantic Council (NAC).

Through the Agreement, the non-EU European members of NATO,[15] such as Turkey, received a green light to participate in crisis management activities conducted under the ESDP framework when such operations employ NATO assets and capabilities. From the end of 2002 until May 2004, the EU–NATO coordination was managed rather smoothly.[16] Subsequently, through Council Joint Action 2004/551/ CFSP of July 12, 2004, the EU announced that it would "assimilate" or "incorporate" the WEAG into a new defense agency. On November 22, 2004, the defense ministers of the WEAG decided to dissolve the WEAG[17] and transfer all defense cooperation to the EDA before the middle of 2005 (Van Eekelen 2005).

In the WEU, Turkey used to enjoy having an equal say with the other WEU members, when it came to parliamentary scrutiny of European security and defense affairs. With the formation of the EDA, Turkey, like all non-EU WEAG countries, lost the privilege to enjoy an equal say with other WEU members on parliamentary scrutiny of European security and defense affairs, i.e. decision-making in EU crisis management operations.[18] Even though both the WEU (from 1992 to 1997) and the EU (from 1997 onward) continuously assured the non-EU NATO members that they would not be excluded from the decision-making processes

---

[15] Estonia, Latvia, Lithuania, Slovenia, and Slovakia were admitted into the EU in May 2004, shortly after their accession into NATO at the end of March 2004. In 2007, Romania and Bulgaria became EU members, leaving Iceland, Norway, and Turkey as the remaining non-EU European NATO members until 2009. In April 2009, Albania and Croatia became members of NATO and joined Iceland, Norway, and Turkey in the non-EU European members of NATO list. With the accession of Croatia into the EU in July 2013, and the membership of Montenegro in NATO in 2017, Iceland, Norway, Turkey, Albania, and Montenegro are the only remaining non-EU European members of NATO. Following the United Kingdom's official withdrawal from the EU, it will join this group of countries.

[16] Despite occasional diplomatic tensions between Turkey and Greece, two EU crisis management operations – Operation Concordia in the Former Yugoslav Republic of Macedonia and Operation EUFOR-ALTHEA in Bosnia and Herzegovina – were conducted under the Berlin-Plus framework.

[17] WEAG was terminated in May 2005.

[18] Participation agreements establishing the parameters for the participation of non-EU European members of NATO in the EU crisis management operations were signed in advance of the date of transfer in May 2005 with all relevant countries except for Turkey. Only in June 2006 did Turkey and the EU sign a similar agreement (*Official Journal of the EU* 2006), which was later ratified by Turkish Parliament in July 2007.

of a future armaments cooperation organization, with the admission of the Republic of Cyprus into the EU the whole picture has changed. Since 2004, the Republic of Cyprus vetoes Turkey's participation in the successor defense agency to the WEAG – the EDA. Consequently, Turkey, unlike Norway,[19] is still not able to secure an Association Agreement with the EDA. This contributes to grievances that Turkish policymakers have toward the EU and spurs Turkey's mistrust against the EU's intentions.

Perception of motives is very important in soft balancing (Pape 2005). As Art (2005, p. 182) indicates, the "influence motive" constitutes a case for soft balancing. Turkey certainly seems to have the influence motive vis-à-vis the EU. Many Turkish officials interviewed express that as one of the main contributors to European and transatlantic security, Turkey's exclusion from the decision-shaping mechanisms within CSDP causes "bitterness"[20] and "resentment"[21] toward the EU. Illustrating the lack of trust toward the EU, a Member of Turkish Parliament from the AKP notes that the situation since 2004 represents "violation of promises."[22] Another Turkish policymaker notes that Turkey's "constant frustration" with the EU led to a "revision of its constructive attitude."[23] A Member of the Turkish Parliament notes that the fact that Turkey is "not allowed to be an equal partner in European security decision-making and decision-shaping mechanisms" creates a significant grievance in Turkey.[24] As another interviewee puts it, as a country with the second-largest military

---

[19] Norway signed the Administrative Arrangement agreement with the EDA on March 7, 2006, which made it possible for the country to collaborate on defense equipment, joint defense research and technology projects, and joint development of future military capabilities in Europe. It also created a Consultative Committee for Norway and the EDA "to exchange views and information on matters of common interest falling within the scope of the Agency's mission" and aimed at ensuring that the Norwegian Ministry of Defense is kept fully informed of opportunities for future co-operation". Additionally, on May 26, 2008, Norway has further associated with the EDA through its participation in the Regime on Defence Procurement. Norway cooperates with all EDA directorates (Lindbäck 2009, p. 8).

[20] Interview with a former Turkish foreign minister, then Member of Turkish Parliament, Ankara, July 15, 2011.

[21] Interview with a Member of Turkish Parliament, Ankara, July 14, 2011; Interview with a former Turkish foreign minister, then Member of Turkish Parliament, Ankara, July 15, 2011; Interview with a Member of Turkish Parliament from the AKP, Ankara, July 13, 2011.

[22] Email correspondence with a Member of Turkish Parliament from the AKP, July 20, 2011.

[23] Interview with a Member of Turkish Parliament from the AKP, Ankara, July 14, 2011.

[24] Interview with a Member of Turkish Parliament from the AKP, Ankara, July 13, 2011.

forces in NATO, Turkey simply wants to "voice its concerns about a small country [Cyprus] holding the rest of the EU hostage."[25] Broken promises constitute one of the main reasons behind the mistrust at both the public and the elite levels toward the EU and its CSDP. This seems to fit well into the signaling behavior identified in the soft balancing literature that "cooperation cannot be taken for granted to the point that [a country is] repeatedly shortchanged in the decision-making process" (Kelley 2005, p. 168). Using its veto, Turkish policymakers signal to the EU that they want to be treated as equals.[26]

This situation contributes to the feeling of alienation from the West, leading to blunt criticism of the EU by Turkey. The Turkish Ministry of Foreign Affairs (2019c) underlines that there is a "restrictive philosophy on the part of the EU" when it comes to the involvement of non-EU European allies in the CSDP. The ministry requests the reinstatement of this imbalance, which works to the disadvantage the non-EU European allies (Turkish Ministry of Foreign Affairs 2019c). It criticizes the EU for "narrowly" interpreting the Nice Implementation Document and using the document "as a restrictive tool, rather than a mutually beneficial, progressive one" (Turkish Ministry of Foreign Affairs 2019c).

The Turkish veto since 2004 has been a persistent headache for EU–NATO security relations. In line with the expectations of soft balancing, Turkey's veto over the EU's assured access to NATO planning facilities for crisis management and blocking of the sharing of sensitive intelligence information between the EU and NATO impose real military costs for the Union. Through its veto, Turkey seeks to delay, complicate, and increase the costs of EU's military coordination with NATO. As defense budgets continue to shrink across Europe, the EU cannot afford to pursue independent security and defense policies outside of NATO. The lack of coordination between the two institutions further causes operational problems and leads to material and personnel costs, leading a number of European leaders to accuse Turkey of playing with peacekeepers' lives in Kosovo, Afghanistan, and elsewhere (EurActiv.com 2009, *Hürriyet Daily News* August 28, 2009, *Official Journal of the EU* 2010, E/69).

---

[25] Interview with a former Turkish foreign minister, then Member of Turkish Parliament, Ankara, July 15, 2011.
[26] Interview with a former Turkish foreign minister, then Member of Turkish Parliament, Ankara, July 15, 2011; Interview with a Member of Turkish Parliament from the AKP, Ankara, July 13, 2011; Interview with a Member of Turkish Parliament, Washington DC, September 30, 2016.

In preparation for NATO's Lisbon Summit in 2010, then NATO Secretary General Rasmussen came up with a proposal for "the EU to conclude a security agreement with Turkey, give Turkey special status with the [EDA], and involve it in decision-making on EU security missions" (Vogel and Brand 2010). However, such attempts have been in vain, mainly because of the opposition from the Republic of Cyprus. Therefore, through strategic noncooperation, i.e. not letting NATO further collaborate with the EU, and imposing real costs on the EU, Turkey seeks to restore the balance to its advantage and increase its future influence vis-à-vis the EU.

Entangling Diplomacy

Besides strategic noncooperation, Turkey engages in entangling diplomacy and attempts to use the rules and procedures of NATO to influence the EU's policies, especially regarding the resolution of the Cyprus conflict. As indicated by many Turkish, Greek Cypriot, and European interviewees, "The resolution of the Cyprus problem and the current impasse transatlantic relations are inseparable."[27] As a German NGO official astutely observes, "As long as the Cyprus issue is unresolved, the cooperation between EU and NATO will remain interrupted."[28]

As a NATO official indicates, the resolution of the Cyprus issue is "a pre-condition to closer structural cooperation between NATO and the EU," which "in turn would allow formal NAC-PSC meetings, replacing the informal meetings which have become the norm in recent years."[29] As stated by another interviewee, the solution of the Cyprus problem cannot be delayed forever, as "the stakes are getting higher."[30] By using its veto power in NATO, Turkey seeks to put pressure on the EU to help resolve the Cyprus problem in line with its key interests.

Although Turkey has accepted to extend the Customs Union Agreement to the newly admitted EU countries (including the Republic of Cyprus) by signing the 2004 Ankara Protocol (commonly referred to as the Additional Protocol), it refuses to implement the terms of the protocol to the Republic of Cyprus,[31] until a negotiated settlement is reached in

---

[27] Interview with a Greek Cypriot academic, Nicosia, July 20, 2011.
[28] Interview with a German NGO official, Belgrade, October 2, 2015.
[29] Author's email exchange with a NATO official, February 27, 2017.
[30] Interview with a Greek Cypriot diplomat, Nicosia, July 22, 2011.
[31] Interview with a European Union official, Nicosia, July 20, 2011.

favor of the Turkish Cypriot community in the north and the Republic of Cyprus allows direct trade with the Turkish Cypriots and removes its economic isolation of the "Turkish Republic of Northern Cyprus."[32] Turkey's refusal to extend the Additional Protocol to the Republic of Cyprus constitutes another instance of the use of strategic noncooperation. It is a result of a deliberative cost–benefit analysis on the part of Turkey, as Turkey uses its veto power over EU–NATO security relations as political leverage over its EU accession negotiations.

An overwhelming majority of the Turkish elites interviewed seems to hold the opinion that some countries in the EU want to use the unresolved Cyprus problem as an "excuse" to delay the resumption of Turkey's accession negotiation process.[33] A Member of the Turkish Parliament from AKP questioned the seriousness of the EU's intentions for having Turkey as a member and noted that if it were serious it would have put pressure on Cyprus to remove its veto over accession negotiation chapters.[34] This may be regarded as cheap-talk diplomacy, as Turkish authorities try to verbally convey the message that the status quo is unacceptable.

Nevertheless, several European and Greek Cypriot interviewees characterize the Turkish unwillingness to implement the Additional Protocol as "arrogant behavior"[35] and add that it is a legal obligation for Turkey to implement the Additional Protocol.[36] The implementation of the Additional Protocol has been added to Turkey's EU accession negotiations framework, even though it was not originally a part of it. Unless Turkey implements the Additional Protocol, it has no chances of getting admitted into the EU. The issue remains unresolved to this day despite diplomatic initiatives attempting to resolve the issue of the ports and airports.[37]

In response to Turkey's demands for greater involvement in CSDP decision-making and decision-shaping processes, one Greek Cypriot

[32] Interview with a Member of Turkish Parliament from AKP, Ankara, July 13, 2011; Interview with a Turkish diplomat, Ankara, July 18, 2011; Interview with an international NGO official, Istanbul, July 11, 2011.

[33] Interview with a former Turkish foreign minister, then Member of Turkish Parliament, Ankara, July 15, 2011; Interview with a Member of Turkish Parliament from AKP, Ankara, July 18, 2011.

[34] Interview with a Member of Turkish Parliament from the AKP, Ankara, July 18, 2011.

[35] Interview with a Greek Cypriot academic, Nicosia, July 21, 2011.

[36] Interview with a former Minister of the Republic of Cyprus, Nicosia, July 20, 2011; Interview with a Greek Cypriot academic Nicosia, July 21, 2011.

[37] Interview with an international NGO official, Istanbul, July 11, 2011.

diplomat emphasizes that third-party countries (like Turkey) may not have the same role and responsibilities in CSDP processes unless they become a full member of the EU.[38] Providing a legal explanation for the Cypriot veto against Turkey's association with the EDA, a Greek Cypriot official notes that countries need to sign a security of information agreement with the EU in order to become an Associate Member of the EDA.[39] Besides this technical/legal explanation, there is a political motivation behind the Cypriot veto as acknowledged by many Greek Cypriot interviewees, i.e., to compensate for the power asymmetry between Turkey and the Republic of Cyprus. Many Greek Cypriot elites state that by blocking the Turkish Associate Membership in EDA, Cyprus "gains leverage internationally."[40] This, in turn, is expected to help put pressure on Turkey to diplomatically recognize the Republic of Cyprus.

According to a Member of the Turkish Parliament from the AKP, "The opening of ports and airports by Turkey is possible but it would require the Republic of Cyprus to stop unilaterally freezing the six chapters in Turkey's accession negotiations."[41] In the words of another Turkish interviewee, "[t]here is a vicious cycle" here: "The EU says that within the Ankara Protocol, you should open up ports and airports to the Republic of Cyprus; and Turkey says that you accepted Cyprus into the EU without a diplomatic solution [–] how can Turkey be expected to unilaterally implement the Additional Protocol, without the resolution of the Cyprus problem[?]"[42]

One Greek Cypriot interviewee suggests a "simple solution to this problem" and notes that Cyprus would lift its veto on Turkey's affiliation with the EDA if Turkey allows Cyprus to join the PfP program."[43] According to the Turkish officials, however, since it was the EU that made the promise that Turkey would be affiliated with the EDA as soon as the WEU is terminated, the responsibility to convince the Republic of Cyprus to remove its veto on Turkey's Associate Membership into the EDA falls on the Union.[44] They underline that this outcome would be in

[38] Interview with a Greek Cypriot diplomat, Nicosia, July 21, 2011.

[39] Interview with a Greek Cypriot diplomat, Nicosia, July 21, 2011.

[40] Interviews with Greek Cypriot diplomats, Nicosia, July 21, 2011.

[41] Interview with a Member of Turkish Parliament from the AKP, Ankara, July 14, 2011.

[42] Interview with a Member of Turkish Parliament from the AKP, Ankara, July 18, 2011.

[43] Interview with a Greek Cypriot academic, Nicosia, July 20, 2011.

[44] Email correspondence with a Member of Turkish Parliament from the AKP, July 20, 2011; Interview with a Turkish diplomat, Ankara, July 18, 2011.

the strategic interest of the EU.[45] Many Turkish interviewees add that the country is legally on sound ground according to the Berlin-Plus Agreement and acknowledge that Turkey uses strategic noncooperation in an attempt to serve Turkish interests better in the future.[46]

Additionally, there seems to be a technical excuse used by Turkey for preventing the intelligence information exchange with non-NATO EU member states. Some Turkish policymakers voice concerns that there might be a "misuse of sensitive information by some countries" if such information were to be shared with non-PfP/non-NATO members of the EU.[47] Cyprus is the only such country, following Malta's signature of PfP agreement with NATO in 2008. A retired Member of the Turkish Parliament notes, "If Turkey would allow a non-NATO EU member state to have access to sensitive intelligence, then the way for other third parties to have access to such information would have opened," and it would set a "dangerous precedent" in security affairs.[48]

Uncertainties regarding its EU accession further exacerbate Turkey's lack of trust toward the EU and its CSDP and motivate the blockage of NATO–EU security relations, which allows for an increased bargaining position against the EU by pursuing boundary challenging. Turkey signed the Ankara Agreement with the European Economic Community in 1963 and became a candidate country in 1999. With the opening of EU accession negotiations in October 2005, Turkey's unease with the plans for an autonomous European security infrastructure outside of NATO was temporarily alleviated. The prospects of EU accession provided strong incentives for Turkey to approach such ambitions with more tolerance. Nevertheless, as noted in the Introduction, despite an initial period of momentum and optimism the Turkey–EU accession negotiations have reached a stalemate over the past few years. Moreover, as noted earlier in this chapter, the relationship between Turkey and the EDA is not normalized, and it is expected to remain so unless the veto from the Republic of Cyprus is alleviated. As indicated by a NATO official, "[t]he Office of the NATO Secretary General continues

[45] Interview with a Turkish diplomat, Ankara, July 18, 2011.
[46] Interview with a Turkish NGO official, Istanbul, July 12, 2011; Interview with a former Turkish foreign minister, then Member of Turkish Parliament, Ankara, July 15, 2011; Interview with a Member of Turkish Parliament from the AKP, Ankara, July 18, 2011.
[47] Interview with a Member of Turkish Parliament, Ankara, July 14, 2011.
[48] Interview with a former Turkish foreign minister, then Member of Turkish Parliament, Ankara, July 15, 2011.

to raise the issue at high-level meetings with the Turkish government to resolve this blockage."[49]

As Turkey's hopes for becoming an integral part of the EU and its security infrastructures grow dim, the country tries not to lose any more diplomatic, political, and military clout. One of the most effective venues where Turkey may exercise such clout is NATO (Dursun-Özkanca 2017). As such, the country opposes NATO's sharing of sensitive intelligence information with non-NATO EU members that did not sign a bilateral agreement with NATO on protecting classified information. On that topic, the official website of the Turkish Ministry of Foreign Affairs (2019c) proclaims:

There is dire need for renovated thinking in the EU ... Turkey is a hard and soft security provider at a geostrategic location of significant relevance for the EU. She is also a NATO ally willing and able to provide considerable support for ESDP undertakings. The consideration that is justifiably given within NATO to the need to be open and transparent with Partners contributing to Alliance operations should be of relevance to the EU as well ... Furthermore, despite its commitments, the EU has neither finalized cooperation arrangements between Turkey and the European Defence Agency, nor signed an agreement for [an] exchange of classified information with Turkey, due to the objection of some EU members (including Cyprus).

In response to the Cypriot veto, Turkey threatens to use its veto power against a possible application for the PfP from the Republic of Cyprus, even though Turkey traditionally favors the expansion of NATO membership. According to one Member of the Turkish Parliament from the AKP, the reason why Turkey does not allow Cyprus to enter into NATO is due to its "skepticism that the current situation with the Cypriot veto preventing Turkey's integration with the EU CSDP infrastructures would then be repeated within NATO," which would significantly change the dynamic of the relationship between the two countries in such a way that Cyprus, as a new NATO member, would hold the same veto power Turkey holds within NATO.[50] As mentioned by another interviewee, "Should Cyprus become a PfP member, it would no longer be classified as a country without a security agreement with NATO," and "Turkey would no longer be able to prevent Cyprus' involvement in NATO–EU coordination meetings."[51]

---

[49] Email exchange with a NATO official, February 27, 2017.
[50] Interview with a Member of Turkish Parliament from the AKP, Ankara, July 14, 2011.
[51] Interview with a Turkish NGO official, Istanbul, July 12, 2011.

Therefore, in retaliation to the Cypriot veto against its EDA affiliation, Turkey blocks NATO's sharing of intelligence information with the EU, when Cyprus is present at joint EU–NATO meetings. Turkey essentially signals an important message to the EU by making a direct connection between its EDA affiliation and the sharing of sensitive intelligence information between the EU and NATO. In other words, it engages in issue-linkage bargaining. In return, the EU does not allow engaging in broader discussions with NATO without all of its members present at meetings.[52] As noted at the 2007 Annual Session of NATO Parliamentary Assembly, "this situation has created a stalemate in which the two institutions can only formally discuss 'Berlin-Plus' operations ... More problematically, as a result of this situation, the organizations as a whole cannot formally discuss non–'Berlin-Plus' missions ... at all at the ambassadorial level" (NATO 2007). As cautioned by a NATO official, "Turkey may [eventually] adopt a less constructive stance in the Alliance towards the implementation of the NATO–EU cooperation agenda agreed at the [Warsaw] Summit depending on the status of the EU–Turkey relations."[53]

Turkey's Issue-Linkage Bargaining and Inter-institutional Balancing against the EU Using NATO

As established in the literature, soft balancing is especially effective in power asymmetries. As one foreign policy expert points out, "The worst-case scenario for conflict resolution is when one country is in and another one is out of the international institution."[54] This worst-case scenario seems to come to life, since Turkey is a member of NATO and not of the EU, and the Republic of Cyprus is a member of the EU and not of NATO.

One interviewee notes that, while "for some observers looking from the outside, it might seem like Turkey wants to create problems within NATO, this is not an accurate understanding."[55] In order to level the playing field against the EU, through its veto power in NATO, Turkey utilizes the inter-institutional balancing tool to increase its future leverage vis-à-vis the EU. The Turkish veto over the EU–NATO security exchange is mainly due to the fear of loss of influence in crisis management activities as a result of more operations being conducted under the autonomous EU framework, rather than

---

[52] Interview with a Greek Cypriot academic, Nicosia, July 21, 2011.
[53] Email exchange with a NATO official, February 27, 2017.
[54] Interview with an Austrian scholar, Belgrade, September 29, 2015.
[55] Interview with a Turkish NGO official, Istanbul, July 12, 2011.

under the NATO command structure, where Turkey enjoys equal status with other allies. As a non-EU member of NATO, Turkey is concerned about the decline of NATO's role vis-à-vis the CSDP in the European context (Dursun-Özkanca 2008) and "pursues a NATO-first policy."[56] It opposes the dominance of the EU in European security, especially if it is expected to come at the expense of Turkey in particular and NATO in general.[57] In retaliation for its exclusion from the EDA, Turkey engages in inter-institutional balancing using its institutional veto player position within NATO and vetoes sharing of sensitive intelligence information at the joint NATO–EU meetings. The Turkish veto may, therefore, be explained as a signaling of resolve (Pape 2005) to challenge the boundary of its relations with the EU.

Turkish policymakers interviewed underline that Turkey's exclusion from European defense frameworks represents a violation of the "no discrimination against the non-EU European members of NATO" principle. They hold the opinion that it presents evidence of an anti-Turkish bias in the current EU framework and note that the EU is willing to break its promises by leaving Turkey outside of the EDA as well as the EU and go against Turkey's key interests in the Cyprus conflict. So long as the prospects for its EU accession remain low and its exclusion from developments in European security infrastructures continues, Turkey will most likely "remain skeptical of the EU and its CSDP initiatives"[58] and continue soft balancing against the EU (Dursun-Özkanca 2017).

In line with the definition of institutional binding (Ikenberry 2001), weaker states seek to restrain stronger states through institutional agreements. Accordingly, the Turkish veto provides an excellent illustration of "institutional binding," as Turkey seeks to achieve outcomes favorable to the country's strategic interests, while mitigating power asymmetries (Ikenberry 2001, p. 14). By projecting its own security/foreign-policy issues into NATO, Turkey hopes to engage in inter-institutional balancing against the EU, in order to increase its diplomatic leverage against the EU. As Turkey officially warns, if the Cyprus problem remains unresolved and Turkey's concerns with regard to its participation in the CSDP are not addressed, "no further movement should be expected on the NATO-EU dossier" (Turkish Ministry of Foreign Affairs 2019b).[59]

---

[56] Interview with a Member of Turkish Parliament from the AKP, Ankara, July 13, 2011.
[57] Interview with a Turkish diplomat, Ankara, July 18, 2011.
[58] Interview with an official at the Delegation of the EU to Turkey, Ankara, July 15, 2011.
[59] On the resolution of the Cyprus problem, many interviewees voiced optimism for the negotiations that occurred in 2017 (Interviews with a Member of Turkish Parliament,

Illustrating the issue-linkage bargaining aspect of the topic, one Turkish interviewee argues that it would not be strategic for Turkey to remove its blockage unless the Cyprus conflict is resolved and there is a clear calendar for Turkish membership in the EU.[60] In other words, Turkey holds this veto card as a "quid pro quo for its membership into the EU."[61] This is indicative of Turkey's attempts to test and challenge boundaries with the EU. A NATO official interviewee maintains:

Starting formal NAC-PSC meetings could mean a broader range of issues being discussed, opportunities for more frequent exchange of information at the institutional level and harmonization of political agendas. However, the political problems that have impeded the two organizations from reaching the full potential in their cooperation are still there and not likely to disappear in the near future. Turkey will continue to have a major influence on the pace and scope of NATO–EU cooperation (including maritime issues linked to migration), even if a solution to the Cyprus issue is reached.[62]

Turkey may be convinced to allow for increased inter-institutional cooperation if the EU offers Turkey an association agreement with the EDA and removes some of the frozen chapters to allow for a renewed momentum in the country's EU accession negotiations. The Turkish policymakers interviewed in this book seem to believe that the responsibility to convince Cyprus to remove its veto on Turkey's EDA associate membership falls on the EU, since "it was the EU that failed to keep its promise [of integrating the country in European defense and procurement infrastructures]."[63] They consistently remind the EU that the removal of the Cypriot veto is in the strategic interest of the Union.[64] The Ministry of Foreign Affairs of Turkey (Turkish Ministry of Foreign Affairs 2019c) similarly adopts an accusatory tone and states:

a former US diplomat, and an EU official, Washington DC, September 30, 2016; Interview with a US NGO official, Belgrade, October 2, 2015). Others, however, warned against being "overly optimistic," underlining the potential spoiler role of Russia in preventing the resolution of the conflict due to its interests in the gas future for Europe (Interview with a former US diplomat, Washington DC, September 30, 2016) or the long track record of unsuccessful negotiation rounds on the island (Interview with a British journalist via Skype, October 14, 2016). The negotiations came to an end in 2017 without the resolution of the conflict.

[60] Interview with a Turkish security advisor, Ankara, July 15, 2011; Interview with a Turkish-American academic, October 21, 2016.
[61] Interview with a Turkish-American academic, October 21, 2016.
[62] Email exchange with a NATO official, February 27, 2017.
[63] Email correspondence with a Member of Turkish Parliament from AKP, July 20, 2011; Interview with a Turkish diplomat, Ankara, July 18, 2011.
[64] Interview with a Turkish diplomat, Ankara, July 18, 2011.

Greek Cypriots have hindered the approval of the [implementation] document [between Turkey and the EDA] at the EU meeting at the technical level, held on 14 April 2005 in Brussels, by emphasizing it was based on "political considerations." The approval of the implementation document, which would establish the relations between Turkey and EDA, would help contribute to the development of European defense capabilities. The EU is yet to honor its commitments. This is not only about complying with the basic principle of *pacta sunt servanda* but also a necessity for a fruitful cooperation between NATO and the EU in the field of capacity building.

In 2014, at the thirteenth annual Berlin Security Conference, the then Turkish Defense Minister İsmet Yılmaz similarly complained about Turkey's exclusion from the EDA and failure to sign agreements on exchanging classified information, and added, "We strongly believe that non-EU NATO allies [in Europe] should be involved in the EU defence initiative, and be part of the decision making process" (Jennings 2014). Turkish elites also point to a sizable capabilities/expectations gap with regard to the CSDP[65] and maintain that the multiple crises that the EU has to deal with hinder the development of autonomous CSDP capabilities due to the decreasing defense budgets of many European countries.[66] Many emphasize that it is not in the interest of the EU "to exclude such a strong military country [Turkey] from the CSDP."[67]

Turkish foreign policymakers also realize that the EDA is not a decision-making agency and that it only makes recommendations, limiting the Agency's practical influence. They recognize that "there are many ongoing procurement fora within the NATO Alliance."[68] Therefore, from Turkey's perspective, it may not be worthwhile for Turkey to lose important political and diplomatic leverage against the EU by relinquishing its EU–NATO security exchange veto over the EDA associate membership issue. Accordingly, at least in the short to medium term, it is reasonable to expect Turkey to continue signaling of resolve to maintain a more equitable relationship with the EU through its veto power in NATO. Using issue-linkage bargaining, Turkey seeks to test the boundaries with the West, increasingly challenging such boundaries in an attempt to save face diplomatically.

---

[65] Interview with a Turkish scholar, Ankara, July 16, 2011.
[66] Interview with a Member of Turkish Parliament from AKP, Ankara, July 18, 2011.
[67] Interview with a Turkish scholar, Ankara, July 16, 2011.
[68] Interview with a Turkish NGO official, Istanbul, July 12, 2011.

CONCLUSION

As this chapter illustrates, through the use of a number of foreign policy tools, including strategic noncooperation, entangling diplomacy, issue-linkage bargaining, and inter-institutional balancing, Turkey uses its veto power in NATO as a way to expand the number of stakeholders on the Cyprus problem and increase pressures on the Greek Cypriots for resolving the conflict. Through its veto, Turkey engages in strategic noncooperation, and seeks to strengthen Turkey's negotiating position vis-à-vis the EU in its accession process. As the relationship between Turkey and the EDA is not normalized, Turkey continues to engage in boundary testing and boundary challenging against the EU, to gain leverage vis-à-vis the EU, in hopes that it would eventually be integrated into EDA. Put simply, "by using the mechanisms for mutual regulation or for the containment of member states by not cooperating" (Saltzman 2012b, p. xxviii), Turkey hopes that its "voice will be heard during the various deliberations and activities of the institution" and that its "position will have an effect on the final outcomes" (Saltzman 2012b, p. xxviii). The resolution of the Cyprus conflict would have positive spillover effects on security in the Eastern Mediterranean, Turkey–EU relations and EU–NATO security coordination.

Having said all this, the EU is still perceived to be "a major source of public goods" that "cannot simply be replaced" (Paul 2005, p. 59). Accordingly, at least for the time being, despite its blockage of NATO–EU security relations, Turkey continues to contribute troops to EU-led operations, such as EUFOR/ALTHEA, European Union Police Mission (EUPM) in Bosnia and Herzegovina, and EULEX in Kosovo. Turkey still aspires to enhance its military cooperation with CSDP and continues to have economic cooperation through the Customs Union Agreement. The official position provided by the Turkish Ministry of Foreign Affairs is that for Turkey, the strategic partnership between the EU and NATO is "very valuable" and that Turkey strongly supports the efforts to improve the cooperation between the two institutions.[69] As stated by a diplomat at the Turkish Ministry of Foreign Affairs, "Even though there are attempts to prevent Turkey from contributing to CSDP operations in Kosovo and Afghanistan, Turkey strongly supports the relationship between EU and NATO."[70]

---

[69] Interview with a Turkish diplomat, Ankara, July 18, 2011.
[70] Interview with a Turkish diplomat, Ankara, July 18, 2011.

Turkish authorities want greater involvement in CSDP decision-making and defense procurement and deem the ability to engage in decision-shaping in CSDP as vital.[71] Many interviewees hold the opinion that it is in Turkey's strategic security interests "to continue being an integral part of the European security infrastructures" and affiliated with the EDA.[72] They emphasize that this affiliation would also be beneficial for European defense procurement, since "Turkey is already involved in a number of defense industry collaboration projects with its European counterparts."[73] Many Turkish interviewees note that it is in the interest of the West to have an ally like Turkey in the region. As noted by an interviewee, an active Turkish involvement in Euro-Atlantic security frameworks would contribute to the stability in the Middle East and North Africa, Afghanistan, Pakistan.[74]

Only time will tell whether Turkey would be willing to lift its veto, so that the transatlantic allies could resume their strategic exchange and coordination, or choose to pursue boundary breaking against the EU. The analysis here leaves us with cautious pessimism about the removal of Turkey's veto. As long as the uncertainties around Turkey's EU accession and EDA associate membership prevail and the Cyprus conflict remains unresolved, Turkey's boundary testing against the EU – through entangling diplomacy, cheap-talk diplomacy, and issue-linkage bargaining – and boundary challenging – through strategic noncooperation and inter-institutional balancing – will likely continue.

[71] Interview with a Turkish NGO official, Istanbul, July 12, 2011.
[72] Interview with a Member of Turkish Parliament from AKP, Ankara, July 18, 2011.
[73] Interview with a Member of Turkish Parliament from the AKP, Ankara, July 18, 2011.
[74] See, for instance, interview with a Member of Turkish Parliament from the AKP, Ankara, July 18, 2011.

4

The EU–Turkey Deal on Refugees

Turkey functions as a major transit country for refugees en route to Europe fleeing from civil wars and instability in the Middle East and North Africa. As noted in the Introduction and the previous chapter, Turkey's relations with the EU have become tense over the lack of progress in its EU accession negotiations and its exclusion from European security and defense infrastructures, despite assurances from the EU. The EU–Turkey relationship has become even more controversial due to the refugee deal brokered between the two parties on March 18, 2016.

This chapter examines the EU–Turkey refugee deal and situates it under the proposed intra-alliance opposition framework. It demonstrates that, by using tools like compellent threats, Turkey takes advantage of the urgency of the refugee crisis as leverage to extract important benefits from the EU – such as bringing momentum to its accession negotiation talks, acquiring visa liberalization with the EU, and revising its Customs Union Agreement with the EU – and, more importantly, to bring the bilateral relations on a more equal footing. The chapter ends with an exploration of the factors that jeopardize the deal – such as the domestic political factors, Turkey's non-application of certain provisions of the UN Refugee Convention, and difficulty of implementing the legal changes that the EU requires – and analyzes the implications for Turkey's relations with the West.

AN OVERVIEW OF THE EU–TURKEY REFUGEE DEAL

The EU has been experiencing the biggest refugee crisis since World War II, as a result of a large influx of refugees and immigrants from the civil wars in the Middle East and North Africa and the lack of economic opportunities in those regions. Starting in 2015, the refugee crisis has escalated, presenting a major challenge for the EU to manage. Turkey has been following an open-door policy since the beginning of the Syrian civil war (Tolay 2014). Hosting close to three million Syrian refugees since the beginning of 2017, Turkey has emerged as a key actor in dealing with the refugee/immigration crisis, acquiring a substantial leverage vis-à-vis the EU in the longer term.

The EU has a long track record of externalizing migration policy to third countries (Lavenex and Uçarer 2004). The EU–Turkey deal on the refugee crisis is no exception to this. In the words of an interviewee, instead of developing a common approach, "the EU tried to externalize the [refugee] crisis to third countries, especially to Turkey."[1] The European Council adopted the EU–Turkey Joint Action Plan on November 29, 2015. The European Commission announced that the Joint Action Plan is the outcome of an understanding and a "spirit of burden sharing" between the EU and Turkey to "step up their cooperation on support of Syrians under temporary protection and migration management in a coordinated effort to address the crisis created by the situation in Syria" (European Commission 2015a).

For Turkey–EU relations, the Joint Action Plan provided "concrete actions with associated timelines . . . such as regular high-level meetings, the opening of new chapters, further dialogue in energy cooperation, and upgrading of the Customs Union . . . [and] the possibility of visa-free travel for Turkish citizens as early as 2016" (Şenyuva and Üstün 2015). The Plan announced that Turkey's EU "accession process needs to be re-energized" through the opening of Chapter 33 on "Financial and Budgetary Provisions" in accession negotiations and the provision of "an initial 3 billion Euros of additional resources" by the EU for the welfare and protection of Syrian refugees in Turkey (European Commission 2015b). It also announced that both sides welcome "the announcement to hold the Intergovernmental Conference on December 14, 2015 for opening Chapter 17 [on Economic and Monetary Policy]" (European Commission 2015b). Through the Joint Action Plan, the EU announced that it commends Turkey's commitment "to accelerate the fulfillment of the Visa Roadmap benchmarks vis-à-vis all participating Member States" (European Commission 2015b). The document reiterated the need for the establishment of a High Level Economic Dialogue Mechanism for the

---

[1] Exchange with a Turkish scholar, Berlin, December 16, 2016.

enhancement of bilateral economic relations, and the establishment of a High Level Energy Dialogue and Strategic Energy Cooperation, as well as the upgrading of the Customs Union between Turkey and the EU (European Commission 2015b).

Building on and updating the November 2015 Joint Action Plan, Turkey and the EU finalized a deal on March 18, 2016, referred to as the "EU–Turkey Statement," designed to stem the flow of refugees to Europe. The negotiated deal became operational on March 20, 2016 (European Council 2016). It announced the following nine measures: the return of all irregular migrants crossing from Turkey into Greek islands, as from March 20, 2016, to Turkey; the "1:1 scheme" – the resettlement of one Syrian from Turkey to the EU (taking into account the UN Vulnerability Criteria) for every Syrian returned to Turkey from Greek islands – up to a limit of 72,000; prevention of new sea or land routes for illegal migration from Turkey to the EU; the activation of a Voluntary Humanitarian Admission Scheme; the acceleration of the fulfillment of the visa liberalization roadmap vis-à-vis all participating member states with a view to lifting the visa requirements for Turkish citizens by the end of June 2016, "provided that all benchmarks have been met" through the fulfillment of seventy-two criteria; the speeding up of the EU's disbursement of the initially allocated 3 billion EUR under the Facility for Refugees in Turkey and funding of further projects for persons under temporary protection; the continuation of the efforts for upgrading of the Customs Union; the re-energizing of the Turkish accession process as set out in the joint statement of November 29, 2015; and a joint endeavor to improve humanitarian conditions inside Syria, in particular near the Turkish border (European Council 2016). The European Parliament (2016) also made the removal of the emergency rule a precondition for its review of visa liberalization.

Issue-Linkage Bargaining

The EU–Turkey refugee deal provides an excellent illustration of Turkey's employment of issue-linkage bargaining, compellent threats, and blackmail to effectively bolster its hand vis-à-vis the EU and have an increased bargaining position against the EU in the future. As Turkey does not want to be locked in an "asymmetric bargaining relationship" (Kelley 2005, p. 159), it sought to restructure the status quo by using the imminence of the refugee crisis to level the playing field and force the EU to undertake more intensive cooperation with the country. As noted by an interviewee, in the EU–Turkey refugee deal the motivation of the EU is the increasing popularity of far-right political parties and the containment of the refugee crisis, while the motivation of the Turkish government is the financial support along with other perks to be derived from the EU.[2] The next section delves into detail about such perquisites.

As Ian Lesser, vice president for Foreign Policy at the German Marshall Fund of the United States, puts it, "The [EU–Turkey refugee] deal signals a return to pragmatic, transactional diplomacy" (quoted in Dempsey 2015). As Neils Annen (2016), a Member of the German Bundestag, notes, "The EU has a very narrow interest in engaging in the refugee flows ... We know that there is only a political solution, and we know that it involves Turkey." Similarly, in the words of a European Commission staff member:

The Turkey–EU deal was fundamental [for the management of the refugee crisis] ... [Refugees and immigrants] saw that there is no longer border control in Europe. Organized crime was burgeoning in Turkey. It was important to send the signal to the refugees that the door to the EU was closed. We are extremely grateful for the enormous generosity of Turkey to accept Syrian refugees ... to provide schooling and grant access to its labor market. (Vicini 2016)

In addition to a pledge to release 3 billion EUR, the speeding up of the visa liberalization process, and the revitalization of the accession negotiations, under the March 2016 deal Turkey was able to have the EU announce the potential release of an additional 3 billion EUR to Turkey by the end of 2018 and acknowledge that the Customs Union Agreement with Turkey is in need of modernization.[3] In response, Turkey agreed that it would readmit all asylum seekers – who either opt out of the asylum process in Greece or whose asylum application is judged "inadmissible" based on "first country of asylum" or "safe third country" criteria – and prevent the flow of refugees from Turkey to the EU.

One important perquisite that Turkey was able to secure from the EU was the prospect of an earlier implementation of visa liberalization for Turkish citizens. For Turkey, visa liberalization talks are a part of the larger Readmission Agreement negotiations with the EU. The negotiating

---

[2] Phone interview with a US academic, October 15, 2016.
[3] Turkish authorities have been raising their concerns about the increasing number of Free Trade Agreements (FTAs) that the EU was signing with third parties such as South Korea, Mexico, Japan, and Canada, as such countries' exports compete with Turkish exports. In other words, Turkey faces greater competition in the EU market as well as in its own market, without enjoying preferential access to third-party markets.

directives for a readmission agreement between Turkey and the EU were adopted back in 2002, and the negotiations were formally started in 2005. But due to the European Council's decision to suspend the opening of new chapters with Turkey, the negotiations came to a halt in 2006, only to be restarted in 2009 (European Commission 2012a). As one scholar sees it:

The issue of readmission became very symptomatic of the deepening mistrust in EU–Turkish relations. Turkish officials feared the country would become a buffer zone and a dumping ground for unwanted migration to the EU, while the EU resented Turkey's uncooperative stand on a highly sensitive issue for many member countries. (Kirişci 2014)

The Readmission Agreement was signed in December 2013 and came into force in October 2014. Nevertheless, it covered only the return of Turkish nationals, with the third-country national clause expected to apply from October 2017 on. The request for visa liberalization with Turkey led to a battle within the EU, between Directorate-General for Migration and Home Affairs (DG Home) and for Neighbourhood and Enlargement Negotiations (DG Near) on the one hand, which consistently backed the agreement, and the Justice and Home Affairs Council and Germany and France, on the other (Dimitriadi 2016). For the European Council, visa liberalization represents "a domestically contentious concession that – if granted – would leave the EU without leverage" (Dimitriadi 2016, p. 6). For Turkey, the visa liberalization issue has been a very important agenda item in its relations with the EU. Therefore, from the Turkish official perspective, visa liberalization constitutes an important part of the package that serves to balance the readmission agreement, "which was widely viewed [in Turkey] as an imbalanced deal that would turn Turkey into 'Europe's warehouse for migrants'" (Dimitriadi 2016, p. 6). Accordingly, Turkey's ability to tie visa liberalization to the readmission agreement is a good illustration of its effective use of standard bargaining strategies such as issue-linkage bargaining.

The visa liberalization talks with Turkey began back in 2012, and the Visa Liberalization Dialogue with Turkey was launched on December 16, 2013, in conjunction with the signature of the EU–Turkey Readmission Agreement. The Visa Liberalization Dialogue is based on the Roadmap Towards a Visa Free Regime with Turkey document, which lists a set of seventy-two benchmarks in five categories: document security, migration management, public order and security, fundamental rights, and readmission of irregular migrants (European Commission 2017a). The refugee crisis brought the two sides back to the table and provided momentum to the stalled progress on the Roadmap for Visa Liberalization. In the words of one expert, "This time . . . the EU is the side with the more urgent needs" (Dimitriadi 2016, p. 6). The urgency of the crisis arguably bolsters the hand of Turkey vis-à-vis the EU.

The refugee crisis was effectively used as a bargaining chip by the Turkish government to hasten the visa liberalization process. Turkey accordingly managed to get the EU to declare March 2016, and later June 2016, as a deadline for the implementation of visa liberalization, provided that it successfully applies all the benchmarks identified in the Visa Liberalization Dialogue. In its May 2018 report, the European Commission underlines the following seven outstanding benchmarks that remain to be implemented by Turkey: issuing biometric travel documents compatible with the EU standards, adopting measures to prevent corruption, concluding an operational cooperation agreement with Europol, revising legislation and practices on terrorism in line with European standards, aligning legislation on personal data protection with EU standards, offering effective judicial cooperation in criminal matters to all EU member states, and implementing the EU–Turkey Readmission Agreement in all its provisions (European Commission 2018b).

Regarding the implementation of the visa liberalization benchmarks, Annen (2016), a Member of the German Bundestag, notes that "[t]he ball is in Turkey's court" and recommends the EU to "incentivize Turkey to set its course back to Europe." For the implementation of the visa liberalization agreement, the revision of Turkey's anti-terror legislation in line with the European *acquis* and the jurisprudence of the European Court of Human Rights are of key importance (Ülgen 2016). Turkey has the highest number of journalists in jail in the world, mainly due to the anti-terror legislation in the country (*The Economist* 2019). The EU officials therefore regularly encourage the Turkish government to follow the highest judicial standards with regards to the treatment of journalists.

Under the Visa Liberalization Dialogue, Turkey and the EU are also negotiating on whether to institute a civilian border control unit. Turkey's concerns on forming a civilian border control unit stem from the fact that "Turkey's eastern borders are vulnerable to terrorism," and the "regional unrest and violence in neighboring countries" (European Commission 2017a). Turkey is also required to comply with the EU legislation on data privacy – through giving more independence to the Data Protection Authority and implementing increased restraints on government agencies in terms of access to personal data on grounds of national security and public order – and enhance democratic transparency and accountability

(Ülgen 2016). Upon the lifting of the state of emergency, some of the barriers against the visa liberalization process are eliminated.

As noted by EU Commission Vice President Jyrki Katainen in February 2019, there are still four benchmarks out of seventy-two that remain to be met by Turkey (*Daily Sabah* February 28, 2019). Because of the lack of progress on these outstanding benchmarks, the visa liberalization was still not implemented as of June 2019. The European Commission continues to emphasize the importance of having a dialogue with Turkey to find solutions on the outstanding benchmarks (European Commission 2018b).

As one scholar underlines, in order to address Turkey's concerns that the country is not gaining anything from the agreement, Turkey was given "the right to suspend the [Readmission Agreement] if the EU does not meet the terms of the visa liberation roadmap" (Yılmaz 2011, p. 24). As illustrated in the next section, this right is effectively used as a bargaining chip by Turkish officials in putting further pressure on the EU to extend visa liberalization to Turkey. The Turkish government remains concerned about Turkey becoming the main receiver of all refugees headed toward the EU. Therefore, Turkey remains skeptical about removing the geographical limitation, which was adopted in the 1951 Geneva Convention on the Status of Refugees. The 1951 Geneva Convention originally recognized refugees as those who seek asylum as a result of "the incidents that happened in Europe before 1951." While other signatories of the Convention lifted the geographical limitation in 1967, Turkey is the only signatory that retains it.

Besides visa liberalization negotiations, a second benefit that Turkey has secured from the EU is financial support for taking care of the Syrian refugees in Turkey. The EU's Facility for Refugees in Turkey became operational in February 2016. In 2018–2019, the total amount disbursed for the Facility for Refugees in Turkey was 2.09 billion EUR (European Commission 2019a).

A third important benefit that Turkey was able to extract from the EU is the attempts at modernization of the Customs Union Agreement between the EU and Turkey. The Customs Union Agreement entered into force in December 1995. The Agreement covers all industrial goods but excludes agriculture (with the exception of processed agricultural products), services, and public procurement. The European Commission proposed "extending and deepening" the Customs Union in November 1996, and the European Council agreed to negotiating guidelines on the liberalization of services and public procurement between the two parties. Nevertheless, negotiations on this were suspended in 2002 (European Commission 2019b).

Despite its benefits, the Customs Union membership of Turkey without its full membership into the EU was proven to be against Turkey's economic and political interests. It reduced the country's leverage in its interactions with the EU, and, in the event of new tariff-free deals concluded between the EU and third countries, the third countries would gain tariff-free access to the Turkish market without reaping the same benefits with regard to entering the markets of third countries. For years, the Turkish government had been complaining about some of these imbalances in the system but had been unable to get the EU to renegotiate the Customs Union Agreement.

By 2015, Turkey has managed to bring momentum on the negotiations using the salience of the European refugee crisis. A member of the Turkish Parliament notes that upgrading the Customs Union Agreement would be in line with "the common interests" of both parties and ensure an increase in the bilateral trade volume.[4] Turkey is the EU's fourth-largest export market and fifth-largest provider of imports. The EU is Turkey's top import and export partner (European Commission 2019b). Turkey had realized a total of 76.1 billion EUR in exports to the EU in 2018, while receiving 77.2 billion EUR in imports under the same period (*Daily Sabah* February 28, 2019). Turkey represents 4 percent of the EU's total foreign trade (European Commission 2016a). For Turkey, the EU is the most important trading partner, representing 41 percent of Turkey's global trade. Moreover, two-thirds of FDI in Turkey originates in the EU (European Commission 2016a).

It is now commonly agreed that the Customs Union Agreement has important deficiencies in dealing with the modern-day challenges of trade integration (European Commission 2016a, Hakura 2018b). First and foremost, as noted earlier, Turkey is concerned about its obligation to follow the EU's commercial policy with third countries, without legal means to convince the EU's Free Trade Agreement (FTA) partners to conclude FTAs with it, in parallel. Nor does the Customs Union Agreement contain an effective dispute settlement mechanism. Largely due to these deficiencies, both sides have been unable to find appropriate ways to solve an increasing number of trade and market access problems (European Commission 2016a, p. 6). Similarly, Turkey wants to simplify the complex procedures

---

[4] Interview with a Member of the Turkish Parliament, Washington DC, September 30, 2016.

for the Turkish trucks carrying goods when crossing the borders to Greece and Bulgaria and transiting between different EU member states (Hakura 2018b).

Signaling a change in the stalemate, following the EU–Turkey refugee deal the European Commission published the Impact Assessment document in December 2016. In the document, the Commission proposed draft negotiating directives to the Council in order to modernize the existing Customs Union Agreement to deepen EU–Turkey trade and economic relations. The document proposed extending the bilateral trade relations to services, public procurement, and sustainable development (European Commission 2019b). The Impact Assessment document recommended further liberalization of trade in agricultural and fisheries products, extensive coverage of services, public procurement, and rules to support business and investment. It also advocated improving the consultation mechanisms, aligning Turkey's trade policy and technical legislation with that of the EU, and equipping the Customs Union with a modern dispute settlement mechanism to address existing trade barriers. The Council started examining the Commission's proposal in mid-2017. However, negotiations on modernizing the Customs Union have still not been launched as of June 2019, mainly due to political tensions between Turkey and the EU and the lack of political will on both sides (Hakura 2018b).

A fourth important benefit of the EU–Turkey deal for Turkey was the reenergization of its EU accession process. This is a good illustration of the implementation of a future-oriented strategy, à la Art (2005, p. 183–184), who notes that, in a "future-oriented strategy," actors attempt "to augment assets so as to produce better outcomes the next time," whereas bargaining "is the attempt to produce favorable outcomes with current assets." Through the promise of reenergization of its accession process, Turkey seems to be able to increase its future leverage vis-à-vis the EU.

In the key areas of judiciary and fundamental rights and of justice, freedom, and security, the technical work continues. Accession negotiation Chapters 23 and 24 cover a range of critical issues, including fundamental rights such as freedom of speech, judiciary, anti-corruption policy, migration and asylum, visa rules, border management, police cooperation, and the fight against organized crime and terrorism. The EU expects Turkey to respect the highest standards when it comes to democracy, rule of law, and fundamental freedoms, including freedom of expression (European Commission 2017a). In spring 2016, the Commission submitted preparatory documents to the Council on energy (Chapter 15), education and culture (Chapter 26), and foreign, security, and defense policies (Chapter 31). As the Fifth Progress Report concludes, "Progress has been made on all the elements of the EU–Turkey Statement, however, the implementation requires continuous efforts and commitment. Successful implementation depends mainly on the political determination of all sides to take the necessary action" (European Commission 2017a, p. 14). That political determination seems to be missing. All in all, the issue-linkage bargaining tactic was influential in the signing of the refugee deal.

Compellent Threats and Blackmail

The refugee crisis undoubtedly tilted the negotiation advantages toward Turkey. In the aftermath of the signature of the refugee deal, Turkey has switched to compellent threats and blackmailing to extract a number of concessions from the EU. As Turkey has already been accustomed to dealing with a number of unfavorable policies and obstacles in its relations with the EU, compellent threats appear as a low-risk strategy for the country to utilize.

As established in the literature, countries with limited relative internal sources of power may build up a "blackmail power" (Meerts 2015, p. 29). Nevertheless, Walt (2013) warns that giving in to one state's threats "might convey weakness" and invite demands by others or additional demands from the same actor. Greenhill (2011) notes that refugees may be used as "weapons of mass migration," to achieve "coercion by punishment" through threats to overwhelm a target's capacity to accommodate a refugee influx. Accordingly, the immense political, economic, and social costs of the refugee crisis for Europe made Erdoğan "grasp that the EU is no longer dealing from a position of strength" (Çandar 2016). Affirming this sentiment, a Member of the Turkish Parliament from the AKP notes:

[Turkish authorities] suddenly saw the European leaders coming to Turkey ... During 8 years of Barroso's term as the President of the European Commission, he came to Turkey only twice. But since the refugee crisis, Tusk, Junker, Merkel came to Turkey five times. This is a clear indication that Europe is looking at the picture differently ... The number of refugees from Turkey to the EU has decreased from 8,000–9,000 a day to single digits.[5]

[5] Interview with a Member of the Turkish Parliament, Washington DC, September 30, 2016.

Didier Billion, the president of the French Institute for International and Strategic Affairs, notes, "The EU finally understands that Turkey is a country that is indispensable" for the management of migration (*Euronews* 2015). This realization might be said to have empowered Turkey through a blackmail capacity. Turkey used the imminence of the refugee crisis and built up a blackmail power when it came to realize that some of the perquisites it extracted from the EU, such as the promise of visa liberalization or further progress in its accession negotiations, might not materialize. This is an excellent illustration of Turkey's future-oriented strategy, when it was willing to reach a deal with the EU on the refugee crisis.

While initially, Turkey may have wanted to become a member of the EU or to get further integrated with the EU through the revision of its Customs Union or visa liberalization, as soon as it realized that these are unrealistic given the domestic limitations its motivation has switched to defeating the EU or reducing the EU's capacity to further humiliate or harm Turkey. Regarding the rest of the payment that was pledged by the EU for the refugee deal, Erdoğan said: "The promises made to us have not been kept ... They said they would give 3 billion EUR plus another 3 billion EUR of support, but so far 850 million EUR have entered our safe." He added, "If you're going to give that money, then do it. This nation has pride and you can't toy with our pride" (quoted in *Reuters* March 19, 2018).

In the words of a former EU ambassador and Head of Delegation to Turkey, Turkish authorities saw a "historic opportunity to play hard-ball with a weakened Europe and attempt to weaken it further" through the deal (Pierini 2016a). In July 2016, Erdoğan is quoted as saying, "The European leaders are not sincere [in implementing the EU–Turkey refugee deal] ... Of the 3 billion Euros pledged, the EU has paid a token 1–2 million Euros" and Turkey has already spent nearly 11 billion Euros on the Syrian refugees (*BBC* July 26, 2016). Illustrating the compellent threats strategy Turkey uses, in November 2017 Erdoğan made explicit threats to the EU that he would allow three million refugees into Europe, in the face of EU criticism following the clampdown on opponents following the failed coup attempt (Pitel and Beesley 2016). The effectiveness of Turkey's compellent power is made very clearly visible when the EU showed its willingness to ignore the serious violations of human rights in Turkey in exchange for stemming the refugee flow to Europe. Pierini (2016d) warns:

Linking Turkey's refugee controls to the opening of accession negotiation chapters is a deadly trap for the EU, because it amounts to exonerating Turkey from the EU's political criteria for membership. By making progress on accession contingent on Turkey's refugee containment policy, Brussels has given Ankara massive leverage.

Indicative of this leverage, in response to a 2016 call from the European Parliament to suspend Turkey's EU accession talks to protest Turkey's harsh response to the failed coup attempt, Erdoğan "responded angrily ... saying he could open the floodgates to Europe" (Pitel and Beesley 2016). He is quoted as saying, "We are the ones who feed 3–3.5 million refugees in this country ... You [the EU] have betrayed your promises. If you go any further those border gates will be opened" (quoted in Pitel and Beesley 2016). With the EU accession process losing its credibility, Turkey increasingly sees the EU as a threat rather than a partner or a potential organization to bargain with in order to improve its prospects to join it.

The compellent threats become more apparent in the case of non-implementation of the items in the negotiated deal. Turkish officials frequently accuse the EU of breaching "the deal to stem the exodus of immigrants from Syria and elsewhere ... because it is not fulfilling promises of visa-free travel for Turks in Europe" (Peterson and Miller Llana 2017). Similarly, a Member of the Turkish Parliament from the AKP emphasizes, "Many of the [EU's] promises have not been fulfilled," especially the visa liberalization aspect, which is "a very important process for the Turkish public."[6] The same interviewee maintains, "We made all necessary changes to the anti-terror law in 2014 ... [Turkey] worked very hard to fulfill the 72 criteria ... but in the last moment, the [anti-terrorism law] became the center of attention ... whereas [it] was never mentioned in our discussions [with the EU]."[7] Pointing to the surprising nature of EU's last-minute requests for a change in the anti-terror law, the same Member of the Turkish Parliament likens them to "a nuclear bomb" and asserts that "the European Parliament is hiding behind the [anti-terrorism law], which wasn't among the 72 criteria."[8] Turkish officials regularly emphasize the lack of a political will on the side of the European countries to implement

---

[6] Interview with a Member of the Turkish Parliament, Washington DC, September 30, 2016.

[7] Interview with a Member of the Turkish Parliament, Washington DC, September 30, 2016.

[8] Interview with a Member of the Turkish Parliament, Washington DC, September 30, 2016.

visa liberalization.[9] Reaffirming the use of compellent threats by Turkey, a Member of the Turkish Parliament notes, "Visa liberalization is a critical issue, because we don't have any intention to put [the EU–Turkey refugee deal] into effect without [it]."[10]

Providing another excellent illustration of the use of compellent threats, in March 2017 Turkish Foreign Minister Mevlüt Çavuşoğlu announced that "deals with the European Union, including an agreement on stemming the flow of migrants, would be jeopardized if the bloc failed to implement promised visa liberalization for Turks" and that Turkey would present a final text to the bloc "and either it will all be canceled, including the visa liberalization and migrant deal, or it will all be implemented" (*Reuters* March 11, 2017). This announcement came in response to the constitutional amendment referendum campaign scandal with some European countries, including Germany and the Netherlands, during which Erdoğan accused these countries of "fascist actions" reminiscent of Nazi times (*Daily Sabah* March 15, 2017).

Turkey conducted diplomatic initiatives to gauge whether European institutions could demonstrate some flexibility regarding the outstanding conditions for visa liberalization. But the President of the European Parliament stated that the Commission's "recommendation to lift visas will not be forwarded to the relevant Parliamentary committee for deliberation until Turkey fulfills all the remaining conditions" (Ülgen 2016). In response, "Ankara stated clearly that it would suspend the Turkey–EU Readmission Agreement unless it receives visa freedom from Europe, potentially leading to the collapse of the whole refugee deal" (Ülgen 2016). The then Turkish Defense Minister Fikri Işık notes, "The EU is not fulfilling its responsibilities for the [EU–Turkey readmission agreement] to come into force," and adds, "We are disturbed by this and ... have the right to cancel this agreement for this reason. But Turkey certainly doesn't desire this" (quoted in *Al Jazeera* 2017). Answering a question whether Turkey feels "let down by the EU on the refugee issue," Işık maintains:

Well of course ... As you know visa-free travel was one of the conditions of the readmission agreement. Although Turkey has fulfilled all requirements as part of

---

[9] Interview with a Member of the Turkish Parliament, Washington DC, September 30, 2016.
[10] Interview with a Member of the Turkish Parliament, Washington DC, September 30, 2016.

this agreement, Europe has made excuses and not fulfilled its responsibilities, and right now this distresses us as a country. (Quoted in *Al Jazeera* 2017)

Many interviewees underline that Erdoğan's threats to allow the flow of refugees to the EU empower Turkey with blackmail power.[11] As one interviewee accurately notes, immigration is a "joker card in Erdoğan's hand, as he threatens the European partners that he would send 3 million refugees back to Europe" if they do not comply with the terms of the agreement.[12] Similarly, Steven Cook of the Council on Foreign Relations notes, in the context of the Turkish threat to send a large number of refugees toward Europe, "Turkey has the EU over a barrel" (quoted in Serwer 2016). This ensures that Europe remains silent over the massive purge of academics, police officers, and military officers that has been taking place in the aftermath of the failed coup attempt in Turkey. As Kati Piri, a member of the European Parliament Committee on Foreign Affairs, notes, the EU "has given the impression its silence can be bought in exchange for stemming the flow of refugees crossing the Aegean Sea" (quoted in Dempsey 2015). Erdoğan is reported to have said that the EU "had woken up too late to his country's importance" (*Euronews* 2015). In March 2017, Ömer Çelik, Turkey's minister of EU Affairs, is quoted as saying that Ankara might consider relaxing its controls over land crossings with Greece and Bulgaria (*The Telegraph* March 14, 2017). Bill Frelick of Human Rights Watch observes that refugees are being used as "bargaining chips" (Human Rights Watch 2016). Alluding to the blackmail potential of Turkey, *The Economist* notes, "Mr. Erdoğan, who once boasted of being able to flood Greece and Bulgaria with refugees, may use his leverage over the EU to press for still more concessions" (*The Economist* 2016).

CONCLUSION

This chapter illustrates that the EU–Turkey refugee deal was at first used by the Turkish authorities for boundary testing against the EU through the utilization of issue-linkage bargaining strategies to extract significant benefits from the EU. Ankara has been able to secure the promise of reversal of a number of unfavorable policies and extract concessions from the EU in return for its cooperation on stemming the flow of

---

[11] Interview with a British journalist via Skype, October 14, 2016; Phone interview with a US academic, October 15, 2016.

[12] Exchange with a Serbian NGO official, Berlin, December 15, 2016.

refugees, such as the reenergizing of the stalled accession negotiations process, a commitment to visa liberalization and modernization of the Customs Union, and payment of financial support from the EU to help alleviate the costs of hosting Syrian refugees in Turkey. Upon realizing that the perks secured through the deal were not going to become materialized, Turkey then switched to compellent threats and blackmail power and engaged in boundary challenging and boundary breaking against the EU. The country was initially able to ensure that, through its newly acquired leverage, it could prevent the EU from being severely critical of its track record on human rights and rule of law.

The odds for the long-term success of the implementation of the deal are low, as there are a number of problems with it. As a Serbian academic notes, the "refugee crisis is far from being solved."[13] Nevertheless, one might still argue that Turkey effectively uses it to threaten the EU. The outcome of the EU–Turkey deal on refugees will serve as a good litmus test on whether Turkey will switch from challenging to breaking its boundaries with the EU. If the deal falls through, there will be important ramifications for both European security and Turkey–EU relations. Thus far, the Turkish officials only utilized the threat of revoking the refugee deal. The fact that the deal remained operational since 2016 decreases the credibility of such threats, creating an impression of cheap-talk diplomacy. If such threats become reasonably credible or actually materialize, then it is possible to talk about a switch in Turkish foreign policy behavior to boundary breaking.

---

[13] Exchange with a Serbian academic, Berlin, December 16, 2016.

5

Turkey's Energy Policies

This chapter focuses on Turkey's energy policies in light of the country's relations with the West, with a particular emphasis on Turkey's refusal to become a full member of the EU's Energy Community Treaty (ECT), collaboration with Russia on energy projects, and evasion of sanctions against Iran. Through its energy policies, Turkey mainly engages in boundary challenging against the West through the use of informed strategic noncooperation and collaborative balancing with Russia. It also engages in boundary breaking, mainly against the United States, through the evasion of sanctions against Iran.

TURKISH REFUSAL OF FULL MEMBERSHIP IN ECT

Turkey has become a pivotal actor in European energy security, especially in the aftermath of the Russia–Ukraine crisis, and increasingly positions itself as a central player by connecting the energy producers with European consumers. However, studies that examine Turkey's position in energy security in light of its relationship with the EU and the West are scarce in the literature (for notable exceptions, see Önsoy and Udum 2015, Ekinci 2013). Through both rejecting its full membership into the ECT without its full accession into the EU and the revived Turkish Stream (commonly referred to as TurkStream) project with Russia, Turkey engages in challenging the boundaries of its partnership with the EU in the energy sector, using strategic noncooperation, cooperative balancing with Russia, and economic statecraft.

Informed Strategic Noncooperation

Energy is arguably one of the most important subjects in Turkey–EU relations. Turkey is a key partner for Europe's energy security and diversification, especially as a means to reduce European dependence on Russian gas imports (Bechev 2017). Since the foundation of the Energy Community in 2005, the EU has been trying to persuade Turkey to align itself with the energy *acquis* through joining the ECT. The Energy Community was established with the goal of having an integrated energy market supporting the competition between the EU members and non-EU members of Southeast Europe as well as other neighboring countries. It is "primarily a platform for exporting the relevant *acquis* in the fields of electricity, gas, and oil to create a homogeneous regulatory environment and push for infrastructure development" in the EU's immediate neighborhood (Bechev 2017, p. 13). It is very similar to the process that takes place within the EU under the framework of the Connecting Europe Facility (CEF), which aims at promoting growth, employment, and competitiveness at the EU level by supporting the "development of high performing, sustainable and efficiently interconnected trans-European networks in the fields of transport, energy and digital services" (European Commission 2017b).

Turkey initially displayed enthusiasm for the possibility of energy market integration with the EU in Southeast Europe, briefly supported the idea of its full membership in the Energy Community, and provided feedback during the organization's foundation stage. Nevertheless, to the surprise of many, at the eleventh hour Turkey declared that it would not take part in the organization as a full member (Kopač and Ekinci 2015). It instead decided to limit its involvement to an observer status, which it acquired in 2006, in an attempt to continue emphasizing the importance it assigns to regional energy cooperation.

Here, the Turkish foreign policy behavior seems to be informed by its Customs Union experience with the EU, as explained in detail in the previous chapter. That is to say, Turkey's rejection of a full membership application to the ECT should be interpreted as the country's attempt at not repeating the mistake it made by signing a Customs Union Agreement with the EU before becoming a full member of the EU.[1] Turkey does not want to adopt a significant portion of the *acquis* without receiving a commitment from the EU that its full membership prospects are realistic.

---

[1] Phone interview with a Turkish academic, March 8, 2017.

Turkey therefore engages in informed strategic noncooperation with the EU on ECT full membership and refuses to initiate its full membership application in the ECT. Further integration projects with the EU without the realistic prospects of full membership are frequently interpreted by the Turkish authorities in terms of limiting the country's potential leverage vis-à-vis the EU and weakening its negotiating position in the EU accession process (Kopač and Ekinci 2015). Accordingly, Turkey's EU candidate status hinders rather than helps EU–Turkey energy cooperation.

Moreover, the stalled EU accession negotiations and the lack of trust toward the EU help further explain the use of informed strategic noncooperation by Turkey when it comes to the issue of avoiding full membership in the Energy Community. Turkish authorities make the argument that Turkey's membership in the ECT might be interpreted as Turkey's implicit acceptance of a "privileged partnership in the energy field" (Barysch 2007, p. 6). In the words of a long-time observer of Turkish politics, "Turkey has a point when it says that it wants the EU energy *acquis* as part of its accession negotiations, not as part of some alternative process that is also available to countries that have not yet achieved official candidate status" (Barysch 2007, p. 6).

Turkey therefore engages in boundary challenging through strategic noncooperation with the EU in energy market integration, in an attempt to increase its future leverage against the EU in its accession negotiations and to keep its options open. It wants to avoid a situation where it would lose its decision-making autonomy on energy policies and have its policies dictated by the Energy Community. Finally, as explained in this chapter, the country further aims to complicate the energy market integration efforts of the EU, seeks to increase the EU's costs in the energy market, and engages in issue-linkage bargaining.

Issue-Linkage Bargaining

Here, an additional factor seems to be particularly influential in explaining Turkey's reluctance to join the ECT as a full member: the unilateral veto of the Republic of Cyprus on the opening up of accession negotiations on Chapter 15 – the Energy Chapter. Even though the screening process for Chapter 15 was completed in 2007, it has been frozen since December 2009 due to a veto from the Republic of Cyprus. A Member of the Turkish Parliament expresses a commonly held frustration among the Turkish officials when he notes that "a relatively small EU member state" (i.e. Cyprus) is capable of freezing the negotiations on the Energy Chapter, "despite the fact that Turkey plays a very central role in the European energy security sector."[2] Turkish officials contend that for full membership in the Energy Community, it is necessary to open accession negotiations on Chapter 15. This is a good illustration that an issue-linkage bargaining tactic is being used by the Turkish officials.

Should the Energy Chapter be opened through the removal of the veto from the Republic of Cyprus, a very important obstacle blocking Turkey's membership to the Energy Community would be removed. Nevertheless, similar to the results revealed by the analysis in Chapter 3, as long as the Republic of Cyprus continues to veto Turkey's Energy Chapter and there are no credible prospects of Turkish accession into the EU, Turkey can be expected to continue its strategic noncooperation on ECT and CEF and to prefer to remain outside of energy integration frameworks of the EU.

Turkey is also concerned about the ECT's legal framework on the environment, competition, and external energy trade policies and argues that there are technical problems with some of its provisions (Barysch 2007, Kopač and Ekinci 2015). To illustrate, Turkey has been unwilling to reform the state-subsidized BOTAŞ Petroleum Pipeline Corporation, which would be a requirement under the ECT (*The Market Mogul* 2016). The EU, on the other hand, emphasizes that Turkey would benefit from full membership in the Energy Community, as it would lead to a more predictable investment climate in the country's energy sector, allowing the country to acquire a key position as an energy hub (Barysch 2007, Kopač and Ekinci 2015).

In an attempt to convince Turkey to become a full member of the Energy Community, the EU engaged in a round of negotiations with Turkey in 2009 and stressed the potentially positive outcomes of Turkey's full membership.[3] Illustrating the importance of energy in the EU accession negotiations process, this topic was included as an agenda item in the Positive Agenda that was initiated by the European Commission in 2012 to enhance the cooperation between Turkey and the EU and to promote reforms in areas of joint interest (European Commission 2012b). Again, in order to alleviate concerns that Turkey's full membership in the Energy Community would hinder the prospects of

---

[2] Interview with a former Turkish foreign minister, then Member of Turkish Parliament, Ankara, July 15, 2011.

[3] Kopač and Ekinci (2015) argue that full ECT membership would enhance Turkey's leverage in accession negotiations with the EU.

its full membership in the EU, the Energy Community published a report in 2015 stating that "transposition and implementation of the relevant *acquis* would be smooth as a result of the advanced development of the Turkish energy market" (Energy Community 2015, p. 7). Moreover, on March 16, 2015, the Turkey–EU High-Level Energy Dialogue was launched, which was followed by the second High-Level Energy Dialogue meeting on January 28, 2016 (Turkish Ministry of Foreign Affairs 2019d). The goal of these High-Level Energy Dialogue meetings was to bring "renewed political momentum" to energy cooperation between the EU and Turkey, which was expected to lead to "concrete actions and projects" that were mutually beneficial (European Commission 2016b).

Turkey, nevertheless, continues to stay out of the ECT. Turkish officials do not want to unilaterally agree to "a big chunk of the *acquis* without being able to ask anything in return" (Barysch 2007, p. 6). As a consequence of Turkey's strategic noncooperation on the ECT, the EU lacks incentives to encourage Turkey to join the sanctions against Russia. Furthermore, as made clear in the following section, Turkey, ever since the recent rapprochement with Russia, has been operating from a position of strength due to its key position in the dialogue regarding the future of European energy security. As The Energy Governance in Turkey report published by the Energy Community states, "Turkey is bound to become the gateway to Europe's diversification strategy through pipeline connections to be built in the Southern Gas Corridor [SGC]" (Energy Community 2015, p. 7). Turkey's rekindled relations with Russia in the energy sector could potentially mean an increase in European dependence on Russia. As an article in *The Market Mogul* (2016) maintains:

Brussels is in an extremely delicate position, as a possible failure to include Turkey in the energy alliance will most likely result in a widening gap between Turkey and the EU ... [which] will provide Russia with an opportunity to delay Ankara's much-anticipated energy diversification and more importantly, the supply of Azeri gas for Europe.

Many EU officials argue that energy is a very salient issue for waiting for the accession talks to make progress. Others maintain that energy should be decoupled from the Turkish accession process in a way to prevent Turkey from using "its strategic location to get concessions from the EU" (Barysch 2007, p. 7). The concern shared by many is that this could "set a dangerous precedent," where, once energy links are in place, "Turkey could try to use them to get ahead in negotiations with its

EU partners in unrelated areas" (Barysch 2007, p. 7). In other words, the fear is that, just as it did with the EU–Turkey refugee deal, Turkey may be tempted to use its newly acquired leverage as a blackmail tool in the future on the energy security issue.

In order to alter the status quo, the EU needs to incentivize Turkey to cooperate more closely in the energy sector. One way of doing so is through the Energy Union initiative that was proposed by then Polish Prime Minister Donald Tusk in April 2014 to "move beyond the internal energy market towards a true European energy union" (Erbach 2015, p. 4). In February 2015, the European Commission published a framework strategy for the proposed Energy Union, which would integrate the continent-wide energy system to achieve "secure, sustainable, competitive, affordable energy for every European" (European Commission 2015c). It is "based on competition and a free flow of energy across borders" (Erbach 2015, p. 2). It is expected to "benefit the region by helping to deepen functional integration and giving a boost to market liberalization and infrastructure development" (Bechev 2017, p. 16). It may help to potentially "blur the lines between members and non-members by bringing 'third countries' onboard through flexible arrangements" (Bechev 2017, p. 16). One expert recommends the EU offer a seat to Turkey at the table through "some form of association [with the Energy Union], and a voice in decision-making," and make it clear that "non-EU states which seek association with the Energy Union are not expected to harmonize their legislation with the *acquis*" (Bechev 2017, p. 16). However, as long as the Turkish policy-makers have concerns regarding the prospects of their full membership in the EU, this does not seem to be a feasible option for Turkey.

TURKISH STREAM PROJECT WITH RUSSIA

Cooperative Balancing with Russia

Turkey increasingly aspires to turn itself into a European energy hub and seeks "to diversify its energy deals."[4] The EU is interested in diversifying its energy supply and increasing its energy security in a way to decrease its dependence on Russian energy. In this context, the SGC, a system of interconnected pipelines running from the Caspian region through Turkey to Southern Europe, has become an important strategic energy project for the EU. The SGC is projected to expand the infrastructure that

---

[4] Interview with a Turkish-American academic, October 21, 2016.

transfers natural gas from the Caspian Basin, Central Asia, the Middle East and the Eastern Mediterranean Basin to the EU. When the route opens in 2019–2020, it will allow around 10 billion cubic meters (bcm) of gas to flow along the route, possibly increasing to 80–100 bcm in the long term. Therefore, it has the potential to meet up to 20 percent of the EU's gas needs (European Commission 2016b).

Turkey seeks to maintain a central role in the projects that transport Caspian and Middle Eastern gas into Europe. A significant component of the SGC project is the construction of the Trans-Anatolian Pipeline (TANAP). While Turkey initially supported the Nabucco Project to deliver the Persian and Caspian gas to Europe, with the waning of the European enthusiasm for the project it decided to move on with the construction of TANAP instead (Ekinci 2013). Through TANAP and the Trans-Adriatic Pipeline (TAP), "Russia will be less and less in a position to dictate the terms," and "Gazprom's long-term contracts will be more flexible – especially with regard to the price-setting formula" (Bechev 2017, p. 15). Therefore, TANAP is projected to help Turkey gain significant leverage with the EU and enable Turkey to play an even more central role in European energy security. TANAP started operations in 2018 and is expected to be connected soon to Europe through TAP. TAP is expected to deliver gas to European markets by mid-2020 (*Daily Sabah* November 21, 2018).

For Russia, on the other hand, its war with Ukraine and the sanctions from the EU have caused significant problems. Therefore, bypassing Ukraine has become an important strategy for Russia. The South Stream project was found to be in noncompliance with the Third Energy Package, which aimed at introducing competition into the European energy market by breaking up energy monopolies (Dempsey 2014). Despite announcing that it might challenge the decision of the European Commission legally, Russia abandoned the South Stream project in the end (Dempsey 2014) and claimed, "The European Commission and Bulgaria unlawfully and deliberately killed it" (*The Market Mogul* 2016). Russia consequently turned toward Turkey, which has not signed the EU's competition and energy legislation and decided to replace the South Stream project with Turkish Stream (Bechev 2017). Additionally, the projections for the doubling of the demand for natural gas in Turkey in the next ten years make the Turkish market very appealing for Russia (*The Market Mogul* 2016).

During Russian President Vladimir Putin's visit to Turkey in December 2014, a memorandum of understanding was signed between Russian Gazprom and Turkish BOTAŞ for the construction of this new project. Turkish Stream envisioned delivering 31.5 billion bcm of natural gas a year from Russia to Turkey via the Black Sea and then further to Europe. It "is supposed to redirect no less than 40% from Ukraine's grid" (*The Market Mogul* 2016) and is expected to "empower Turkey," as "Ankara would play a central role in its construction, and it would use that role to improve its relationships with countries that would receive Turkish Stream natural gas" (Stratfor 2015). Turkey was also able to negotiate a price reduction from Russia (*The Market Mogul* 2016). Many analysts note that Turkish Stream would compete against the TAP and TANAP projects, which envisage transporting Azerbaijani gas to Turkey (Gurbanov 2015).

The Turkish Stream project was put on hold following the crisis in Turkey–Russia relations caused by the downing of a Russian jet by the Turkish military in November 2015. The subsequent sanctions from Russia inflicted a heavy blow to Turkey–Russia bilateral economic relations, the tourism sector, and a number of collaborative projects such as the nuclear energy facility in Akkuyu, Turkey. For instance, Turkey's exports to Russia dropped by 40 percent between 2014 and 2015 and by 60 percent in the first four months of 2016 (Kirişci 2016).

In June 2016, Erdoğan, eager to recover the economic relations with Russia and to seek Russian backing against the Kurds in Syria, sent a letter of apology to Russia and blamed the downed Russian jet on coup plotters within the military. Referring to Turkey's apology to Russia in June 2016, one interviewee stresses the significance of its timing and notes that Russia played Turkey to "undermine Western solidarity" just before NATO's Warsaw Summit in July 2016, against the background of tensions between Russia and the West.[5] He notes, "Putin is being clever: by mending relations with Turkey, he makes NATO look like it is not united," adding that Erdoğan "does not see this."[6]

Following the failed coup attempt in July 2016, Erdoğan declared a state of emergency and started a crackdown on domestic opposition, which was heavily criticized by the EU and the United States. In the immediate aftermath of the failed coup, Putin was one of the first foreign leaders to express sympathy to Erdoğan (Bremmer 2017a). Erdoğan and Putin met on August 9, 2016, to "open 'a new page' in bilateral relations and reverse the damage sustained by sanctions imposed by Russia" (*EurActiv.com* 2016). With the Turkey–Russia rapprochement, the

[5] Interview with a British journalist via Skype, October 14, 2016.
[6] Interview with a British journalist via Skype, October 14, 2016.

presidents of both countries agreed to resume the Turkish Stream project in August 2016. Turkey and Russia signed the Turkish Stream Agreement on October 10, 2016.

Many experts and interviewees express their skepticism about the rapprochement between Turkey and Russia, as it was "with startling speed" that "Russia became Turkey's 'friend and strategic partner'" (Bremmer 2017a). One interviewee maintains that the mending of Turkey–Russia relations should be viewed as a result of Erdoğan's "desperate need for some good news amidst purges, no extradition of Gülen, continued fight against the PKK, setbacks in Iraq and Syria, and the economy slowing down."[7] The same interviewee notes that Erdoğan acted "tactically and very short-term" by rekindling Turkey's relations with Russia, just due to Putin's promise to reduce the price of the Russian gas sold to Turkey.[8]

As Turkey's prospects of EU accession dim, in order to strengthen its hand in the accession negotiations with the EU, Turkey signals to the EU that it has other alternatives to the SGC project, such as the Turkish Stream project, which would inflict heavy costs on European energy security by diminishing the likelihood of the EU's independence from Russia in the energy sector. In the words of a former EU ambassador and Head of Delegation to Turkey, "The [Turkish Stream] deal represents a tactical advantage to Turkey ... [as Turkey hopes to reinforce] its position as a gas hub on the EU's doorstep" (Pierini 2016c). As mentioned by another expert, Turkey seeks to acquire more "leverage by positioning [itself] as a critical geography for the rest of the world" (Karakullukçu 2014). Put simply, Turkey is tempted to use Turkish Stream and TANAP against each other, in order to "make [the] most of the energy game as a leading transit country" (Sönmez 2015, p. 24).

As a transit country, Turkey has the potential to "weaken a key pillar of the EU's Energy Union and its Energy Security Strategy, which aim at diversifying supplies away from Russia and avoiding the potential disruption resulting from tensions between Russia and Ukraine" (Pierini 2016c). Over time, transit countries have evolved from being "just dependent service providers" to having "a profound influence on the market share of a supplier," increasing their leverage "to negotiate higher transit fees depending on the available flexibility of switching between markets and suppliers on both sides" (Fischer 2016). Accordingly, Turkey is likely to

---

[7] Interview with a British journalist via Skype, October 14, 2016.
[8] Interview with a British journalist via Skype, October 14, 2016.

use its enhanced position as a transit country to extract more benefits from the EU. As one expert warns:

Once a pipeline is constructed, the temptation for rent-seeking in transit countries – and transit control power – is huge ... The threat of Turkish influence over how much Azeri or (some of the) Russian gas would enter European markets and the potential for rent-seeking in transit fees looks troubling in the current political environment. The willingness of Turkey's government to link issues, such as refugee treatment, visa liberalization, and financial transfers, as has happened recently, should serve as a warning. (Fischer 2016)

Turkey's cooperative balancing with Russia against the EU is a "leveling strategy" used by Turkey to restructure the situation by increasing its alternatives (Kelley 2005). The goal is to undermine the EU's power without direct (military) confrontation and increase the political and economic costs to the EU (Pape 2005, He and Feng 2008).

Economic Statecraft

In addition to cooperative balancing, Turkey engages in economic statecraft, using its energy policies and its geostrategic position as a transit country as both a carrot and a stick. In the words of a Turkish-American academic interviewee, "From the Western perspective, rapprochement between Turkey and Russia enabled Putin to have an energy policy to block natural gas to Ukraine and sell to Western Balkans and Italy."[9] While by seeking to cooperate with the EU via the SGC, Turkey engages in positive economic statecraft, i.e. "the extension of economic incentives or rewards"; by seeking to cooperate with Russia via the Turkish Stream project, Turkey engages in negative economic statecraft against the EU, i.e. "the use of economic sanctions, coercion or punishment" (Alves 2014, p. 3). While the positive economic statecraft constitutes boundary testing, the cooperation with Russia on TurkStream constitutes boundary challenging. The crucial question here is whether Turkey is capable of playing this "delicate energy game" with the two leading actors, the EU and Russia (Sönmez 2015, p. 24).

It is important to acknowledge that a number of interviewees voice skepticism about the feasibility of the Turkish Stream project. For instance, one interviewee notes that it is not realistic to "sign an agreement for the Turkish Stream with Russia, and expect Europe to buy the gas."[10]

---

[9] Interview with a Turkish-American academic, October 21, 2016.
[10] Interview with a British journalist via Skype, October 14, 2016.

Another interviewee maintains, "At a time when the West is trying to push for more sanctions against Russia, the improvement of Turkey and Russia trade and energy relations goes against the spirit of transatlantic relations."[11] One interviewee maintains that, while TANAP is very desirable for Europe, "Turkish Stream doesn't make any sense financially" due to the fact that Europe would be unwilling to buy it.[12] The same interviewee adds, "Turkish Stream will probably go the way of Nabucco. Turkish authorities should think more thoroughly as to what Turkish Stream would imply for the country's relations with the West, due to more tensions with Russia."[13]

Presenting a slightly more optimistic perspective on the feasibility of the Turkish Stream project, a former Turkish ambassador to Azerbaijan notes that "Turkish Stream can become a viable partnership between Turkey and Russia only if it does not present a challenge to the SGC" and recommends the construction of the Turkish-Bulgarian Interconnector facility, "with a view to connecting it to Turkish Stream" (Çeviköz 2016, p. 75). Nevertheless, it is highly unlikely that the Bulgarian government and the EU would be willing to allow for the construction of an interconnector facility, due to tensions with Russia. The rapprochement in Turkey–Russia relations since summer 2016 and the revival of the Turkish Stream pipeline project provide good evidence for Turkey's increasingly boundary challenging behavior against the EU through the use of economic statecraft and cooperative balancing.

TURKEY'S EVASION OF IRAN SANCTIONS

Economic Statecraft

In May 2018, President Trump announced the US withdrawal from the Joint Comprehensive Plan of Action (JCPOA). This accompanied the announcement on the reintroduction of sanctions on Iran as well as the decision to punish any nation or entity that cooperates with it. The latter is referred to as "secondary sanctions," as it involves a ban from doing business "not only with sanctioned companies and people but also with any third parties dealing with them" (Lew and Nephew 2018). The initial sanctions kicked in on August 4, 2018, on the Iranian automotive

---

[11] Interview with a Turkish-American academic, October 21, 2016.
[12] Interview with a British journalist via Skype, October 14, 2016.
[13] Interview with a British journalist via Skype, October 14, 2016.

sector as well as trade in gold and other metals. In November 2018, additional sanctions became effective, targeting Iran's energy sector.

Following the Trump Administration's announcement, the Turkish authorities repeatedly denounced sanctions against Iran, calling them "not appropriate" (Smith 2018). Turkey is heavily dependent on Iran for energy imports. As a result, the reimposition of sanctions against Iran would have a drastic impact on the Turkish economy. Consequently, the Turkish authorities regularly announced that Turkey would not abide by the sanctions. In 2017, Iran surpassed Iraq as the second-largest provider of energy for Turkey, following Russia. Iran provides half its total oil supplies and a fifth of its gas supplies (Erdemir and Tahiroğlu 2018).

On the topic, Turkish Foreign Minister Çavuşoğlu said, "We buy oil from Iran and we purchase it in proper conditions," and Turkish President Erdoğan asked, "Who will heat my country throughout the winter?" (The Associated Press July 25, 2018). President Erdoğan continued, "Iran is both our neighbor and our strategic partner," and added that severing ties with Tehran on America's whim goes against Turkey's "sovereignty" (*RT* July 25, 2018). This book holds that the evasion of sanctions constitutes negative economic statecraft, as it deliberately undermines the goals behind sanctions.

The use of economic statecraft in the form of evasion of sanctions serves as good evidence of Turkish boundary-challenging behavior against the United States. As an ally, Turkey was expected to abide by the sanctions imposed by the USA. The fact that Turkey undermined these sanctions from 2010 to 2015 is a good indication that it does not value its alliance with the USA as much as it does the calculated costs of the violation of sanctions.

During the period from 2012 to 2015, Turkey had secured a number of exemptions for its companies doing business in Iran and for Halkbank's activities (Yinanç 2018). Despite that, Turkey has still gotten around the US sanctions against the Islamic Republic from 2010 to 2015. Between 2012 and 2013, Iran is alleged to earn at least 13 billion USD due to the sanctions-evasion scheme (Erdemir and Tahiroğlu 2018). Reza Zarrab, an Iranian-Turkish gold trader, and Mehmet Hakan Atilla, one of the top executives of the Turkish state-owned Halkbank, were both sentenced to prison. Zarrab was charged with conspiring to defraud the United States, conspiring to violate US sanctions law, bank fraud, and money laundering. He pleaded guilty and cooperated with the authorities. In his testimony, he provided evidence for bribing key Turkish officials, such as Minister of Economy

Zafer Çağlayan and other officials in the inner circle of Erdoğan. He also claimed that then Prime Minister Erdoğan had personally ordered in 2012 that two banks to be allowed to participate in an oil-for-gold scheme that violated US sanctions on Iran (Weiser 2017). Atilla was found guilty of conspiring with others to evade US sanctions, using the US financial system to conduct barred transactions on behalf of the Iranian government, and defrauding US financial institutions by concealing the true nature of these transactions (Yinanç 2018).

In June 2019, the US Department of the Treasury was still in the process of deciding on the amount of fines it would determine for Halkbank, which is expected to have a massive impact on the Turkish banking sector. In order to increase pressure on Turkey to release Andrew Brunson, in the beginning of August 2018 the US Department of the Treasury announced its decision to impose sanctions on two Turkish ministers – the minister of Internal Affairs and the minister of Justice. The imposition of sanctions on a NATO ally by the United States is a rather rare phenomenon, indicating the seriousness attributed to the Brunson case. Brunson was released in October 2018. In return, analysts anticipate minimum fines for Halkbank (Erdemir and Tahiroğlu 2018).

In the aftermath of the Trump Administration's withdrawal from the JCPOA, Turkey receives a greater spotlight due to multiple lawsuits and arrests of Turkish nationals in the United States as a result of a high-profile sanctions-busting scheme uncovered by the US Department of the Treasury. On July 7, 2018, US Department of State Director of Policy Planning Brian Hook announced the determination of the US administration to punish foreign companies that do not comply with the Iran sanctions. During a time when the Turkish economy goes through major difficulties and the Turkish Lira loses its value against all major currencies, the possibility of sanctions against Turkish companies is not an appealing option for Turkey. Due to the fact that Turkey is heavily dependent on Iran for its oil and gas demand, Turkey is left between a rock and a hard place.

As already noted, sanctions against the Iranian energy sector became effective in November 2018. However, as a result of the thawing of relations between Turkey and the USA following the release of Brunson as well as the investigation into the murder of Saudi journalist Jamal Khashoggi, Turkey secured an exemption from the Iranian oil sanctions, and the sanctions against the two Turkish ministers were lifted (Lake 2018). Accordingly, Turkey is allowed to import limited quantities from Iran. Even with the exemptions, Turkey will still need to look elsewhere, most likely Iraq and the Gulf states, for its additional oil and gas imports, which will prove to be more expensive due to higher transportation costs (Bakeer 2018). Given the condition of the Turkish economy, higher transportation costs will be burdensome for the country.

Despite the exemptions, Turkish President Erdoğan announced that the country will defy the US sanctions on Iran (Gauthier-Villars 2018). On March 3, 2019, Turkish Foreign Minister Çavuşoğlu announced that the sanctions have an important economic effect on Turkey and declared that the Turkish government is seeking to extend the timeframe of exemptions beyond May 2019 (*Mehr News Agency* March 3, 2019). Shortly thereafter, at the end of March 2019, the US Department of the Treasury announced that a "vast network" of twenty-five people, firms, and Iranian government agencies will be hit by sanctions for evading sanctions against Iran and transferring about 1 billion USD (Lee 2019). Among those were some Turkish firms with ties to Iran.

That a key US ally evaded the US sanctions against Iran from 2010 to 2015 and publicly refuses to implement the renewed sanctions against Iran marks a significant moment in the history of bilateral relations. Nevertheless, it is important to note that Turkey is not alone in its dismay against the renewed sanctions or attempts to seek waivers. The EU member states and Turkey collaborate about the availability of alternative arrangements to be made with Iran to enable them to import Iranian oil and gas.

CONCLUSION

The first half of this chapter provides an illustration of Turkish boundary testing through the use of issue-linkage bargaining and economic statecraft. It further illustrates that Turkey also engages in boundary challenging against the EU in the energy sector through the case studies of the Turkish rejection of full membership status in the ECT and the recently revived Turkish Stream pipeline project with Russia. These indicate Turkey's use of informed strategic noncooperation, economic statecraft, and cooperative balancing with Russia. The EU is well advised to work on putting a renewed emphasis on its accession negotiations with Turkey in the energy area, if it would like to see Turkey's continued engagement in its energy policies.

The second half of the chapter offers an analysis of Turkey's evasion of sanctions against Iran from 2010 to 2015, illustrating a shift from boundary challenging to boundary breaking behavior on the part of the Turkish government. With the renewal of sanctions against Iran, and the imposition of secondary sanctions, all eyes are once again on Turkey. Having said that, the European countries are similarly concerned about the renewed US sanctions against Iran. Therefore, there seems to be a potential venue for collaboration between Turkey and the EU members on the negotiation of exceptions to the renewed sanctions against Iran.

6

Turkish Rapprochement with Russia in Security

As noted by a number of commentators, "Turkey under the AKP is increasingly resolute in its turn away from the West and toward eastern friends such as Russia" (Peterson and Miller Llana 2017). This chapter delves into detail about the security- and defense-related implications of the recent Turkey–Russia rapprochement. Turkey is increasingly alienated from the Western alliance. Accordingly, the country gradually charts an independent course, which puts it further at odds with the United States, the EU, and NATO. Illustrating the Turkish boundary-breaking behavior against the USA, the EU, and NATO, this chapter analyzes two case studies: Turkey's declared intent of becoming a member of the Shanghai Cooperation Organization (SCO) and its agreement signed with Russia to buy a missile defense system. It argues that Turkey employs compellent threats, costly signaling, and cooperative balancing with Russia, leading to a break in its boundaries with the West.

TURKEY AS A FULL MEMBER OF THE SCO?

As a corollary to the rapprochement with Russia, Turkish elites increasingly proclaim that Turkey is considering full membership in the SCO and seeks to portray SCO full membership as an alternative to the EU, if not NATO. In the words of an expert, Erdoğan sees international institutions as "entities to be manipulated" and as a means to "internationalize problems" in international fora (Ünver 2014b). Illustrating that SCO membership is being portrayed as an alternative to EU membership, during his remarks on the possibility of Turkey joining the SCO as a full member Erdoğan "urged Turks to be patient until the end of [2016] over relations with Europe, and said a referendum could be held on EU membership in 2017" (*Reuters* 2016). Through its proclamation of its intention to become a full member of the SCO, Turkey employs compellent threats and engages in boundary challenging against the West. If it goes through with these threats, it would best be considered as engaging in boundary breaking against the West.

Compellent Threats for Alternative Alliances

The SCO has its origins in the Shanghai Five (which included China, Russia, Kazakhstan, Kyrgyzstan, and Tajikistan), which was founded in 1996. The Shanghai Five organization was renamed in 2001, following Uzbekistan's membership into the organization. It was originally established as a confidence-building forum to demilitarize borders. Since 2001, the SCO's goals and agenda have "broadened to include increased military and counterterrorism cooperation and intelligence sharing" (Albert 2015). In June 2016, India and Pakistan signed accession agreements with the SCO and became full members in 2017.

Turkey joined the SCO as a Dialogue Partner in 2012. At the signing ceremony, then Foreign Minister Davutoğlu noted, this occasion marks "a declaration of 'common fate' and also the beginning of a long road where Turkey and SCO walk hand in hand" (Turkish Ministry of Foreign Affairs 2017). Dialogue Partners are entitled to take part in ministerial-level and some other meetings of the SCO but do not have voting rights (*Reuters* 2016). On November 23, 2016, Turkey was granted chairmanship of the SCO Energy Club for the 2017 period, making it the first nonmember to chair the Energy Club. The SCO Energy Club brings together some of the world's largest energy producers with the world's largest energy consumers. It seeks to deepen energy cooperation and improve energy security. According to a Turkish newspaper, "The members of the SCO cover some 36% of the world's electricity, 23% of natural gas, 20.8% of crude oil and 60.2% of coal production. They also consume some 28% of natural gas, 25.2% of crude oil and 65.1% of coal" (*Daily Sabah* November 23, 2016).

On multiple occasions, such as during his speech in November 2016, Erdoğan stated the possibility of abandoning EU candidacy in return for full membership in the SCO (*Reuters* 2016). Back in 2013, then Prime Minister Erdoğan jokingly said to Putin, "If we get into the SCO, we will say goodbye to the European Union" (quoted in Wang 2016). This is best considered as an attempt to signal to the EU that Turkey has other options (Chulkovskaya 2017). Similarly, in November 2016, Erdoğan was quoted as saying, "Turkey did not need to join the European Union 'at all costs' and could instead become part of a security bloc dominated by China, Russia and Central Asian nations" (quoted in *Reuters* 2016). This may be labeled as a compellent threat or as an attempt to increase the leverage or maneuvering space for Turkey vis-à-vis the EU or even NATO (as the SCO increasingly acquires a security/defense dimension).

Some argue that Erdoğan looks for alternative venues for foreign policy cooperation, where his domestic policies would not be heavily scrutinized or condemned (Bertrand 2016). Turkey is increasingly realigning itself with Russia, China, and Iran, among others. According to Aykan Erdemir, a Senior Fellow at the Foundation for Defense for Democracies and a former Member of the Turkish Parliament from the Republican People's Party (*Cumhuriyet Halk Partisi*, CHP), "Erdoğan feels much more comfortable and at home among the authoritarian regimes of the Shanghai Cooperation Organization rather than facing the scrutiny and criticism of the European family of nations" (quoted in Bertrand 2016).

Nevertheless, the jury is still out on the feasibility of such threats. Michael Koplow, a Middle East analyst and policy director of the Israel Policy Forum, warns that a possible Turkish membership in the SCO would "drastically alter relations with the US and NATO" and "be viewed as a rejection of the Western alliance" (quoted in Bertrand 2016). Michael Kofman of the Wilson Center is quoted as saying that the SCO is "not a cohesive economic or political bloc" and hence a possible membership in the SCO would only serve to "instill the perception that the West is some-how 'losing Turkey'" (quoted in Bertrand 2016). As illustrated in Chapter 4, the refugee deal between the EU and Turkey further complicates the situation by making it very costly for the EU to "lose" Turkey.

In the words of Ian Bremmer, president of the Eurasia Group, "SCO membership would not require Turkey's exit from NATO" but would severely damage Turkey–NATO relations (quoted in Bertrand 2016). Many in Turkey do not view the SCO as an alternative to NATO (Chulkovskaya 2017). Turkish Prime Minister Binali Yıldırım denounces the claims that the SCO is being presented as an alternative to the EU by noting, "Shanghai is not an alternative to the EU ... We are not using [the SCO] to scare the EU. [But] Turkey cannot disregard the threats and opportunities it faces. We do not have the luxury to say, 'The EU is our only option and we will be there whenever it wants us to be there'" (quoted in Chulkovskaya 2017).

Others argue that the statements that Turkey would like to become a member of the SCO go beyond just "an idle bluff" and maintain that

Turkey could benefit economically from joining the organization after the country is "repeatedly" alienated by its Western allies (Oruç 2016). They predict a continuation of Turkey's drift from NATO. From the Russian perspective, Turkey's potential full membership in the SCO is viewed positively due to both the central role Turkey plays in the European energy sector and the fact that it would increase Russia's leverage vis-à-vis the West (Chulkovskaya 2017). Vladimir Zhirinovsky, the leader of the Liberal Democrats in Russia, predicts further drifting of Turkey toward Eurasia and the Middle East and potential withdrawal of Turkey from NATO (Chulkovskaya 2017). Zhirinovsky is reported to have said that Erdoğan personally asked for his help with Turkey's membership in the SCO (Chulkovskaya 2017). Nevertheless, on this topic, one expert maintains, Putin "knows that as a rogue and dysfunctional NATO ally, Turkey is of greater use to Moscow than as a defector to the Shanghai Cooperation Organization" (quoted in Bertrand 2016).

Others underline that Turkey cannot be a member of both the SCO and NATO (Oruç 2016, Chulkovskaya 2017). For instance, Leonid Ivashov, one of the founders of the SCO, is reported to state that the accession of a NATO member into the SCO is not feasible (Wang 2016). In the words of an interviewee, "Erdoğan sadly thinks Russia, the SCO, or the Middle East are alternatives, but there is no alternative to Turkey–EU relations."[1] As the SCO continues its expansion and attracts considerable attention from the international circles as a counterbalance to Western influence, it remains to be seen whether Turkey will ever materialize on its declared intentions of becoming a member. If it does, this would constitute boundary breaking with the West. However, as it stands now, the country's threats to become an SCO member should be considered as boundary challenging rather than boundary breaking. In other words, through its threats to become an SCO member, Turkey only signals its intentions to acquire an increased independence from within the Western alliance.

THE PURCHASE OF AN S-400 MISSILE DEFENSE SYSTEM FROM RUSSIA

Cooperative Balancing with Russia against the West

Thus far, the strongest case to illustrate Turkey's potential to break its boundaries with the West is observed in defense matters. Since 2016, the

---

[1] Interview with a British journalist via Skype, October 14, 2016.

Turkish government has been negotiating with Russia to purchase a missile defense system. The two parties signed an agreement at the end of December 2017 (Gümrükçü and Toksabay 2017). Such an agreement is best explained in the context of Turkey's recent tensions with the EU, the United States, and NATO and increased alienation from the West. This chapter makes an argument that the Turkish government uses cooperative balancing and compellent threats to engage in boundary breaking against the USA, NATO, and the EU in security/defense affairs. As illustrated in the following paragraphs, the eventual purchase of an S-400 missile defense system from Russia would not only create problems with regards to interoperability but also expose the alliance's defense networks to potential intelligence infiltration from Russia, as "any datalinks that were patched together with S-400 batteries" may compromise NATO's defensive networks (Roblin 2018).

Ever since 2007, Turkey has been simultaneously working on developing a national long-range ground-to-ground missile system (Bekdil 2017), while considering the acquisition of long-range air and missile defense systems with an estimated cost of 4 billion USD (Yavuz 2011, Alirıza and Brannen 2013). Turkey already has a shorter-range missile defense system developed nationally (*Al Jazeera* 2017). But it currently relies on a Cold War-era US system – Nike-Hercules (MIM-14) – for its long-range air defense and NATO ballistic missile system (Alirıza and Brannen 2013). In 2008, the tender for the acquisition of a missile defense system was postponed until 2011, "due to NATO's missile defense system project" (Yavuz 2011).

In 2013, Ankara finalized the long-postponed tender, declaring that the Chinese HQ-9 missile defense system produced by the China Precision Machinery Import and Export Corporation (CPMIEC) won the tender, due to its price advantage and generosity in terms of transferring technology. CPMIEC agreed to allow for Turkey to acquire the blueprints for the system for over 50 percent local co-production of missile parts (Alirıza and Brannen 2013, Kucera 2015). Nevertheless, the deal caused great controversy with NATO allies because of the integration problem with the Chinese missile system and the NATO air defense umbrella, as it would compromise the security of NATO data (Alirıza and Brannen 2013, Kucera 2015, Oruç 2016). In response to criticism from the USA and NATO that a Chinese missile system would not be compatible with the NATO system, Erdoğan was reported to say:

There are Russian missiles in NATO countries. We have evidence that there are seven or eight countries whose military forces have Russian missiles . . . There is no stipulation that you cannot buy weapons or that you cannot enter into co-production outside of NATO. (Quoted in Alirıza and Brannen 2013)

In response, in 2013, a US State Department representative announced that the USA has "serious concerns about the Turkish Government's contract discussions with a US-sanctioned company for a missile defense system that will not be interoperable with NATO systems or collective defense capabilities" (quoted in Alirıza and Brannen 2013). To discourage Turkey from awarding the tender to China, US lawmakers inserted a provision into the National Defense Authorization Act (NDAA) for Fiscal Year 2015 stating that no US Department of Defense funds could be used to integrate Chinese missile defense systems into US or NATO systems (United States 2014). Consequently, the Turkish government yielded to pressures from the transatlantic allies and declared that the 3.4 billion USD program with China was canceled in 2015 (Kucera 2015).

Back in 2011, Russia was quickly eliminated from the tender, as Turkey raised serious concerns about the fact that an older model – S-300 missiles – was possessed by Greece and the Republic of Cyprus and that the Russian defense company Rostec did not make any commitments for joint production (Yavuz 2011). Nevertheless, Turkey has been seriously considering purchasing a Russian missile defense system since 2016. In their meeting in March 2017, Putin and Erdoğan reaffirmed their agreement on that, and the Turkish and Russian authorities negotiated the terms of financing since Turkey asked for a loan (Ünal 2017b, PressTV 2017). Turkey and Russia reached a 2.5 billion USD agreement in July 2017, which encompasses the selling of two S-400 missile batteries. In December 2017, the two sides signed an agreement for the purchase of the missile defense system.

Similar to the case when Turkey was negotiating with China to acquire a missile defense system, the negotiations with Russia caused controversy with the NATO allies. The fact that a NATO member country seriously considers reinforcing its defense systems by agreeing to purchase Russian S-400 missiles raises serious questions about whether Turkey's defense posture is shifting. One interviewee warns that acquiring a missile defense system from Russia would be "a bigger mistake than to acquire it from the Chinese."[2] Similarly, as a former member of the Turkish Parliament from the CHP cautions:

---

[2] Interview with a British journalist via Skype, October 14, 2016.

There are a lot in DC who have argued that "it's just a bargaining tool, or it's just posturing. The Turks will never buy Chinese or Russian equipment. They are committed to NATO. Wait and see." Is it a risk that we are willing to take? Because it takes only one round of procurement from outside NATO, and, trust me, the game will forever be changed. A Turkey that starts buying its military equipment from China or Russia is both politically and militarily a different Turkey and will have wider consequences for the US and the EU. (Erdemir 2017)

In response to allegations that purchasing a Russian missile defense system means Turkey is turning its back to NATO, Turkish officials repeatedly deny that Turkey is "breaking ties with NATO" and state that Turkey simply feels the pressing need to defend itself against the backdrop of the threats from ISIS, the Syrian civil war, Kurdish terrorism, and other regional threats (quoted in *Al Jazeera* 2017). Yet, on the question of whether Turkey feels let down by NATO allies on the acquisition of a missile system, then Turkish Defense Minister Işık noted, "NATO member states could have been more frank and more sincere" (quoted in *Al Jazeera* 2017). In the words of an analyst, "Being abandoned by its NATO partners, again and again, Turkey now knows that it needs to protect itself. In order to become self-sufficient with regards to security, Turkey now asks for technology transfer when it buys high-tech weaponry systems" (Oruç 2016).

Moreover, Turkish authorities repeatedly bring up their complaints with other NATO allies' support for certain groups that threaten Turkey's security. Then Turkish Defense Minister Işık, in his interview with *Al Jazeera* in March 2017, notes that "we have serious complaints" in terms of the origins of weapons given to terrorist organizations, such as the PKK and PYD, and adds, "We state our disturbance on weapons of German origin coming to the hands of PKK and PYD whenever possible in the most clear manner to our counterparts ... [T]hey should avoid acts that may pose a threat to Turkey's security" (quoted in *Al Jazeera* 2017).

Turkish authorities consistently "stand firm against NATO pressure" and signal Turkey's determination to pursue the deal with Russia (Ünal 2017a). For instance, in July 2018, Turkish Foreign Minister Çavuşoğlu claimed that the missile defense system poses no threat to the alliance members (Sprenger 2018). They repeatedly point to other NATO members, such as Greece and Cyprus, who "have been using systems purchased from countries outside of NATO" (Işık, quoted in Ünal 2017a). They also emphasize that Turkey attempted to purchase a missile defense system from the NATO allies first but faced challenges on pricing and on technology sharing (Sprenger 2018). Turkish Presidential Spokesman

Ibrahim Kalın emphasizes that Turkey uses three criteria, "price, technology transfer, and time of delivery," when making a decision on purchasing the missile defense system (quoted in Ünal 2017a).

In July 2018, Turkish Foreign Minister Çavuşoğlu announced that Turkey tried to procure missiles from NATO sources but was rejected (Wemer 2018). He underlined Turkey's frustration that the NATO defense system may only cover 30 percent of Turkey's airspace and asked, "Who is going to protect my nation, my people, from the missiles coming from Syria or any other countries?" (Çavuşoğlu, quoted in Wemer 2018). Çavuşoğlu also argued the purchase was necessary after Germany "withdrew" its Patriot missiles from Turkey's southern border (Wemer 2018).

As was the case with the Chinese tender, integration and compatibility issues with NATO defenses are once again on the table. The acquisition of the Russian missile system potentially undermines the Connected Forces Initiative (CFI) of NATO, which "aims to enhance the high level of interconnectedness and interoperability" of Allied forces on operations through a comprehensive training, exercise, and assessment program "with the use of cutting-edge technology" (NATO 2016a). As indicated by an interviewee, it is "worrisome for NATO to see a country like Turkey talking about purchasing an anti-missile system from Russia or China, when it is clear that only an American system would be interoperable with NATO."[3] There are serious concerns on the US side about the capability of the S-400 system to "spy on Turkish territory exposing sensitive details of the F-35 performance, such as capturing minor patterns of F-35 flights" and to monitor the operational activities at İncirlik Air Base (Erkuş 2019).

In response to compatibility and integration criticisms, Turkish officials emphasize that Turkey has no intention to integrate the Russian missile systems into the NATO system (Ünal 2017b). Turkish authorities frequently reaffirm that Turkey's main goal is to develop its own air and missile defense system program that can "capture missiles earlier, or determine such threats earlier and eliminate them" (Işık, quoted in *Al Jazeera* 2017). The Turkish government officials deny that the negotiations with the Russians are a bluff or simply a "negotiating tactic to put pressure on NATO allies to say if you don't give us NATO missiles, we have other options" (Işık, quoted in *Al Jazeera* 2017).

Indicating that the acquisition of the missile defense system from Russia is not a simple bluff, in April 2018 Erdoğan and Putin agreed to

[3] Interview with a Turkish-American academic, October 21, 2016.

expedite the delivery of the S-400 missile defense system. The first delivery is scheduled to take place in July 2019 and the system is expected to become operational in October 2019 (Erkuş 2019). With the implementation of the agreement to purchase S-400 missile defense systems from Russia, Turkey would clearly engage in boundary breaking against the West, particularly the USA and NATO. It would specifically indicate collaborative balancing between Turkey and Russia on defense matters against the West. Given the ongoing tensions between the West and Russia, this move represents a significant turning point in Turkish foreign policy behavior.

Costly Signaling

US policymakers have long warned that the purchase of a S-400 missile defense system would constitute an act that is sanctionable under US law. Under Section 231 of the Countering America's Adversaries Through Sanctions Act (CAATSA) passed by the US Congress and signed by US President Trump in August 2017, sanctions will be imposed to those entering into transactions with Russian intelligence and military entities (United States 2017). Therefore, the acquisition of the S-400 missile defense system will carry significant costs for Turkey.

Nevertheless, as already noted, the Turkish authorities went ahead with signing the purchase agreement with Russia in 2017, and the system is expected to become operational in October 2019 (Erkuş 2019). From the perspective of the USA, it jeopardizes the integrity of the NATO alliance, due to reasons outlined in the previous section, especially at such a critical time, when the alliance needs to adopt a unified front against the threats posed by the Russian Federation. In order to discourage Turkey from the purchase, US authorities have been taking some concrete steps, attaching real costs to Turkey's planned acquisition of the S-400 missile defense system.

One such important step has been the threat to remove Turkey from the F-35 JSF program. Turkey has been a partner on the F-35 program since 2002 and was scheduled to purchase 100 F-35s from the USA over multiple years, starting in 2018. As part of the F-35 JSF consortium, Turkish industries were eligible to become suppliers to the global F-35 fleet, creating industrial opportunities of about 12 billion USD for Turkish companies (F-35.com 2019). A Turkish facility in Eskişehir was already designated for the F135 engine production and sustainment as well as for overhaul capability (F-35.com 2019).

A second important step has been the introduction and signing into law of the NDAA for Fiscal Year 2019. The US House of Representatives passed its own version of the NDAA for Fiscal Year 2019 in May 2018, and the US Senate did so in June 2018. US President Trump signed it on August 13, 2018 (Garamone 2018). The NDAA for Fiscal Year 2019 identified the sale of S-400 to Turkey as a threat to the NATO alliance and enforced a freeze on F-35 deliveries until the secretary of defense, in consultation with the secretary of state, submits a report to the US Congress about the US relationship with Turkey and the risks involved in this purchase (United States 2018). The tying of Turkey's participation at the JSF consortium with the purchase of S-400 illustrates the use of an issue-linkage bargaining tactic on the US side.

In response to threats to cease Turkey's involvement in the JSF consortium, then Turkish Defense Minister Nurettin Canikli accused the US of "blackmailing" Turkey to call off the finalized deal with Russia on the S-400 air defense missile systems and noted that "it is not right to tie the two issues together" as Turkey fulfilled all responsibilities as a part of its F-35 program participation, including the payment of over 800 million USD toward the total of 11 billion USD (*Sputnik News* June 14, 2018). Canikli added, "[T]he S-400 system does not at all threaten the F-35s," and the prevention of Turkey from acquiring F-35s as previously agreed would create a "dangerous trust problem" in bilateral relations (Sputnik News June 14, 2018). Turkish Foreign Minister Çavusoğlu in an interview with PBS NewsHour in June 2018 noted, "In the last 10 years, we tried to buy [the missile defense system] from the United States, which is our ally, but it didn't work," leaving Turkey with no other choice but to purchase the missile defense system from Russia (quoted in interview with PBS NewsHour June 4, 2018). Turkish authorities also emphasize the costs that the USA would incur in case of the removal of Turkey from the F-35 JSF consortium. The US Department of Defense estimates that it would take about two years to replace Turkish firms with new suppliers (Seligman 2018).

The US Department of Defense (2018) submitted the requested report to the US Congress in late November 2018. The unclassified Executive Summary of the report underlines that Turkey's desire to acquire S-400 should be interpreted in light of the country's perception of "growing regional security threats from aircraft and ballistic missiles" and its frustration "with its protracted, decade-long search for an air and missile defense system" (US Department of Defense 2018, p. 1). It warns that the purchase would have "unavoidable negative consequences for US–Turkey bilateral relations" (US Department of Defense 2018, p. 1).

The purchase of the S-400 air defense missile systems represents a major breaking point in Turkey's relations with the West. By repeatedly signaling its willingness to go ahead with the purchase, Turkish authorities engage in costly signaling and are indicating that they are willing to incur significant costs, such as possible sanctions and the prevention of the transfer of F-35s, along with further "damaging" complications in the USA–Turkey bilateral defense industrial cooperation, such as Turkish acquisition programs of "Patriot missile defense system, CH-47F Chinook heavy lift helicopter, UH-60 Black Hawk utility helicopter, and the F-16 Fighting Falcon aircraft" (US Department of Defense 2018, p. 2). In March 2019, the US Department of Defense made its first direct warning to Turkey and announced that there will be "grave consequences" for the military relationship between Turkey and the USA with implications on Patriots and F-35s, if Turkey goes ahead with the purchase (Karam 2019). Therefore, in this case, costly signaling is best categorized under boundary breaking, as the costs have been significantly increased and there is every indication that Turkey will move forward with the purchase, potentially burning bridges with the West on defense cooperation. On March 29, 2019, Turkish Foreign Minister Çavuşoğlu once again reiterated that the agreement with Russia "is a done deal" (DeYoung 2019). Consequently, in the beginning of April 2019, the USA suspended Turkey's participation in the F-35 JSF program (DeYoung 2019).

CONCLUSION

This chapter provides an examination of the implications for Turkey's relations with the West of the rekindled relationship between Turkey and Russia in security/defense. Turkey's repeated announcement of intentions to join the SCO constitute boundary challenging, and the purchase of the S-400 missile defense shield from Russia represent boundary breaking with the West. Through the use of costly signaling, compellent threats for alternative alliances, and military cooperative balancing with Russia, Turkey increasingly signals its resolve to engage in boundary breaking against the EU, NATO, and the USA.

According to Pape (2005, p. 37), if states cooperate on a repeated basis, "they may gradually increase their trust in each other's willingness to cooperate against the unipolar leader's ambitions." The analysis in this chapter demonstrates that increasing Turkey–Russia cooperation in

security/defense matters is a harbinger of the attempts on these two countries' side to "demonstrate resolve in a manner that signals a commitment to
resist" the West's ambitions (Pape 2005, p. 37). In fact, affirming this, in
March 2019, Turkey and Russia announced that they will hold joint patrols
in Syria and a joint naval drill in the Black Sea (Karam 2019). From 2018 to
2019, Erdoğan consistently announced that Turkey is also considering
acquiring a S-500 missile defense system from Russia, adding that joint
production with Russia is also on the table.

As explained in the next chapter, while it is important to acknowledge
that a number of factors might adversely affect the rapprochement
between Turkey and Russia, such as the developments in the Syrian civil
war and the Russian support for Syrian Kurdish forces, the case studies
examined in this chapter effectively illustrate that Turkey increasingly
resorts to costly signaling, compellent threats for alternative alliances,
and collaborative balancing with Russia against the USA, NATO, and
the EU. Therefore, this chapter concludes that Turkey progressively
engages in boundary breaking against the West.

Referring to the effectiveness of Turkey's collaborative balancing strategy with Russia in attracting an increased attention to Turkey's strategic
importance by its Western allies, a Member of the Turkish Parliament
interviewee notes, "[Then US Vice President] Biden visited Turkey three
times [in 2016]: first two times, he criticized human rights violations in
Turkey, but on the third time, after the apology from Turkey to Russia,
there was no criticism of human rights violations from Biden on his third
visit."[4] Another illustration of the effectiveness of this strategy is the fact
that the US Department of State approved a possible sale of the Patriot
Surface-to-Air Missile (SAM) system with an estimated cost of 3.5 billion
USD in December 2018 (Erkuş 2019). The US made a formal sale offer to
Turkey in January 2019, which expired at the end of March 2019. Upon
the expiration of March 2019 deadline, the US Department of Defense
announced that Turkey's participation at the F-35 program was suspended until Turkey cancels its planned purchase of S-400 (DeYoung
2019).

Due to lack of financing and joint production possibilities, the offer
from the USA does not seem to be particularly appealing to Turkey (Erkuş
2019). While the Turkish authorities have been announcing that Turkey
considers buying both the US and the Russian systems, this does not seem

---

[4] Interview with a Member of Turkish Parliament from AKP, Washington DC,
September 30, 2016.

to be feasible from military, technical, or financial perspectives. In the very short term, Turkey will have to make a choice, one which will have significant repercussions on its status within the Western alliance. Some argue that Turkish authorities used the S-400 issue as a political weapon in the prelude to the March 31 local elections in Turkey (Karan 2019). Nevertheless, at the time of writing, there was no indication from the Turkish side that the S-400 deal with Russia would be canceled.

Indicating the use of issue-linkage bargaining by the Turkish side, on April 4, 2019 – in response to US Vice President Mike Pence's warning that "Turkey must choose. Does it want to remain a critical partner in the most successful military alliance in history or does it want to risk the security of that partnership by making such reckless decisions that undermine our alliance?" – Turkish Vice President Fuat Oktay noted, "The United States must choose. Does it want to remain Turkey's ally or risk our friendship by joining forces with terrorists to undermine its NATO ally's defense against its enemies?" (Jones 2019). Consequently, Turkey and the USA may reach an agreement on the S-400 issue, if the two sides find a mutually agreed solution to the Syrian quagmire following the US withdrawal from the region. If the S-400 issue is not resolved, then the rift between Turkey and the West is likely to become too wide to mend, pushing Turkey further under the sphere of influence of Russia. The subsequent chapter examines the spillover of the Turkish-Russian rapprochement in defense/security affairs to the Middle East, making the use of blackmail power and issue-linkage bargaining more evident.

7

Turkey's Foreign Policy on Syria and Iraq

Walt (2009, p. 104) holds that states balance when they "coordinate action, augment their power, and take on new commitments with others, because they are worried about the unipole's dominant position and/or are alarmed by the actions it is undertaking." As Chapters 5 and 6 demonstrate, Turkey already engages in a number of energy and security/defense initiatives with Russia, increasingly breaking its boundaries with the West on some issues while running the risk of breaking its boundaries on others. This chapter examines an additional venue with significant implications for Turkey's relations with the West, by focusing on Turkey's foreign policy on Syria and Iraq. It first examines the motivations behind Turkish boundary breaking against the West in Syria and Iraq and then delineates the tools utilized by Turkey against the West. It concludes with a discussion of the effects of Turkish foreign policy in the Middle East on Turkey–USA and Turkey–NATO relations.

INCOMPATIBLE INTERESTS BETWEEN TURKEY AND THE USA

Turkey and the United States had significant disagreements on the courses of actions to be taken in Syria and Iraq due to a multiplicity of reasons, including Turkey's concerns regarding the future balance of power in the region, the priority assigned to the removal of Bashar al-Assad from power, and the involvement of Syrian Kurds in the fight against the IS. The domestic political factors have also created a hospitable environment for Turkish boundary-breaking behavior against the West in Syria and Iraq. As many interviewees indicate,

Erdoğan increasingly emphasizes the importance of "Turkey's independence from the West."[1]

In Syria, whereas Turkey prioritized the removal of Assad from power, the USA prioritized the fight against the IS. US officials often made the argument that the Kurds are the best-organized force on the ground in the fight against the IS in Iraq and Syria. Turkey's biggest fear is to have an independent Kurdish state on its southern borders. Turkey is concerned that an independent Kurdish state in northern Syria might embolden its own Kurdish minority, constituting about one-fifth of Turkey's population, to pursue a similar goal, jeopardizing the territorial integrity of Turkey (Abramowitz and Edelman 2015, Afanasieva and Dziadosz 2014). In Iraq, Turkey is worried about the increased influence of Iran and its proxies, which has the potential to disrupt the regional balance of power to Turkey's disadvantage.

The main breaking point in the bilateral relations goes back to the IS's siege of Kobane. In early October 2014, Turkish Kurds protested the Turkish government's lack of action in a series of violent protests that caused twelve deaths (Cockburn 2014). Many experts agree that the US support for the Kurdish forces in the fight against the IS creates a significant amount of tension and mistrust in USA–Turkey relations (Tol and Pearson 2016, Abramowitz and Edelman 2016, Harris 2017, Robinson 2017, McLeary 2017).[2] One interviewee characterizes the Kurdish problem as the "main driver of anti-Americanism in Turkey."[3] Despite Turkey's pleas, following the failure of the US attempts at training and funding "moderates" in Syria in October 2015 the Obama Administration decided to support the YPG and formed the Syrian Democratic Forces (SDF), a 50,000-strong umbrella rebel group in Syria, which is mainly dominated by the YPG forces, in the fight against the IS.

The Kurdistan Workers' Party (*Partiya Karkeren Kurdistan*, PKK), recognized as a terrorist organization by Turkey, the EU, and the USA, has been pursuing military insurgency in Turkey since 1984, which has led to a death toll of over 40,000 in Turkey (International Crisis Group [ICG] 2019). Turkish officials consistently make a case that the Democratic

---

[1] Interview with a Turkish academic, Washington DC, September 30, 2016.
[2] Interview with a Turkish academic, Washington DC, September 30, 2016; Interview with a US journalist, Washington DC, September 30, 2016; Interview with a Turkish-American academic, October 21, 2016.
[3] Interview with a Turkish academic, Washington DC, September 30, 2016.

Union Party (*Partiya Yekitiya Demokrat*, PYD) and its military wing the YPG are extensions of the PKK terrorist organization. On the topic, then Turkish Defense Minister Fikri Işık underlined:

> The YPG is a terrorist organization. Those giving orders to the YPG and the PYD are the seniors of the PKK. The YPG has direct organic ties with the PKK ... The whole world sees that there is an indirect support [of terrorist organizations through support for the PYD]. We are disturbed by the ambivalence of the West. (Quoted in *Al Jazeera* 2017)

The USA, however, does not recognize the YPG as a terrorist organization and relies on the SDF (McLeary 2017). The arguments that the USA utilizes for its support for the Syrian Kurds create an "unprecedented" degree of disagreement between the USA and Turkey.[4] Turkish officials regularly maintain that "the PKK has deployed the YPG's Syrian man-power, resources, tactics and newly acquired battle skills in military operations within Turkey" (ICG 2017, p. 5). One interviewee adds, "It is no longer a conspiracy theory that the US is using one terrorist organization [the YPG] to fight against another terrorist organization [IS]."[5] Another interviewee characterizes the argument that the PKK and the YPG are separate as "fiction" and notes that this approach "enrages the Turkish public opinion."[6] In an op-ed in the *New York Times*, President Erdoğan complained:

> My government has repeatedly shared our concerns with American officials about their decision to train and equip the PKK's allies in Syria. Unfortunately, our words have fallen on deaf ears, and American weapons ended up being used to target civilians and members of our security forces in Syria, Iraq, and Turkey. (Erdoğan 2018)

Since summer 2012, the PYD has begun to fill the void created by the Syrian regime's forces retreating from the mostly Kurdish-majority towns in northern Syria (Dalay 2017). Despite its concerns about the PYD's consolidation of power in northern Syria, Turkey initially did not react militarily due to the start of its own Kurdish peace process at the end of 2012 (Dalay 2017). By November 2013, the PYD established an interim Kurdish government composed of three autonomous cantons in northern Syria, adding to the unease on the part of the Turkish authorities (Park 2015). The expansion of the IS influence in Iraq and Syria in 2014

---

[4] Interview with a Turkish-American academic, October 21, 2016.
[5] Interview with a Turkish academic, Washington DC, September 30, 2016.
[6] Interview with a US journalist, Washington DC, September 30, 2016.

facilitated the PYD's expansion of territory and acquisition of international legitimacy and military equipment (Dalay 2017).

Since 2014, despite strong objections from Turkey, the USA has relied on the PYD and the YPG in the fight against the IS. The USA airdropped ammunition, small arms, and medical supplies to the YPG in its fight against the IS in Kobani as early as 2014 (Schmitt 2014). On the topic, then US Secretary of State John Kerry noted, "We understand fully the fundamentals of [Turkish] opposition and ours to any kind of terrorist group and particularly obviously the challenges [Turkey] faces with respect [to] the PKK" (quoted in Chulov et al. 2014). Despite this reassurance, the USA continued to provide logistical support to the Syrian Kurds in the counterterrorism campaign against the IS.

Nevertheless, there were a number of positive developments in the meantime. In October 2014, giving in to the pressure from the USA, Turkey agreed to allow the Iraqi Kurdish fighters (known as *peshmerga*) to cross its borders to northern Syria in the war against the IS in Kobani (Chulov et al. 2014). Most of these *peshmerga* forces were the ones that were affiliated with Barzani's Kurdistan Democratic Party (KDP), with which Turkey maintains a close relationship (Abramowitz and Edelman 2015). Following multiple rounds of negotiations, in February 2015, Turkey and the USA also signed a deal for Turkey to train and equip moderate Syrian rebels. However, even then, the two sides had different goals in mind. Whereas the USA intended for the program to train fighters to combat the IS, Turkey had an additional goal of ousting Assad from power (Abramowitz and Edelman 2015).

Adding a further complication to the bilateral relations between the USA and Turkey, the Kurdish peace process in Turkey collapsed with the renewed fighting between the Turkish military and the PKK in July 2015, putting an end to a two-and-a-half-year-long ceasefire. The PKK initiated a new round of terrorist attacks against Turkish security forces. In response to the urban warfare campaign that the PKK started in major Turkish cities, the Turkish military engaged in a more intensive military campaign against the terrorist organization (Abramowitz and Edelman 2016).

The deployment of Turkish troops near Mosul toward the end of 2015 created additional tensions in USA–Turkey relations. Mosul is traditionally a Sunni-Turkmen city in Iraq. Turkey insists on taking part in the Mosul offensive against the IS, while Iraq and the USA object to a direct Turkish involvement. A central concern for the Turkish authorities is the question of who will fill the vacuum in Mosul after the removal of the IS from the area. Turkey is concerned that the Shiite extremists will take advantage of the vacuum and "attempt to modify the demographic structure of Mosul" and Tal Afar (Işık, quoted in *Al Jazeera* 2017). Turkey's sensitivities about the future of Mosul and Tal Afar are directly related to its concerns about the regional balance of power. As then Turkish Defense Minister Işık maintained:

We are advising the Iraqi government to take a tough stance and display astuteness in preventing the modification of the demographic structure in Mosul and Tal Afar. Tal Afar is a Turkmen city. There are Shia Turkmens and Sunni Turkmens. The modification of this demographic structure would greatly discomfort Turkey ... Everyone needs to know that Turkey will not remain silent to a demographic restructuring in Tal Afar [and Mosul]. (Quoted in *Al Jazeera* 2017)

In the words of an interviewee, "Turkey wanted to play a more visible role in Mosul, but Iraq and the US sidelined Turkey."[7] While the Turkish Parliament passed a resolution in October 2016 "to extend its military presence in Iraq [and Syria] for a year to take on what it called 'terrorist organizations,'" Iraqi Prime Minister Al-Abadi "warned Turkey that it risks triggering a regional war" (Tol and Pearson 2016, p. 2). Turkey is concerned about the rise of Iran's influence in Iraq and Syria and consistently makes a case that "the PKK and Shiite militias are acting in concert," a concern shared by the Kurdish Regional Government and Barzani's KDP (Zaman 2017). Nevertheless, the USA was hesitant to allow Turkey to participate in the Mosul operation as it could not only potentially "spark clashes between Turkish forces and Iranian-backed Iraqi Shiite militias" but also lead Turkey to use the Mosul operation in launching attacks against the PKK camps in northern Iraq (Tol and Pearson 2016, p. 2).

The military operation in Raqqa, Syria put additional strains on the USA–Turkey relationship (Pearson 2016, Jeffrey 2016). Turkish officials frequently warn the USA that the Kurds seek to seize the opportunity to change the demographic nature of Raqqa in an attempt to create a "Kurdish federation" (İlnur Çevik, quoted in Peterson 2017). The key question was whether the USA would rely on Kurdish forces in the war against the IS (Harris 2017). While the USA advocated for the deployment of the SDF led by the YPG, Turkey advocated for using a non-Kurdish Syrian proxy force and accused the USA of supporting "terrorists" that would jeopardize the territorial integrity of Syria. Turkey feared that the

---

[7] Interview with a Turkish-American academic, October 21, 2016.

US support for PYD/YPG "would facilitate a PYD-dominated northern Syria" after the IS is defeated (Jeffrey 2017).

Accordingly, Turkey and the USA continued negotiations about potential Turkish involvement in the military offensive in Raqqa (De Luce and McLeary 2017). In order to prevent USA–YPG collaboration, Turkey demanded that the USA should sever ties with the YPG/PYD, offered to take part in the operation through ground troops, and threatened not to take part in the battle of Raqqa if the YPG/PYD are involved in the operation. While the USA indicated its willingness to collaborate with Turkey, since Turkey strongly opposed the involvement of the YPG and the PYD in the military operations and requested the Turkish forces to be allowed to go south of Al-Bab, the two sides could not reach an agreement. Turkey was concerned that the YPG's lead role in Raqqa would deepen its alliance with the USA and add to its international legitimacy, strengthening the PKK's strategic hand (ICG 2017, p. 5).

Turkish authorities warned that if PYD dominates Raqqa after the IS is cleaned out of the city, it would lead to "a huge conflict ... between the people of that region and the Kurds" (Işık, quoted in *Al Jazeera* 2017). Referring to the involvement of PYD/YPG in the Raqqa offensive, Turkish Prime Minister Binali Yıldırım threatened, "If [the USA] insists on carrying out this operation with terrorist organizations, then our relations will be harmed" (quoted in Harris 2017). On the same topic, Erdoğan repeatedly criticized the USA and was reported as stating, "We don't consider [the USA's] business with a terrorist organization appropriate, taking into account our strategic partnership and alliance in NATO" (quoted in Peterson 2017).

The Turkish government advocated for the USA to rely on Turkish troops and the Free Syrian Army, "a largely untested Arab Force" (De Luce and McLeary 2017). Then Turkish Defense Minister Işık maintained that the OES proved "that a force consisting of the locals of that region [which includes the Free Syrian Army] could achieve success in a short time" and added that the merging of the East and West cantons of the PYD is "a red line" for Turkey (quoted in *Al Jazeera* 2017). The USA, however, was not "convinced that Turkey [could] commit enough ground troops to replace the Kurdish forces" (Tol and Pearson 2016, p. 2). Therefore, it maintained its support for the use of the SDF in the Raqqa offensive. A Pentagon official is reported as saying, "Kurds occupy almost all of the leadership positions" in the SDF (quoted in De Luce and McLeary 2017), as it is generally accepted that "the Syrian Arabs recruited for the SDF lack much, if any, military experience" (Robinson 2017). The concern on the part of the USA was that introducing "the Turkish-backed militias would complicate the [Raqqa] operation," as they have a history of attacking the Kurdish fighters in northern Syria (De Luce and McLeary 2017). One analyst warns that launching the Raqqa offensive without an agreement with Turkey would "jeopardize larger US regional and even global geo-political objectives" (Robinson 2017), noting:

While arming the Syrian Kurds might be the easiest way to maintain momentum in the campaign against the Islamic State group, this option courts two significant risks. Turkey may attack Syrians and the US forces working with them, or stop flights and related counter-Islamic State group activity on Turkish bases, severely complicating the campaign against the group … The second risk is that Syrian Arabs will reject the use of the Kurdish-dominated force to liberate their areas.

In an attempt to ease Turkey's concerns about the YPG using "US-supplied weapons to create an independent state," US officials noted that they are looking at options including rationing ammunition and weaponry supplied to the YPG (De Luce and McLeary 2017, Robinson 2017). As noted by Lieutenant General Stephen Townsend, the top US battlefield commander in the fight against the IS, another alternative is that "the US could serve as a guarantor by cementing its long-term influence over the Syrian Kurds" so that "they are not a threat to Turkey" (quoted in Robinson 2017). But it is not clear how this would be implemented in practice. Following this discussion of the drastic differences between Turkish and US national interests, the next section discusses the different tools of statecraft that Turkey utilized on the topic.

TURKEY'S INTRA-ALLIANCE OPPOSITION TOOLS OF STATECRAFT IN THE MIDDLE EAST

Compellent Threats

The presence of US and Russian personnel in YPG-held areas was origin-ally thought to have the potential to deter a possible attack from Turkey. Nevertheless, indicating how volatile USA–Turkey relations could get very quickly, Turkish warplanes bombed Kurdish-controlled areas in northern Syria and northwest Iraq on April 25, 2017, killing "twenty YPG fighters and, in an apparent mistake, five members of the KDP's peshmerga force, which split control of Sinjar with rival PKK-backed forces in a tense cohabitation" (ICG 2017, p. 5). On May 1, 2017, Turkey conducted further air strikes on Kurdish positions in Syria and

Iraq, indicating a collision of interests between the United States and Turkey. The attack site was very close to where the US Special Forces were stationed.

Turkey issued a warning to the USA about the upcoming bombing only half an hour before the attack (McLeary 2017), demonstrating that it is a risky strategy to deploy American forces next to Kurdish forces (ICG 2017). The USA consequently sent an "additional detachment of US Army Rangers to the border as a buffer" between the Kurdish and Turkish forces (De Luce and McLeary 2017). In response to the US move, İlnur Çevik, chief advisor to Erdoğan, used very strong words to threaten the US forces in northern Syria, saying that, if the Kurds and Americans continue to work together, "we won't be considering the fact that there are armored American vehicles . . . All of a sudden, by accident, a few rockets can hit them" (quoted in McLeary 2017). This substantiates a major change in the approach by Turkey, signaling that the country is willing to engage in boundary breaking with the alliance through the use of such harsh compellent threats. As noted by an ICG report (2017, p. 5), "More extensive Turkish military action could seriously hamper a US-backed [SDF] offensive on Raqqa city by forcing the YPG to divert resources toward its own defense," as "the Syrian territory the YPG controls is largely flat and does not lend itself to the guerrilla warfare in which its fighters excel." Turkish authorities seem to be increasingly willing to engage in more military ways of balancing against the unipole in the Middle East.

Despite warnings from Turkey, in May 2017 the Trump Administration announced its decision to provide heavier arms to the YPG in the fight against the IS in Raqqa (Zanotti and Thomas 2017, Anderson 2017). Immediately following this statement, Turkish Foreign Minister Çavuşoğlu announced, "Every weapon in the hands of the YPG is a threat to Turkey" (quoted in Köksal 2017). Such significant divergences between the USA and Turkey in Iraq and Syria seem to motivate Turkey to pursue not only boundary challenging but also boundary breaking against the USA. Moreover, domestic developments in Turkey provide additional motivations to do so. There were legitimate concerns that Manbij, Syria, could become a conflict hot spot between Turkey and the USA. Somewhat alleviating these concerns, Turkey and the USA reached an agreement in early June 2018 with regard to the withdrawal of Kurds from Manbij, endorsing a "road map" for stability and security in Manbij, even though its terms are quite vague (Gall 2018). In March 2019, Turkish Defense Minister Hulusi Akar met with US Special Envoy for Syria James Jeffrey to further clarify the road map, especially in the aftermath of the Trump Administration's declaration of US withdrawal from Syria (*TRT World* March 5, 2019).

On February 13, 2019, then acting US Secretary of Defense Patrick Shanahan announced the USA's intentions to establish a multinational observer force in northeastern Syria. On the topic, an anonymous Turkish official noted that Turkey is given a symbolic place in the observer force so that it is prevented from "having a powerful military presence" in the region. The same official noted that, contrary to its envisioned symbolic role, Turkey "plans to push the YPG/PKK at least 30–40 kilometres south of its border and take military measures to block the terror group" and added that Turkey "opposes figures linked to the YPG/PKK terror group taking posts in administrative units as part of joint USA–Turkey efforts in Manbij" (*TRT World* March 5, 2019). Therefore, at the time of writing, it was still unclear how the road map would be implemented.

Costly Signaling

Through its open-border policy with Syria, Turkey sought to engage in costly signaling – the signaling of resolve to maintain a more equitable relationship with the United States and NATO, which has caused infiltration of IS cells into Turkey. Turkey was a latecomer to military operations against the IS. From the earlier days of the Syrian civil war onward, Turkish foreign policy primarily aimed at ousting Assad from power. Furthermore, the Turkish authorities were adamant about the need to create a safe zone alongside the northern border of Syria to allow for Syrian refugees to return back home. The safe zones concept was seen by Turkey "as a way to block Kurdish ambitions" in its southern border with Syria (Loveluck and DeYoung 2017). However, the USA did not support these goals and instead prioritized the war against the IS.

The US administration officials made recurrent efforts to gain Turkey's cooperation in this war. Nevertheless, Turkey was reluctant to join the anti-IS coalition led by the USA for a very long time. Up until September 2014, Turkey maintained that any Turkish involvement in the war would jeopardize the lives of the forty-nine Turkish citizens that were kidnapped by the IS, when the terrorist organization took control of Mosul in June 2014 (Abramowitz and Edelman 2015). As an effective illustration of Turkey's ambivalent approach toward the fight against the IS, Turkey was also reluctant to tighten its control over its borders with Syria. Turkey has kept its borders open in an attempt to allow Syrian rebels to cross freely between Turkey and Syria to procure logistical support against the Assad government forces.

However, Turkey's open-border policy also allowed IS fighters from around the world to cross freely into Syria and back. The USA and other NATO allies were critical of Turkey's security shortcomings along its borders with Syria and Iraq and put significant diplomatic pressure on Turkey to have a greater control over its borders. Providing evidence for the US frustration with the ambivalent policy of Turkey in the counter-terrorism campaign against the IS, then US Secretary of Defense Ashton Carter announced that "the single most important contribution" Turkey can make in the fight against the IS is to control "their own border" (quoted in İdiz 2016). Some note that, in the beginning phases of the Syrian civil war, Turkey "appears to have actively coordinated with Islamist rebels [affiliated with Jabhat al-Nusra terrorist organization] to provide indirect fire support against Assad regime targets" (Abramowitz and Edelman 2015, p. 14). This is a good indication of costly signaling, because, due to its open-border policy, Turkey now has IS sleeper cells within its territory, something that has not been the case before.

Turkey was certainly concerned about the threat that the IS posed to its national security; however, it was more concerned about the PKK and its affiliates' acquisition of power in northern Syria. Erdoğan is reported as saying that Turkey "will never allow the establishment of a [Kurdish] state on our southern frontier in the north of Syria" (quoted in Almukhtar and Wallace 2015). By prolonging the decision-making process to enter into the war against the IS, Turkish authorities aspired to increase the costs for the USA and its allies and consequently enhance Turkey's leverage vis-à-vis the USA to convince the USA not to choose Syrian Kurds over Turkey. However, for the sake of a timely intervention in the face of Russian and Iranian involvement in Syria and Iraq, the USA decided to take action immediately. This put the USA in a position to choose a convenient and an immediate partner (the Syrian Kurds) rather than an ideal partner (Turkey), a country with the second-largest military in NATO, in the counterterrorism campaign against the IS. Therefore, Turkey's calcula-tions of playing for time and engaging in costly signaling for the sake of increasing its leverage vis-à-vis the USA did not pay off. On the contrary, the IS started conducting more terrorist attacks on Turkish soil (Dalay 2017, Erdoğan 2017). Turkey continues to suffer from terrorist attacks by multiple terrorist organizations, including the PKK and the IS. This under-lines the immense human cost of the ambivalent policy Turkey displayed in the war against the IS.

Territorial/Asset Denial and Blackmail Power

Turkish boundary-breaking behavior is evident not only in Turkey's ambivalent approach in the fight against the IS but also in its denial of the use of İncirlik Air Base by the United States for anti-IS operations from June 2014 until July 2015. The US Air Base in İncirlik is of strategic importance for the US-led military operation against the IS. The USA had been lobbying Turkey to use İncirlik Air Base to launch strikes against the Islamic State in Syria up until the 2015 parliamentary elections in Turkey (Ackerman 2017). For over a year, at the height of the dangers posed by the IS, the Turkish government had denied such requests and also refused to join the US-led coalition against the terrorist organization.

Turkey hoped to use İncirlik "as a bargaining chip to secure US cooperation in fighting Assad" (Abramowitz and Edelman 2015, p. 19). The inability to use İncirlik caused the USA to "fly missions out of the Gulf, a distance of nearly 1,000 miles compared with Incirlik, which is 62 miles from the Syrian border and less than 300 miles from ISIS's capital of Raqqa" (Abramowitz and Edelman 2015, p. 19). Within a couple of weeks of the parliamentary elections in June 2015, Turkey finally allowed US warplanes to base out of İncirlik and joined the air strikes against the IS.

Even after the opening up of the İncirlik Air Base to US warplanes, however, Turkey continued to threaten territorial denial to ensure that its national interests and priorities in Syria and Iraq are respected by the USA and other NATO allies. In fact, the threat of territorial denial served as a compellent threat against the USA, especially in terms of the USA–Kurdish cooperation in the military campaign against the IS. Turkey and the USA may seem to be on the same side in the war against the IS, but, as noted earlier, as the battle of Raqqa loomed on the horizon, "the two NATO allies could not be further apart in their choice of the means to do the job" by supporting competing proxies in Syria (Peterson 2017). In case of the use of SDF/YPG forces in the Raqqa offensive, Turkey could potentially retaliate against the US support for the Syrian Kurds by denying the USA or NATO access to İncirlik. Put simply, Turkey was tempted to play the İncirlik card as a way to prevent the USA from choosing the Syrian Kurds in the battle of Raqqa. In March 2017, late US Senator John McCain, chairman of the Senate Armed Services Committee, "voiced concern about potential Turkish–YPG conflict affecting US interests in Syria – possibly including the use of Incirlik Air Base" (Zanotti and Thomas 2017, p. 5).

Underlining the blackmail power potential of Turkey, a Turkish-American scholar interviewee emphasizes that "[i]f the no-fly zone in Syria" does not materialize, Turkey might have "concerns about the American presence in Incirlik."[8] As one commentator similarly concludes, the USA can no longer "automatically assume it will have access to Turkish facilities in future Middle East contingencies," unless the operations in which these bases will be used "are clearly perceived by Turkish leaders to be in Turkey's national interest" (Larrabee 2011, p. 9). As Harris (2017) warns, "Turkish estrangement could have significant consequences for both the United States, which relies on Turkey's Incirlik Air Base to conduct air operations against the Islamic State, and the European Union, which struck a deal last year for Turkey to limit the flow of Syrian and Afghan refugees."

Another area where Turkey uses İncirlik Air Base as a part of its asset/territorial denial strategy to implement boundary breaking against the West is Turkey's attempt to punish Germany for passing a parliamentary resolution recognizing the Armenian Genocide in June 2016. Turkey banned the German parliamentarians from visiting German soldiers in İncirlik, once because of the Armenian Genocide bill (Bernd 2016) and a second time in May 2017 (Smale 2017) because Germany "granted asylum to a group of Turkish soldiers" who allegedly took part in the 2016 failed coup (Walsh 2017). In response to the German Parliament's search for alternatives to the İncirlik Air Base, such as Cyprus, Kuwait, or Jordan, Turkish Foreign Minister Mevlüt Çavuşoğlu was reported as saying, "If [Germany] want[s] to leave, let's just say goodbye … That's up to them and we won't beg" (quoted in Walsh 2017). One scholar warns that moving the German forces to an alternative air base might put German troops at a greater risk, as the German Air Force uses the same facilities and operates side by side with other NATO member countries that share the same military culture and coordination rules at the İncirlik Air Base (Özcan 2017). German authorities accused Turkey of blackmailing Germany (Walsh 2017). In response, Çavuşoğlu referred to the March 2017 diplomatic skirmish with the German local authorities due to their ban of Turkish officials holding rallies in support of the April 2017 constitutional referendum campaign and noted, "If what we are doing is blackmail, then what was that?" (Walsh 2017). Germany eventually decided to move its reconnaissance and refueling aircraft from İncirlik to Jordan in September 2017 (*Deutsche Welle* September 28, 2017, Smale

---

[8] Interview with a Turkish-American academic, October 21, 2016.

2017). With this move, Turkey can be said to have lost important leverage against this NATO/EU member.

There are additional issues in which Turkey may potentially use İncirlik Air Base as a bargaining chip against the West. As Jeffrey (2016) mentions, "General frictions in bilateral relations can get really nasty on two issues: the extradition request of Gülen, and other alternatives to the Incirlik base in Turkey." Turkey could potentially use the threat to deny the use of İncirlik by US warplanes to successfully bring Gülen back to Turkey for a trial. Illustrating this point, in the immediate aftermath of the failed coup, power was cut at the İncirlik Air Base. Steven Cook, an expert on Turkish politics with the Council on Foreign Relations, suggested that this was done in part "to demonstrate Turks have some leverage over the US" (quoted in Starr 2016). One report emphasizes that İncirlik "has become more of a vulnerability than an asset for Washington" as the fear of losing access to it "paralyzes US policy" (Abramowitz and Edelman 2016, p. 13) and recommends that the USA increase its leverage vis-à-vis Turkey by "looking into alternatives to Incirlik [such as Cyprus, Jordan, or Iraq]" (Abramowitz and Edelman 2016, p. 17). In January 2018, as a result of the restrictions imposed by Turkey, the US air force combat operations at İncirlik have been run down, and a squadron of A-10 Warthog ground attack jets was redeployed to Afghanistan, leaving only the refueling aircraft at İncirlik (Tisdall 2018). This is an ultimate indication of the lack of trust between NATO allies and Turkey and the unbridgeable rift that is taking place within the alliance.

Military and Diplomatic Cooperative Balancing with Russia

The Turkey–Russia crisis from the downing of the Russian jet in 2015 "emboldened the PYD and the PKK" (Dalay 2017). In response to the West's lack of support for its national security concerns in Syria, and being sidelined by its traditional allies, Turkey attempted to rekindle relations with Russia in the second half of 2016 (Kasapoğlu et al. 2017). Turkey's military and diplomatic cooperation with Russia on Syria, specifically its collaboration with Russia on the military operations it conducted in the region as well as its cooperation with Russia and Iran on the Astana peace process, serves as good illustration of boundary-breaking behavior against the West.

As a 2017 study concludes, Turkey could not have maintained "a military presence in Syria without Russia," which controlled Syrian air-space (Han and Özkan 2017). Turkey initiated the OES in August 2016, as a direct result of receiving air support from Russia. Turkey started conducting joint air operations with Russia in Al-Bab in mid-January 2017. Therefore, "the success of OES – and of Ankara's Syria policy in general" was deemed to be "somewhat in the hands of the Kremlin" (Han and Özkan 2017).

As one interviewee maintains, "While in the past, the US and Turkey agreed on strategic objectives, now there is more convergence in the way Russia is approaching the situation with the Kurds."[9] The USA only provided limited air support for some part of the OES. Many experts underline that Turkey's diplomatic and military rapprochement with Russia in Syria is to show the USA that Turkey has other options (Tol and Pearson 2016). One interviewee maintains that the "Turkish intervention in Syria leveled the playing field and demonstrated that the YPG is no longer the only game in town."[10]

The OES began within two weeks of the capture of Manbij by the SDF (Zannotti and Thomas 2017). While the official goal of the OES was to clear Turkey's borders from the IS (which was achieved through Turkey's capture of Al-Bab on February 24, 2017), one of the main goals was to prevent YPG/SDF forces from controlling Manbij or other areas between Afrin in the west and Kobani in the east (Zanotti and Thomas 2017), "as that would give the Syrian Kurds control of most of the Syrian-Turkish border" (Pierini 2017). Turkey wanted to make sure that its border with Syria remains under the control of pro-Turkish elements in Syria, especially the FSA opposition group backed by Turkey. The operation also aimed "to create safe zones for Syrians in Turkey to go to and enable Syrians to maintain their lives on their own land" (Işık, quoted in *Al Jazeera* 2017). Turkey declared the successful conclusion of the OES in March 2017.

Through the OES, Turkey was able to secure "a seat at the table" during the Astana peace talks (Dalay 2017, Kasapoğlu et al. 2017, p. 5). Turkey–Russia military cooperation was reinforced by the Astana talks (Kasapoğlu 2017a), where Turkey and Russia brokered a ceasefire between the Syrian government and the rebels on December 30, 2016. Despite its shaky implementation process, the Astana talks added a diplomatic dimension to the bilateral military cooperation between Turkey and Russia (Kasapoğlu 2017b).

[9] Interview with a Turkish-American academic, October 21, 2016.
[10] Interview with a US journalist, Washington DC, September 30, 2016.

Even though the Astana process was envisioned to complement the UN-brokered Geneva talks instead of replacing them, it "gradually eclipsed" the Geneva process (*France24.com* September 5, 2018). As one analyst notes, the "fact that Russia, Turkey, and Iran are driving the talks – with limited participation from the US as an observer . . . reflects the extent to which the center of gravity in the Syrian war has shifted" (Bonsey 2017). In the fourth round of the Astana talks held in May 2017, Russia, Turkey, and Iran reached an agreement to serve as "guarantor countries" to create "de-escalation zones" across four areas in Syria – Idlib, Eastern Ghouta, Homs, and Syria's southern border with Jordan – and declared a ceasefire, "renewing diplomatic efforts to bring warring parties" around the same table for ending the Syrian civil war, which was hailed by the UN (Loveluck and DeYoung 2017).

In September 2018, Putin and Erdoğan reached an agreement to establish a demilitarized zone 15–20 kilometers long in Idlib, in return for Turkey's pledge to disarm the Hay'et Tahrir al-Sham terrorist group. Nevertheless, in the aftermath of the declaration of US withdrawal from Syria, the Hay'et Tahrir al-Sham terrorist group took control of most of Idlib province, which Russia considered a violation of its 2018 agreement with Turkey.

At the time of writing, the Astana talks were ongoing, with the latest round of negotiations held in April 2019 in the newly renamed capital of Kazakhstan, Nur-Sultan. During the Astana talks in Sochi in February 2019, Turkey tried to buy more time and prevent an attack that could create additional refugee crisis (Kabalan 2019). In the aftermath of the US decision to withdraw from Syria, Russia attaches an even greater role to its collaboration with Turkey in Syria (Kabalan 2019). Turkey has demanded that the USA disarm the SDF before it withdraws and proposed a 30 km buffer zone to the east of the Euphrates (Kabalan 2019). There are disagreements between Turkey on the one hand and Russia and Iran on the other as to what should happen in the US-dominated area after the US withdrawal. Iran and Russia would like to see the SDF-held territories go back under the control of the Syrian government; they ask for Turkey to reactivate the Adana Accord of 1998 with Syria, allowing Turkey to recognize the government in Syria and pursue PKK fighters inside Syrian territory, instead of establishing a permanent military presence (Kabalan 2019). The developments explained here are largely indicative of the existence of cooperative balancing between Turkey and Russia on both military and diplomatic fronts, raising skepticism on the part of the USA and other NATO allies about Turkey's future in the Western alliance.

Nevertheless, some observers are skeptical of the robustness of the Turkey–Russia rapprochement, as they deem it to be more of "an economic marriage of convenience than a deeply rooted political alliance," as the two parties still disagree on important issues on the Syrian conflict, such as the removal of Assad from power (Larrabee 2016). For a brief period of time, as a result of its rapprochement with Russia and involvement in the Astana talks, the weakness of the rebels in the fight against the Assad government's forces, and its emphasis on the threats coming from the Syrian Kurds (Dalay 2017), Turkey seemed to move away from a regime-change goal in Syria. Nevertheless, the US missile attacks against the Syrian air base Al-Shayrat on April 6, 2017, in response to the use of chemical weapons against civilians by the Syrian government, brought renewed hope in Turkey of the possibility of regime change (Pearson 2017) and caused a visible divide between Russia and Turkey on their visions for the future of the Assad government. Moreover, according to a survey conducted in November 2017, only 28 percent of Turks view Russia favorably, versus 63 percent who perceive Russia unfavorably (Hoffman et al. 2018).

More importantly, despite its rapprochement with Russia, "Turkey has been surprised to see Russian forces with Kurdish flags in northern Syria, reportedly side-by-side with the Americans in supporting the SDF-YPG" (Peterson 2017). Russia "has forged some local agreements with the Kurds," alarming the Turkish government (McLeary 2017). Therefore, it still remains to be seen whether Turkey and Russia will continue their cooperation on Syria or move further apart from one another due to their significant differences on the Kurds and the Syrian regime.

IMPLICATIONS OF THE RAPPROCHEMENT FOR NATO

As illustrated by the recent tensions between Turkey and the West in Iraq and Syria, Turkey's relations with the United States, NATO, and the EU are at a very critical stage. In the words of a former US ambassador to Turkey, "We are dealing with the most dramatic transition in Turkey since Kemal Ataturk" (Jeffrey 2016). As acknowledged by a NATO official, "Both EU–Turkey and NATO–Turkey relations are more delicate following the summer of 2016. Turkey has been questioning the West's commitment to friendship and solidarity."[11] Accordingly, Turkey has been exploring alternative venues for partnerships in security and defense.

---

[11] Email exchange with a NATO official, February 27, 2017.

In other words, it has been increasingly engaging in boundary-breaking behavior against the Western alliance.

There are significant trust issues between Turkey and its NATO allies. As noted by a NATO official, "NATO has been portrayed in Turkey as being implicated in the failed coup."[12] Following that failed coup attempt in July 2016, 149 senior military staff, with Western educational background and secular mindset, serving at NATO in Europe and in the USA, were fired (Emmott 2016) and "8 members of the Turkish delegation to NATO have applied for asylum," which arguably adds to the strain in Turkey–NATO relations.[13] As stated by a NATO official, "Misperceptions [that NATO was behind the failed coup], as well as the wider lack of trust and negative public opinion about NATO in Turkey, need to be worked against."[14]

It is important to note that developments since 2003 have led some in Turkey to question the value of NATO. As stated by a Member of the Turkish Parliament, even though "NATO used to be a venue ... in which Turkey completely felt as a part of the Western security infrastructures," when a number of NATO members refused to extend the security umbrella to Turkey to protect the country against a potential attack using weapons of mass destruction from Iraq in 2002–2003, the Turkish security elites started to have serious doubts about solidarity within the alliance.[15]

Subsequent developments in the Middle East further contributed to the Turkish distrust of the West. Turkish authorities frequently argue that Turkey's allies and partners "prioritize their short-medium term interests over Turkey's long-term concerns regardless of how sensible they are" (Kasapoğlu et al. 2017, p. 5). As another indication of the lack of trust, even though Turkey has been advocating for the creation of safe zones in Syria, the Trump Administration's support for the idea caused "mixed reactions from Ankara" due to "the fear that the PYD might emerge as the main beneficiary" (Dalay 2017). Adding to the mistrust, Turkish authorities were not able to convince the USA – or Russia, for that matter – to expand the military campaign into Manbij (Kasapoğlu et al. 2017). Despite Turkish concerns, both the USA and Russia wanted the

---

[12] Email exchange with a NATO official, February 27, 2017.
[13] Interview with a British journalist via Skype, October 14, 2016.
[14] Email exchange with a NATO official, February 27, 2017.
[15] Interview with a Member of the Turkish Parliament from the AKP, Ankara, July 13, 2011.

involvement of the YPG in the battle of Raqqa, as they were deemed to be the most battle-ready among all local forces in the fight against the IS (McLeary 2017). Liberation of Raqqa from the IS without the YPG was deemed to be "next to impossible" (Pierini 2017).

Earlier in 2017, Şamil Tayyar, a Member of the Turkish Parliament from the AKP, called NATO a "terror organization" that "threatens Turkey" (quoted in Bershidsky 2017). Such portrayals of NATO seem to have led to a negative perception of the alliance by the Turkish public, too. According to a poll conducted in late 2017, only 24 percent of Turks viewed NATO favorably, with 67 percent viewing the alliance unfavorably (Hoffman et al. 2018).

One analyst underlines that Erdoğan's "brinkmanship is designed to retain the benefits of formal NATO membership without taking on too many commitments" (Bershidsky 2017). The USA and other NATO allies have so far tolerated this "because a Turkish departure [from NATO] would, in effect, put the Black Sea and the Balkans officially in play as parts of the world where Russia and Turkey can openly vie for influence" and also cause the West to "lose a key Middle Eastern foothold" (Bershidsky 2017).

Indicating a lack of trust toward Turkey, the US military "has been skeptical for some time about Turkish intentions and capabilities" in the aftermath of the purges (Pearson 2017). Another cause of mistrust is due to Turkey's support for rebel groups in Syria with "alleged extremist affiliations" during the initial phase of the Syrian civil war, for which Turkey has been severely criticized by the USA and other NATO allies (Kasapoğlu et al. 2017, p. 5). Turkey has tried to address this by being "more diligent with incorporating only 'moderate at Western standards' indigenous elements to the [OES]" (Kasapoğlu et al. 2017, p. 5).

While it made tactical sense for the USA to engage in a temporary alliance with the PYD to defeat the IS, it did not make sense from a strategic perspective (Jeffrey 2017). The US military "infuriates Turkey by asserting frequently that the PYD can be differentiated from the PKK," despite warnings from former US Secretary of Defense Ashton Carter's Senate testimony in April 2016, documenting the PKK's domination of the PYD and the SDF (ICG 2017). This attitude "feeds Turkish suspicion that, strategically, the United States plans to use the PYD against Turkey" and "could provoke a confrontation between Ankara and Washington in the geostrategic great game looming" in the Middle East (Jeffrey 2017). Turkey has spoiler potential, as highlighted by its air strikes in Syria on April 25, 2017 (ICG 2017).

Turkey's rapprochement with Russia deepens "the already extant rift" with NATO and the USA (Abramowitz and Edelman 2016, p. 19). A further deterioration of Turkey–USA relations "would present opportunities for Moscow to fish in the muddied waters" (ICG 2017, p. 9). As a US academic notes, "We are highly likely to see the deepening of Russia's commitment in the Middle East."[16] Russia is eager to "disrupt the NATO alliance and to exacerbate US–Turkish tensions" (Abramowitz and Edelman 2016, p. 19). One analyst questions Turkey's loyalty toward NATO and concludes that it is dangerous to let Turkey remain in NATO, since it "can play the proverbial Trojan Horse to filibuster any action when crisis looms," and advises the West to "call Erdogan's bluff (Rubin 2018).

Despite the strain in Turkey–NATO relations, many experts indicate that Turkey is expected to remain a member of NATO (Stelzenmueller 2017). For Turkey, NATO still remains a very important venue for pursuing its national interests, as the country increasingly wants to proactively shape the developments in transatlantic security, especially regarding the future direction and the agenda of NATO.[17] One interviewee notes, "If we take Erdoğan out, we would see Turkey still remaining a part of NATO – being problematic on some issues, and useful on other aspects, such as being the only Muslim member of NATO."[18]

As a NATO official maintains, "Turkey is a valued NATO ally" and, through its renewed ties to Russia, "Turkey may effectively contribute to the Alliance-agreed strategy on strength and dialogue vis-à-vis Russia."[19] Turkish authorities may realize that in the face of their dimming prospects for becoming a full EU member, and unstable relations with Russia, Turkey needs the guarantees of NATO membership more than ever. For instance, in the aftermath of the increase in cross-border activities with Russia in 2015, Turkey requested additional military support in the form of "tailored assurance measures" (NATO 2016b). As a NATO official claims, "NATO must live up to its promises and (Treaty) commitments to Turkey, while underlining NATO allies' shared democratic values."[20] Turkey will not go as far as leaving the military wing of NATO but "will try to carve more room for an independent

---

[16] Exchange with a US academic, Berlin, December 16, 2016.
[17] Interview with a Turkish NGO official, Istanbul, July 12, 2011.
[18] Interview with a British journalist via Skype, October 14, 2016.
[19] Email exchange with a NATO official, February 27, 2017.
[20] Email exchange with a NATO official, February 27, 2017.

foreign policy."[21] Nevertheless, if the Eurasianist policy continues, the emergence of "a more independent nationalist Turkish foreign policy" "at the expense of NATO" will be inevitable.[22]

CONCLUSION

As illustrated in this chapter, Turkey runs the risk of completely breaking away from the Western alliance. Turkey's transatlantic partnership has "entered an unstable and unpredictable period, driven by changes on all sides" (Lesser 2017). One study concludes that Erdoğan seeks to create a "new Turkey," where Turkey's "state, society, and position in the world" is "transformed" (Abramowitz and Edelman 2015, p. 5). The lack of US sensitivity to Turkish national interests further exacerbates the rift between the United States and Turkey (Abramowitz and Edelman 2015). Turkey finds itself resisting the policies of the USA and other NATO allies, due to its concerns about threats to its "pre-eminence in the neighborhood" (Whitaker 2010, p. 1116). Turkish authorities increasingly see the West as having "willingness to make gains independently" at the expense of Turkey (Pape 2005, p. 15). This seems to substantially increase the incentives for Turkish boundary-breaking behavior.

This chapter argues that Turkey's divergence from the USA on both the role of the Syrian Kurds in the war against the IS terrorist organization and its involvement in the military operations to liberate Raqqa and Mosul – as well as the adverse domestic climate in Turkey, such as rising anti-Americanism and the increasing authoritarian tendencies of the Turkish government in the aftermath of the failed coup attempt – create motivations for Turkey to break away from the USA and NATO in the Middle East. It provides evidence for boundary-challenging behavior against the USA and NATO in light of Turkey's long-lasting reluctance to join the fight against the IS, its lax control of its border with Syria, and its increasingly boundary-breaking behavior through its denial of the İncirlik Air Base to US warplanes in the military campaign against the terrorist organization up until July 2015. It also makes a case for boundary-breaking behavior as a result of the Turkish rapprochement with Russia leading to the OES mission in Syria, involvement in Astana peace talks, Russian air support to Turkey's ground operation in Al-Bab in

---

[21] Interview with a Turkish-American academic, October 21, 2016.
[22] Interview with a Turkish-American academic, October 21, 2016.

Syria, and the Russia–Turkey–Iran trilateral agreement reached in May 2017 on the establishment of "de-escalation zones" in Syria.

This chapter argues that Turkey engaged in costly signaling through its ambivalent approach in the war against the IS and employed territorial/ asset denial through its threat that it would close down the İncirlik Air Base if the USA continues to choose the Syrian Kurds over Turkey. It utilized compellent threats as well as military and diplomatic cooperative balancing strategy with Russia against the USA and NATO in Syria. As demonstrated by the recent developments in USA–Turkey relations in the Middle East, Turkish foreign policy increasingly shows tendencies for boundary breaking against the USA and transatlantic actors through the use of more traditional tools of balancing such as compellent threats and military cooperative balancing with Russia. Ignoring Turkish sensitivities runs the risk of escalating Turkey–USA/NATO tensions further. Therefore, it is important for Turkey, the USA, and other NATO allies to work together and reinforce the transatlantic partnership for the sake of common strategic goals that affect all transatlantic partners. Otherwise, a significant opportunity will be missed, and Turkey will further align its military and foreign policies with that of Russia. The next chapter summarizes the findings of this book and draws generalizable conclusions about intra-alliance opposition behavior.

Conclusion: Turkey and the West – What Next?

Ever since the collapse of the Ottoman Empire, subsequent Turkish governments understood the importance of taking part in international governance structures, particularly the Euro-Atlantic ones, due to the country's long-term vision of being a part of Western civilization. However, under the AKP rule, especially since 2010, the Western orientation in Turkish foreign policy has been increasingly questioned, creating a need for scholarly analyses of Turkish foreign policy toward the West and its implications for transatlantic and Middle Eastern security. This book contributes to the academic literature by examining the contemporary Turkish foreign policy vis-à-vis the EU, the United States, and NATO and making projections on its future.

Given the urgency of improved transatlantic dialogue on counter-terrorism, Russian aggression, human trafficking, and the refugee crisis, Turkey emerges as a key actor for European security and US foreign policy interests. Turkish authorities have been cognizant of the importance of claiming a more visible role for Turkey in the changing international system. In the aftermath of President Trump's unexpected announcement of the withdrawal of US forces from Syria in December 2018, Turkey's geostrategic importance for the West is further exacerbated. Therefore, the alliances and the informal alignments it will make moving forward will have significant repercussions for transatlantic security interests.

This chapter summarizes the book's findings and elucidates the major factors behind Turkish intra-alliance opposition behavior. It then explores three potential scenarios on the future of Turkey's relations with the West. It finally generalizes its findings to other cases of intra-alliance opposition/conflict and discusses the implications of its findings for the IR literature.

A SYNOPSIS

The case study chapters offer a detailed analysis of a number of key issues – including Turkish foreign policy in the Western Balkans, Turkey's veto over the EU–NATO intelligence information exchange, the EU–Turkey deal on refugees, energy policies, rapprochement with Russia in security and defense, and Turkish foreign policy in Syria and Iraq – in Turkey's relations with the West from 2010 to 2019. While Turkey uses different intensities of tools of statecraft to indicate its intra-alliance opposition ranging from boundary testing to boundary breaking, Table 1 indicates that there is a trajectory in its interactions with the West, as demonstrated by the chronological sequence of the case studies examined in this analysis. Evidence from the case studies suggests that, toward the end of the time period under study, Turkey has been using higher intensity tools of statecraft against the West. While Turkey was at first attempting to bolster its appeal for the transatlantic allies by proving its value added for transatlantic security, the analysis in this manuscript reveals that Turkey has been increasingly switching from boundary testing to boundary challenging from 2014 to 2016 and from boundary challenging to boundary breaking since the failed coup in 2016.

Turkey has been initially experimenting with different foreign policy tools, in an attempt to increase the space of what is acceptable in interactions within the transatlantic community. From 2010 to 2014, it was exploring and testing boundaries, in order both to determine what the expectations of accepted behavior are from its engagement with the Western allies and to assert and reaffirm itself as an accepted member of the alliance. During this process, Turkey was still actively engaged with the West, albeit with certain tensions. Therefore, in the initial stage, when interacting with the EU and NATO members, Turkey had the ultimate goals of becoming a member of the EU and remaining an active member of transatlantic security infrastructures such as NATO and European security institutions, as illustrated in Chapters 2 and 3.

Nevertheless, a general perception of "Western condescension" and resentment against the West seems to gradually dominate the Turkish psyche both at the elites and the public levels (*Reuters* 2016). There is an assessment of not being appreciated by the Western allies and a general sentiment that the West often imposes its expectations on Turkey without much respect to

TABLE 1 *The intra-alliance opposition tools used by Turkey*

	Case study 1: Turkish foreign policy in the Western Balkans	Case study 2: Turkish veto over EU-NATO security coordination	Case study 3: Turkey-EU deal on refugees	Case study 4: Turkish energy policies	Case study 5: Turkish rapprochement with Russia in security	Case study 6: Turkish foreign policy in Iraq and Syria
Process 1: Boundary testing	Active diplomacy, Cheap-talk diplomacy	Active diplomacy, Entangling diplomacy, Cheap-talk diplomacy, Issue-linkage bargaining	Active diplomacy, Issue-linkage bargaining	Issue-linkage bargaining, Economic statecraft		Costly signaling
Process 2: Boundary challenging	Active diplomacy emphasizing regional ownership, Economic statecraft	Inter-institutional balancing, Strategic noncooperation	Compellent threats	Informed strategic noncooperation, Cooperative balancing with Russia, Economic statecraft	Costly signaling	Costly signaling
Process 3: Boundary breaking			Blackmail power, Compellent threats	Economic statecraft	Costly signaling, Compellent threats for alternative alliances, Blackmail power, Issue-linkage bargaining, Military cooperative balancing with Russia	Costly signaling, Compellent threats, Territorial or asset denial, Blackmail power, Hostage diplomacy, Military and diplomatic cooperative balancing with Russia

Turkey's concerns, needs, and sensitivities. For instance, despite Turkey's requests to be involved in it, Turkey was left out of the Butmir process led by the EU and the United States in Bosnia and Herzegovina in 2008–2009. In response, Turkey initiated its own negotiation rounds in the Balkans. Similarly, in response to a veto from the Republic of Cyprus for its EDA associate membership, Turkey engaged in both inter-institutional balancing using its NATO member status and strategic noncooperation against the EU, making it difficult for the EU and NATO to coordinate action.

Consequently, a shift occurred in Turkey's approach toward the West, and the country ultimately decided to challenge the limits of its alliance with the West. As noted in Chapter 1, boundary challenging is an escalated form of intra-alliance opposition that occurs when the actors want to defy the preconceived expectations of behavior within the alliance. It may be summed up as an attempt to acquire more independence within the alliance, against constraints imposed by other members or the unipole. Especially in the period between 2014 and 2016, albeit working within the existing transatlantic frameworks, Turkey occasionally pursued goals that are different from or subversive to those of the West, such as the denial to use the İncirlik Air Base up until July 2015 or the threats to open up the borders to let the influx of refugees into Europe.

Nostalgia and resentment increasingly lead Turkey to pursue a redemptionist foreign policy against the West. There is a temptation to try to increase its standing as a rising state, harking back to the grandeur of the former empire (Zarakol 2011, 2017).[1] Turkish security doctrine is more and more defined through self-help rather than collective security (Aras 2017) and seeks alternative engagements to face its security threats.

Boundary breaking, or independence from without, occurs when Turkey breaks the pattern in its interactions with the West and instead takes on an adversarial relationship against the West. The period following the failed coup exacerbated the intra-alliance security dilemma between Turkey and the West. This is when a transition into boundary-breaking behavior against the West started to become apparent. More and more, Turkey distanced itself from its decades-long goal of becoming a member of the EU and is alienated from its decades-long membership in NATO. The Turkish elites recognize that this foreign policy stance also helps them consolidate power domestically.

---

[1] Zarakol (2011) indicates that the socialization of essentially Eastern states such as Turkey, Japan, and Russia into the Western order following their defeat by the West led these states to aspire to move up rank.

Consequently, Turkey engages in a number of initiatives that indicate hostile intentions toward the West. As noted in Chapters 5, 6 and 7, the country aligns its energy, defense, and general foreign policies with Russia. It signals its resolve to use compellent threats, hostage diplomacy, and other tools of traditional or hard balancing, such as its military collaboration with Russia in Syria, its willingness to join an alternative competitive alliance such as the SCO, or the purchase of an S-400 missile defense system from Russia at the expense of its NATO allies. The following section outlines the major factors behind changes in the Turkish foreign policy.

MAJOR FACTORS BEHIND TURKEY'S FOREIGN POLICY BEHAVIOR

The analysis offered in this book suggests that there are three major factors behind the increasingly confrontational course in Turkish foreign policy vis-à-vis the West: 1) international systemic and regional sub-systemic factors; 2) irreconcilable interests between Turkey and the transatlantic allies, due to lack of progress in its EU accession talks, the US support for Syrian Kurds at the expense of Turkey's key interests in the Middle East, the unresolved Cyprus problem, Turkey's resentment for its exclusion from European and Middle Eastern security developments by its transatlantic partners, and the subsequent lack of trust toward the EU, the USA, and NATO; and 3) domestic factors.

International Systemic and Regional Sub-systemic Factors

Both the international and regional distributions of power seem to motivate Turkey to have a more visible role in international affairs. The current global system allows for maneuvering space for rising powers (Paul 2005, Paul 2016).[2] There is no single hegemonic power in Turkey's immediate neighborhoods, but a multitude of players, such as the USA and Russia in the Middle East, the EU in the Balkans, and Russia in the Caucasus. Each is vying for greater regional influence. Emerging powers may "vindicate the superpowers" using institutionalized consultations, such as BRICS and the G-20 and, consequently, "conquer their respective spaces in the international stage" (Galves Derolle 2015). Turkey sees itself as an increasingly independent global player and likes

---

[2] Exchange with a Turkish scholar, Berlin, December 15, 2016.

to portray itself as an equal partner of the West (Barysch 2011). Many Turkish policymakers acknowledge that Turkey wants to acquire a greater influence in the changing international and regional balance of power, employs assertive diplomacy to shape developments in its immediate neighborhood proactively, and is looking to carve out a regional sphere of influence as a regional power.[3]

While Chapters 2 and 3 generally suggest boundary-testing behavior against the West, Chapter 4 and 5 indicate boundary-challenging behavior. Turkish boundary-testing and boundary-challenging behaviors may partly be explained as a result of Turkey's attempts to have a seat at the table regarding the developments in its immediate neighborhoods, while at the same time proving its relevance as a regional actor to the West. Nevertheless, as suggested by the evidence presented in Chapters 6 and 7, Turkey has become more assertive and hostile against the West and has engaged in boundary-breaking behavior. Turkey seems to perceive the intentions of the EU and the USA as being increasingly at odds with its own national interests at the regional level.

The EU's multiple crises created a regional power vacuum in the Western Balkans. Similarly, the US decision to withdraw from Syria, along with the increasingly isolationist foreign policy of the Trump Administration, is anticipated to create a regional power vacuum in the Middle East. These regional dynamics seem to encourage Turkish boundary-challenging as well as boundary-breaking behaviors. Indeed, many Turkish policymakers interviewed acknowledge that the multiple European crises decrease the allure of Turkish membership into the EU.[4] For instance, one Turkish diplomat notes, "We are not depressed that the [EU accession] chapters are frozen . . . It is not in the EU's interest to make Turkey's EU membership irrelevant."[5]

The case study chapters demonstrate Turkey's attempts at leveling the playing field against the global hegemon and its European allies, taking advantage of the power vacuum in its immediate neighborhood. To illustrate, Chapter 2 makes a case that it is less costly for Turkey to capitalize on its power and leverage in the Western Balkans, when compared to any other of its immediate neighborhoods, due to the country's historical, diplomatic, cultural, and economic links with the region and the power vacuum left by the EU in the region due to its diversion from

[3] Interview with a Turkish NGO official, Istanbul, July 12, 2011.
[4] Interview with a Member of Turkish Parliament from the AKP, Ankara, July 18, 2011.
[5] Interview with a Turkish diplomat, Ankara, Turkey, July 18, 2011.

multiple crises. It demonstrates that Turkey has stepped up its involvement in the Western Balkans, significantly increasing its economic, cultural, political, and diplomatic relations with the countries in the region; demanded that priority to be given to regional ownership initiatives such as SEECP and regional economic zones; and sought to alter the Western Balkans' regional balance of power to its favor. It concludes that Turkey pursues *Realpolitik*, a pragmatic and interests-based rather than ideological foreign policy, in the region to test the boundaries of its relations with the West. Turkey specifically used active diplomacy and economic statecraft to fill in the power vacuum created by the EU in the region, secure economic deals before the countries in the region become EU members, and strengthen its hand vis-à-vis the EU. Chapter 2 concludes that as long as Turkey's accession to the EU remains deadlocked and the Turkish political elites feel alienated from the West, Turkey is tempted to split with the EU to pursue an increasingly independent foreign policy and eventually play a spoiler role in the Western Balkans.

Similarly, as illustrated in Chapter 7, Turkey's concerns with the balance of power in the Middle East seem to guide Turkish foreign policy in Syria and Iraq, leading to Turkey's balancing behavior against the USA. Turkey is mainly concerned about US support for Syrian Kurds, which is considered a significant threat to Turkey's sovereignty. An independent Kurdish state in the southern borders of Turkey is envisioned to further mobilize Turkey's own Kurdish population in search for a similar outcome. In an attempt to better position itself in the Middle East, Turkey uses a number of tools – such as costly signaling, compellent threats, territorial/asset denial, and military and diplomatic cooperative balancing with Russia – to enhance its leverage against the USA and to turn the regional balance of power to its favor. With Russia gaining a bigger foothold in the Middle East, Turkey seems to have become more willing to align its policies with Russia.

Irreconcilable Interests and the Subsequent Lack of Trust

Besides the international systemic and regional sub-systemic factors, the diverging interests, reciprocal biases, and mistrust provide yet another motivation behind the Turkish intra-alliance opposition behavior. Especially the country's dwindling prospects for EU accession, its exclusion from European security developments, and the US support for Syrian Kurds at the expense of Turkey's key interests in the Middle East are presented as evidence of an anti-Turkish bias in the West. This seems to create resentment, widespread perception of Western hypocrisy, and lack of trust toward the transatlantic actors in Turkey. As one interviewee observes, "Turkey's relations with the transatlantic allies are distraught. Confidence is damaged, which in turn affects the economic and political relations with the allies."[6]

Illustrating the overwhelming amount of distrust Turkish government has toward the USA, the Turkish Ministry of Foreign Affairs criticized the Turkey 2018 Human Rights Report published by the US Department of State, announcing that its description of the "supporters of terrorist organizations and circles behind the 15 July terrorist coup attempt as 'political prisoners'" is "clearly biased" (Turkish Ministry of Foreign Affairs 2019e). It further noted, "Prepared by the country that shelters the head of FETO, the report strengthens the perception regarding the identity of those behind the 15 July terrorist coup attempt against our country" (Turkish Ministry of Foreign Affairs 2019e).

Similarly, as a leading journalist on Turkey highlights, Turkish authorities are especially "vengeful" in response to the lack of progress in EU–Turkey relations.[7] The lack of any credible prospects for Turkey's EU accession further exacerbates Turkey's lack of trust toward the EU and its CSDP and motivates a continuation of its veto over the EU–NATO security exchange, a more independent and proactive foreign policy in the Western Balkans, the use of compellent threats on allowing a flow of refugees into Europe, and cooperative balancing with Russia in energy and security/defense affairs. All in all, as long as the hopes for its EU accession remain nil, Turkey is expected to continue approaching EU's policies with skepticism and to seek to demonstrate that it has other alternatives.

Chapter 3 illustrates that one of the venues in which Turkey exercises an important diplomatic weight vis-à-vis the EU is NATO (Dursun-Özkanca 2017). The shared sentiment among the Turkish security elites interviewed for this research is that, despite repeated assurances from the EU, Turkey has been left outside of the process of European defense cooperation. Therefore, Turkey's veto over the NATO–EU security exchange, blocking any formal discussion of issues that are central to the EU and NATO, may best be understood as an attempt to signal that its cooperation cannot be taken for granted in the face of repeated frustrations caused by the EU. Turkey seeks to delay, complicate, or increase the

[6] Phone interview with a Turkish-American academic, May 2, 2016.
[7] Interview a British journalist via Skype, October 14, 2016.

costs of the EU's military aspirations and engages in strategic noncoopera-tion, inter-institutional balancing, entangling diplomacy, and issue-linkage bargaining in hopes of increasing its leverage against the EU in its accession negotiations, resolving the Cyprus problem to its advantage, and getting fully integrated into the EDA. Even though its relations with NATO came under significant strain recently, it is still not in the interest of Turkey to withdraw, as its NATO membership still has key utility for the country's security and also provides an additional venue for the country to exercise leverage against the West.

As revealed in Chapter 4, Turkey has the potential to engage in bound-ary breaking against the EU through the EU–Turkey refugee deal. Here, once again, Turkey's frustration with its prospects for accession into the EU seems to be the main motivation. As Chapter 4 reveals, Turkey managed to use the refugee crisis – and employed issue-linkage bargaining strategies and compellent threats – to get the EU to announce that the country's EU accession process needs to be re-energized through the open-ing of new negotiation chapters and visa liberalization, modernization of the Customs Union Agreement with the EU, and the payment of an additional 3 billion EUR on top of the original 3 billion EUR promised by the EU for the welfare and protection of Syrian refugees in Turkey. Put differently, the EU–Turkey refugee deal seems to "augment" Turkey's "assets so as to produce better outcomes" in its dealings with the EU the next time (Art 2005, pp. 183–184). In the words of an interviewee, immigration is a "joker card in Erdoğan's hand, as he threatens the European partners that he would send 3 million refugees to Europe."[8]

The unresolved Cyprus conflict is yet another factor behind the moti-vations for Turkish boundary challenging against the West. In 2004, the fact that the EU did not make the resolution of the conflict a precondition for the Republic of Cyprus's EU membership raised considerable skepti-cism among Turkish policymakers about the EU's role as an honest broker in the conflict. In the words of an interviewee, by admitting a de facto divided island into the Union, the EU "punished the northern part of the island that voted yes in the referendum for the adoption of the Annan Plan"[9] to resolve the conflict and exacerbated the Turkish resentment toward the EU. This further fuels mistrust toward the EU amongst Turkish policymakers, reinforcing their will to cause frustration to the

---

[8] Exchange with a Serbian NGO official, Berlin, December 15, 2016.
[9] Interview with a Member of Turkish Parliament from the AKP, Ankara, July 14, 2011.

EU on a number of fronts, including the energy, defense, and security sectors.

Unilateral vetoes of a number of EU accession chapters by the Republic of Cyprus seem to further motivate Turkish boundary-challenging behavior against the EU. As demonstrated in Chapter 4, the success of the EU–Turkey Readmission Agreement and visa liberalization agreement are directly related to issues covered in Chapter 23 on Judiciary and Fundamental Rights and Chapter 24 on Justice, Freedom, and Security, both of which are vetoed by the Republic of Cyprus. Therefore, the unresolved Cyprus problem constitutes an important roadblock against the implementation of these agreements. Moreover, as Chapter 5 reveals, Turkey engages in strategic noncooperation against the EU in the energy sector by refusing to become a full member of the Energy Community initiative of the EU. Besides the concerns of weakening its negotiating position in its EU accession process, the unresolved Cyprus problem seems to further motivate Turkey's strategic noncooperation on this issue, as Turkish officials use this tool to force the EU to put pressure on Cyprus to remove its unilateral veto over the opening of accession negotiations on Chapter 15 on "Energy."

Chapter 5 focuses on Turkey's energy policies, particularly its refusal to become a full member of the ECT, rapprochement with Russia in the energy sector through a number of collective projects, and evasion of Iran sanctions. Besides its refusal to initiate its full membership application into the ECT, through the TANAP pipeline (which is envisioned to be a part of the SGC project), Turkey positions itself as a central player in the European energy-security sector, connecting the energy producers with European consumers, and acquires significant leverage vis-à-vis the EU. In order to further strengthen its hand against the EU, Turkey simultaneously considers an alternative project, the Russia-proposed Turkish Stream, which potentially emerges as a competitor to TANAP. Since the EU is interested in diversifying its energy supply and increasing its energy security in a way to decrease its dependency on Russia, the Turkish Stream pipeline project with Russia presents good evidence for Turkey's aspirations to acquire future leverage over the EU. As revealed in Chapter 5, the high-profile sanctions-busting scheme uncovered by the US Department of the Treasury that tied Zarrab with the Turkish government officials illustrated an important boundary-breaking moment in Turkey's relations with the United States. Furthermore, the sanctions imposed on two Turkish ministers for the release of Andrew Brunson further illustrated how bilateral relations hit its lowest point. The renewed sanctions against

Iran therefore present yet another contentious issue in bilateral relations between the USA and Turkey, potentially leading to another boundary-breaking moment.

As illustrated in Chapters 6 and 7, Turkey uses its rapprochement with Russia to check the power of the West. Turkey engages in boundary-breaking behavior in the security/defense sector, through cooperative balancing with Russia, with its planned purchase of a missile defense shield from Russia and declaration of intentions for becoming a full member of the SCO. All of these moves effectively help Turkey signal that NATO and the EU are not its only alternatives when it comes to security and defense and that it is more and more willing to operate from outside of the Western alliance.

Chapter 7 reveals that Turkey uses costly signaling, territorial/asset denial, compellent threats, and cooperative balancing with Russia as a direct result of its frustrations with the USA and NATO allies in the face of the deepening rift between Turkey and the transatlantic allies. Turkey's resentment of the US support for Syrian Kurds in the fight against the IS adds to the frustration of the Turkish officials about the lack of sensitivity on the part of the USA and other NATO allies toward Turkey's national security concerns, since Turkey claims that the PKK and the YPG are affiliated with one another, and causes additional strains for an already troubled relationship between Turkey and the West. The Astana process by Russia, Turkey, and Iran, the subsequent truce and the "safe zones" agreements announced in 2017 (without the direct involvement of the USA and the European allies), and the military collaboration between Russia and Turkey in Syria provide good illustrations of the diplomatic and military cooperative balancing between Turkey and Russia against the West. Turkey and Russia seem to coordinate their diplomatic positions to oppose US policy and obtain more influence together.

Domestic Factors

Domestic factors are similarly effective in explaining the increasing drive for boundary challenging and boundary breaking against the West. States may choose to balance against an external power when "doing so helps them in the domestic power game" (Whitaker 2010, p. 1124). As noted by long-time observers of Turkish foreign policy, Turkish foreign policy is "personalized in Erdoğan's worldview"[10] and has become not only "less

---

[10] Interview with a British journalist via Skype, October 14, 2016.

rule-based, and more discretionary" (Ülgen 2014) but also less predictable (Jeffrey 2017). Following the attempted coup on July 15, 2016, during the prolonged state of emergency, "70,000 were detained, 40,000 arrested, 70,000 suspended from civil service, several companies including educational institutions, media outlets, and hospitals were closed down or transferred to the state" (Erdoğan 2017). Turkey has the highest number of journalists in prison (Gibson 2019).

Increasingly, the USA, NATO, and the EU are presented as "the principal geopolitical threats to Turkey" (Abramowitz and Edelman 2016, p. 11). There is a new nationalism in Turkey due to the spillover effects of the war in Syria, conflict with the PKK, and the coup attempt, which accompanies a sense of victimhood and a confirmation for many nationalist Turks of their fears about Western intentions (Hoffman et al. 2018). According to a poll conducted by Metropoll, 83 percent of Turks held unfavorable views of the USA, and 73 percent of the EU (Hoffman et al. 2018). A majority of Turks (over 55 percent) favor the idea of avoiding relying on other countries, and Turkey producing its own military and industrial goods (Hoffman et al. 2018). In the same poll, when asked whether Turkey should "do more to confront the U.S. or do more to maintain the alliance, even if the two countries don't always agree," 46 percent of respondents said yes and 37 percent said the government should "do more to maintain the alliance" (Hoffman et al. 2018).[11]

Many commentators note that Turkish foreign policy is mostly about consolidating the government's power at home and that the more the government feels threatened, the more it will antagonize its relations with the West (Dağı 2014, Abramowitz and Edelman 2016, Erdemir 2017).[12] A former member of the Turkish Parliament from the AKP notes, as a result of having a "sense of having achieved too much power and potential," the political elites in Turkey "overplay their hands" and "use the international system for manipulation mainly for domestic purposes" (Kınıklıoğlu 2014). Changes in the composition and orientation of the Turkish military, economic problems, political manipulation of public opinion for electoral gain, personalization of Turkish foreign policymaking, increasing slide toward authoritarianism in the aftermath of the failed

---

[11] The AKP supporters chose confrontation over maintenance by 56 percent to 30 percent, while the MHP supporters favored it by 51 percent to 35 percent, the CHP voters by 35 percent to 49 percent, and HDP supporters by 26 percent to 48 percent (Hoffman et al. 2018).
[12] Exchange with a US academic, Berlin, December 15, 2016.

coup in July 2016, and the transition to a presidential system in June 2018 are further conducive to Turkish boundary-breaking behavior against the West.

This finding is in line with the expectations of neoclassical realism and the diversionary theory, which hold that a combination of international systemic factors and domestic politics helps explain foreign policy, drawing attention to the adventurous foreign policies of elites in the face of domestic problems (Levy 1989, Rose 1998, Schweller 2003). As Kupchan (2011, p. 168) maintains, "elite appeals to popular anti-American sentiment" matter in balancing. Nationalism as well as perceived grievances by a rising power contribute to motivations to balance against the great powers (Paul 2016).

Observers underline the distrust Turkish authorities have toward the West and note that there are conspiratorial thinking tendencies with regards to how the West treated Turkey for a long time (Jeffrey 2016, Jenkins 2016). In the aftermath of the failed coup attempt of July 2016, President Erdoğan and other Turkish authorities have been depicting the EU and the USA as major threats to Turkey's national interests, engaging in a series of visible disagreements on the world stage and accusing the West of meddling in Turkish domestic affairs. As noted by an interviewee, Turkey's authoritarian tendencies are putting Turkey on an isolated route internationally, creating an anti-American and anti-European vision in Turkey and "leading to an impression that Turks have no other friends than Turks."[13]

Furthermore, as indicated by a number of interviewees, Turkish elites may be motivated to project power internationally to divert the attention away from the domestic problems, such as declining economic growth or rising inflation.[14] Up until the local elections in March 2019, the Turkish leadership successfully exploited the domestic opposition to the alliance from the nationalist and conservative groups and the general public to its advantage. The results of the presidential and parliamentary elections in summer 2018 is a good evidence of this. Albeit the AKP's loss of major cities in the March 2019 local elections and the re-run of the Istanbul elections in early June 2019, Erdoğan is expected to remain in power in the foreseeable future with the switch to a presidential system. With the narrow approval of the constitutional changes in a referendum in April 2017 and the transition to a presidential system, many are concerned about the insufficient level of checks and balances in the new Turkish

---

[13] Phone interview with a Turkish-American academic, May 2, 2016.
[14] Exchanges with a Slovakian NGO official and a US academic, Berlin, December 15, 2016.

political system. As indicated by a Turkish political scientist, under the new presidential system

[t]he president may declare a state of emergency without parliamentary approval. The decrees issued during the state of emergency are not subject to judicial review. Even under normal conditions, the president enjoys extensive powers to issue decrees, bypassing the parliament ... [T]he president will be able to dissolve the parliament ... – which will automatically trigger early presidential elections – a formidable power to keep the parliament in check. The dismissal of the president by the parliament, on the other hand, is subject to stringent conditions. (Turan 2017)

USA–Turkey relations are further complicated by Turkey's request for the extradition of Fethullah Gülen,[15] whom Turkish authorities characterize as a Western agent that masterminded the failed coup attempt.[16] Turkish political elites repeatedly imply that the USA was behind the failed coup attempt and frequently complain that Turkey did not receive any support from its Western allies in its aftermath. One interviewee notes that Erdoğan has been attempting to portray Turkey as a "victim" and managed to unite Turkey against Gülenists and the PKK by emphasizing that "the West is supporting both of these groups."[17] Another expert concurs, saying that, following the failed coup attempt, "It is common for Erdoğan to talk about 'dark forces,' i.e. the West, who try to destroy Turkey" (Jenkins 2016). These misperceptions play an important role in explaining the rising anti-Americanism and Euroskepticism in the Turkish public opinion.

With serious curbs to political opposition and freedom of the press and the increasingly concentrated power under presidency, and in the face of the economic troubles facing the country, it is reasonable to expect Turkey to engage in more aggressive foreign policies that run the risk of isolating Turkey further from the West. With the installation of an anti-Western mentality, Turkish people are less primed to question the actions of the Turkish government, giving the government more leeway for further isolation from the West. A journalist notes that since "people are frightened to tell Erdoğan about Turkey's weaknesses," "Turkey becomes more isolated in the region, [and] Erdoğan becomes more and more confident that he can go his own way."[18] As a result of its isolation

---

[15] Interview with a European Union official, Washington DC, September 30, 2016; Interview with a Turkish-American academic, October 21, 2016.

[16] Interview with a Turkish scholar, Washington DC, September 30, 2016.

[17] Interview with a Turkish scholar, Washington DC, September 30, 2016.

[18] Interview with a British journalist via Skype, October 14, 2016.

from the West, Turkey seeks to establish close political relationships with Russia and Iran.

The significant changes in the constitution of the Turkish military as a result of the purge of pro-Western/pro-NATO officers in the military following the coup attempt[19] further encourage the adoption of boundary breaking against the West. As one interviewee notes, back in the 1990s, "Turkish officers used to admire the US army and military . . . There used to be a strong bond between the US and Turkish officers . . . The officers saw that membership in NATO and the US military collaboration made them more professional."[20] However, in the aftermath of the failed coup attempt, there are increasingly anti-American and anti-Western ideologies within the Turkish military due to the decommissioning or discharge of the military officers that had training in the USA.

As indicated by many experts, following the failed coup the military has become more submissive to Erdoğan (Jenkins 2016).[21] The coup attempt discouraged any kind of criticism or objections from the military to Erdoğan's rule. To illustrate, while in June 2015 Erdoğan tried to engage in an incursion in Syria and faced opposition from the military generals, following the July 15 coup attempt "he got it his way" (Jenkins 2016). Moreover, the changes made in the aftermath of the failed coup attempt, such as the abolition of military high schools and the lifting of the ban against the graduates of Imam Hatip (religious cleric) schools to become military officers, are expected to have important negative implications on the military ties between Turkey and Western allies.[22] Consequently, a "Eurasianist cohort" among senior officers in the Turkish military "looks to align with Russia and the Central Asian republics" (Lesser 2017). This discussion of the major factors behind Turkish foreign policy vis-à-vis the West requires an assessment of what the future holds for Turkey–West relations.

WHAT NEXT? TURKEY AND THE WEST – ENEMIES?

The analysis in this manuscript demonstrates that Turkey's relationship with the EU, NATO, and the United States is at a critical juncture.

---

[19] Interview with a Turkish scholar, Washington DC, September 30, 2016, Skype interview with a British journalist, October 14, 2016, Interview with a Turkish-American academic, October 21, 2016.
[20] Interview with a British journalist via Skype, October 14, 2016.
[21] Interview with a Turkish scholar, Washington DC, September 30, 2016.
[22] Interview with a British journalist via Skype, October 14, 2016.

Diverging from its traditionally pro-Western foreign policy stance, Turkey has been increasingly emphasizing the importance of its independence from the West and seriously questioning the West's commitment to friendship and solidarity.[23] The frictions in the relations between Turkey and the West are destined to have long-term destabilizing effects. To illustrate, as noted in Chapter 7, the transfer of the German troops stationed in the İncirlik Air Base to an air base in Jordan in 2017 may motivate other NATO allies to follow course, ultimately creating a risk for Turkey to lose its appeal to the NATO allies. Similarly, as illustrated in Chapter 7, military and defense industrial relations with the USA are at a breaking point due to the planned acquisition of a S-400 missile defense system from Russia. It seems that the Turkish authorities concluded that the expected benefits of boundary breaking are greater than its expected costs. With the path-dependent decision to purchase a S-400 missile defense system from Russia, it is reasonable to expect the military and defense industrial ties between Turkey and Russia to gain further momentum at the expense of the security/defense ties between Turkey and its Western allies. Such foreign policy behaviors, in turn, cause growing concerns about Turkey's trustworthiness as a Western ally.

While some may argue that what we are seeing is actually part of a long tradition of cyclical relations in Turkey's relations with the West, this book holds that we are now dealing with a completely different situation. The case studies examined in this book demonstrate that there is now a fundamental gulf between Turkey and the West that is reaching an irreversible point. Turkey has progressively adopted policies that challenged the boundaries of its alliance with the West. The final three case studies illustrate that Turkey has been increasingly engaging in boundary breaking and adopting hostile policies against the USA and European allies.

Especially in the aftermath of the failed coup, many interviewees underscore the emergence of a Eurasianist foreign policy orientation in Turkey, at the expense of its transatlantic alliance.[24] A former Member of the Turkish Parliament from the CHP notes that Turkey is "pivoting" away from the transatlantic allies and values, rather than "posturing" against the West (Erdemir 2017). Others, however, argue that there are no realistic alternatives for Turkey beyond the transatlantic partners in

---

[23] Email exchange with a NATO official, February 27, 2017; Interview with a Turkish scholar, Washington DC, September 30, 2016.

[24] Phone interview with a Turkish-American academic, October 21, 2016; Interview with a British journalist via Skype, October 14, 2016.

its foreign policy orientation, drawing attention to the "60-year legacy of institutionalized cooperation" (Zanotti and Thomas 2017, p. 13, Pierini 2016a, Lesser and Lete 2017) and note that a long-term alliance with Russia is not feasible (Stelzenmueller 2017). Lesser and Lete (2017) similarly argue:

The preference for closer, commercially driven ties to the Muslim world has proven a dead end, as Turkey has become more exposed to the violent sectarian spillovers of a troubled Middle East. Ankara's periodic flirtation with Eurasian alternatives owes more to economic interest and pique at perceived Western neglect than to any serious strategic opening … [The Turkey–Russia rapprochement is] hardly a substitute for NATO as the security situation around Turkey continues to deteriorate.

The developments in Turkey's relations with the EU, NATO, and the USA over the last couple of years raise the question of whether Turkey will completely abandon the West and burn bridges. Accordingly, the next section considers three alternative future scenarios for Turkey–West relations.

Scenario 1: The Continuation of the Status Quo

One possible scenario is the continuation of the current state of relations with the West. Turkey–West relations under this scenario are expected to remain strained without additional escalation or conflict. Under this scenario, Turkish authorities will continue to hold that the country's EU accession is completely unrealistic but will maintain a continued EU candidacy status. They will also remain an official NATO member state, even though many continue to question the value of its membership in the alliance.

It is true that the stalemate in its EU accession negotiations has been going on for a while. It is also the case that Turkey's relations with its NATO allies have been problematic lately. This may lead some to anticipate a continuation of the status quo. While this is possible, it is rather unlikely. This is mainly due to the fact that there are a number of destabilizing forces in place. Turkish voters favor an independent and go-it-alone foreign policy (Hoffman et al. 2018). The multiple crises in the bilateral relations between the USA and Turkey, including the hostage crisis, the request for the extradition of Gülen, sanctions and tariff crisis, the deepening economic crisis in Turkey, and the F-35 crisis and the purchasing of S-400 missile defense system, make the continuation of the status quo unrealistic in the short run. Turkey will face increasing pressures from its transatlantic allies to confirm its commitment to the alliance. The purchase of S-400 missile defense system will have irreversible consequences for the relations between Turkey and its NATO allies, making the continuation of the status quo quite unrealistic.

Scenario 2: The Improvement of Relations with the West

This is the least likely scenario. Given the extremely hostile and conspiratorial public debates in Turkey with regards to the West, any improvement in relations is highly unlikely. Especially since the US administration signaled its willingness to implement secondary sanctions on entities engaging in trade relations with Iran, and the Turkish government unremittingly declared its determination to purchase the S-400 missile defense system from Russia, bilateral relations between Turkey and the USA do not offer any promise of improvement.

Having said that, the Khashoggi case proved that it is possible to renew the ties between the two countries and bring positive momentum to the bilateral relations between Turkey and the USA. Similarly, the good rapport between Presidents Trump and Erdoğan may prove to be instrumental in thawing relations. Nevertheless, given the nature of the problems that continue to haunt the bilateral relationship, a significant improvement of relations with the USA does not seem to be very likely.

On the EU front, it is similarly unrealistic to expect any positive developments for the country's EU accession. Regardless of how realistic an eventual Turkish accession to the EU is, it is in the EU's interest to use a carrot and stick approach to keep Turkey in line with the European stance on international issues. More specifically, the EU should try to entice the Turkish authorities for not completely giving up on its candidacy and to encourage Turkey to engage in further political and economic reforms, however hopeless it may be.

Scenario 3: Burning the Bridges with the West

Many IR scholars draw attention to the potential danger of a transition from soft to hard balancing, especially "when the hegemon's behavior becomes intolerable to the weaker powers" (Fortmann et al. 2004, p. 370, Pape 2005, Paul 2016). Mearsheimer (1983) notes the leaders of weak states may ignore the systemic constraints they face when they believe they possess an asymmetric strategy, i.e., a strategy that allows them to prevail quickly and cheaply in a conflict without facing the full military might of a vastly superior opponent. Paul (1994) further explains how weaker powers might initiate hostilities to obtain limited objectives, such as breaking a deadlock in negotiations or to highlight some perceived injustice in the status quo.

As Paul (2016, p. 19) maintains, if a rising power thinks that the order may accommodate their interests, it may not change it through violence. Nevertheless, if it thinks that "the order is unlikely to be changed without violent challenge," it may resort to conflict if the perceived costs are lower than the perceived benefits. Moreover, Paul (2016, p. 19) adds that "whether the rising power is willing to be accommodated at four levels – ideological/normative, territorial/spheres of influence, economic, and institutional – matters considerably in the eventual outcome." In this process, powerful constituencies and domestic factions may demand a more immediate accommodation, higher benefits, or territorial adjustments from the established powers, especially if there are any perceived historical injustices (Paul 2016).

Turkey is an "example of a potentially hard power emerging state" (Mares 2016, p. 249). Turkish authorities are cognizant of the advantages of having a large military and the latest military technology to defend the country's national interests. With rising nationalism and anti-Western sentiments – and significant grievances against the EU, the USA, and NATO – comes increased antagonism against the West. Turkey might accordingly set off on a hard balancing route against the West and ultimately decide to burn bridges.

Further facilitating a switch to hard balancing, US support for the Syrian Kurds makes Turkey increasingly concerned with the hegemon's military power as it might be perceived to "pose a serious challenge to [its] sovereignty" (Paul 2005, p. 47). While fulfilling this first criterion for hard balancing identified by Paul (2005), Turkish foreign policy behavior does not seem to fit into the remaining two criteria, as Turkey still perceives the USA as well as the EU "as a major source of public goods in both economic and security areas that cannot simply be replaced," and, as things stand right now, Turkey does not have the capabilities or intentions to "directly challenge [the dominant states'] power position with military means" (Paul 2005, p. 47).

However, any perceived threats to Erdoğan's domestic position is expected to "force him to double down on [the anti-Western] rhetoric" and pressure him "to give such rhetoric greater tangible expression in Turkish foreign policy" (Abramowitz and Edelman 2016, p. 11). As noted by an expert, given the rise of populism and nationalism in Turkey, in response to failure of the elites to "compete in a 21st-century globalized economy," it might be tempting for the elites in Turkey to "look for culprits" by steering the "public anger toward other countries, which can easily turn into military conflagrations" (Bremmer 2017b). Developments that occurred after the switch to the presidential system in summer 2018 in Turkey are concerning. The hostage crisis has spilled into the economic realm, as the two countries announced the introduction of new tariffs on each other's imports, such as the decision by the Trump Administration in August 2018 on doubling the tariffs on Turkish steel and aluminum (Hakura 2018a). The Turkish Lira in mid-August 2018 lost about 40 percent of its value against the USD in 2018 (Turak 2018).

In response to the increased sanctions against Turkey, the Turkish government called for a boycott of US electronics products (Reid 2018). President Erdoğan also published an angry op-ed in the *New York Times* on August 10, 2018, calling such sanctions "unacceptable, irrational, and ultimately detrimental" to Turkey's "longstanding friendship," warning that the "unilateral actions against Turkey by the United States will undermine American interests and force Turkey to look for other friends and allies" (Erdoğan 2018). He also accused the USA of "repeatedly and consistently" failing "to understand and respect the Turkish people's concerns" such as the importance of the extradition of Gülen or concerns regarding the partnership between the USA and the PYD/YPG (Erdoğan 2018). He continued to advise, "Unless the United States starts respecting Turkey's sovereignty and proves that it understands the dangers that our nation faces, our partnership could be in jeopardy" (Erdoğan 2018). Erdoğan (2018) further stated, "Turkey has established time and again that it will take care of its own business if the United States refuses to listen" and "take necessary steps to protect [its] national interests." These statements may be interpreted as threats to hard balance against the USA.

On the feasibility of hard balancing, some voice skepticism and draw attention to the capabilities gap between the USA and Turkey.[25] However, as noted in the literature, preponderance of power may fail to generate a deterrent or compellent threat because of the inclination of the weak "to challenge the status quo" due to being risk-acceptant or viewing "the conflict from an asymmetric perspective" (Wirtz 2004, p. 146). Noting the surprise factor as well as the use of a fait accomplis,

---

[25] Interview with a British journalist via Skype, October 14, 2016.

Wirtz (2004, p. 133) explains that the leaders in weaker states may "believe that it will be possible to avoid the full brunt of their opponent's superior capability" and defeat a much stronger opponent. Illustrating this point, Erdoğan (2018) concluded his *New York Times* op-ed with a threat: "Before it is too late, Washington must give up the misguided notion that our relationship . . . [is] asymmetrical and come to terms with the fact that Turkey has alternatives."

Accordingly, despite the military power gap between Turkey and the USA and the EU, Turkey may eventually become more risk-acceptant and decide to engage in hard balancing against the West. This is especially possible if the Turkish authorities make a calculation that the benefits of a more direct confrontation with the West outweigh its costs. Turkish foreign policy's future direction will be determined as much by how the USA and the EU respond to Turkey's increasing demands as by what Turkey's internal dynamics bring forth.

Boundary breaking has so far not been observed in certain areas, such as in Turkish foreign policy in the Western Balkans, in revocation of its alliance with NATO, or in withdrawal of its candidacy to the EU. Nevertheless, since 2016, Turkish authorities have repeatedly threatened to bring back the death penalty and indicated that a referendum may be held on Turkey's EU candidacy. An eventual reinstalling of the death penalty would represent a burning-of-the-bridges moment with the EU, as it would officially disqualify Turkey from being an EU candidate country. In the words of Margaritis Shinas, the European Commission spokesperson, a reinstating of the death penalty would represent "the reddest of the red lines" for the EU (quoted in *The Associated Press* April 18, 2017).

The evidence from Chapters 5, 6, and 7 suggests that Turkey is gradually positioning itself for hard balancing against the West. Turkey's declared intentions to become a full member of the SCO, agreement to purchase a Russian missile defense system, and increasingly hostile policies in Iraq and Syria are cases in point. Chapter 6 illustrates that the acquisition of a Russian missile system would mean that Turkey would choose a path that envisions greater military integration with Russia rather than NATO, as the Russian system would not only be incompatible with NATO's but also would constitute a security risk for NATO's defensive networks. Moreover, Turkey's use of military force against the Kurdish forces in Syria was a watershed event due to the proximity of the attacks to where the US Special Forces were deployed. Chapter 7 concludes with an argument that Turkish foreign policy runs the risk of

shifting further away from its Western orientation and starts showing
tendencies for hard balancing against the West. The blatant threats of the
Turkish authorities against the USA that its forces may be accidentally hit
in Syria aptly illustrate this point. As revealed in Chapters 5, 6, and 7, in
response to its disenchantment with the EU and the USA, Turkey increasingly looks for alternative venues, where its domestic policies would not
be heavily criticized. Against the background of its stalled accession
negotiations and rocky relations with the USA and NATO, Turkish
policymakers acknowledge that Turkey is exploring additional orienta-
tions in its foreign policy.

A key question that emerges from this discussion is how the USA and
the EU will engage a transforming Turkey. Many concur that Turkey's
alienation from the Western camp would be unsettling for the common
strategic interests of transatlantic actors. As one expert indicates, "An
alienated Turkey is not a good Turkey."[26] Turkey, the EU, and the USA
need to collaborate with each other and maintain a close dialogue on
a variety of pressing issues, such as the developments in the Middle East,
trade, energy, counterterrorism, and the refugee crisis (Annen 2016,
Pierini 2016b, Lesser 2017). As illustrated throughout this book, coordination becomes especially important with regard to the refugee crisis,
peace and stability in the Balkans, the Kurdish issue, stability and balance
of power in the Middle East, counterterrorism, and the resolution of the
Cyprus problem.

Because betrayal by one's ally is costly, management of opportunistic
behavior is a central part of alliance politics (Kim 2016, p. 42). In that
sense, an important responsibility falls on the NATO allies for deterring
Turkish foreign policy from additional boundary-breaking behaviors.
Some argue that alliance obligations may help reduce the chances of intra-
alliance conflict (Long et al. 2007). For instance, promises of nonaggres-
sion by alliance members constitute "costly signals of credible intentions
about future behavior" (Long et al. 2007, p. 1106), which in turn gen-
erates audience costs to be incurred in case of violation of these promises
(Fearon 1997). Therefore, in theory, parties may return back to a lower-
intensity intra-alliance opposition behavior at any time.

One commentator warns the West against "pursuing short-term
interests . . . [that seeds] long-term problems by enabling an authoritarian
government and sabotaging one of the region's few democracies"
(Ackerman 2017). As a Member of the German Bundestag puts it,

---

[26] Exchange with a Bosnian NGO official, Berlin, December 15, 2016.

"Turkey's path to Europe is in the interest of not only Turkey but also of other members of the EU," suggesting a return to the "successful path" that Turkey was on during the beginning of its accession negotiations (Annen 2016). Similarly, EU High Representative Mogherini (2016) warns, "If Turkey moves further away from our European Union and from democracy, it would lose part of its own heritage and identity, and culture, and power. This would be in no one's interest." Turkish officials similarly warn frequently that a Turkey outside of the EU will be against the interests of the West.[27] Others emphasize that if Turkey's EU accession process comes to an end, it would have significant negative consequences for Turkey, given the economic advantages of its EU candidacy (Erdemir 2017). It is especially important for Turkey to maintain good relations with the West, as the country went into an economic recession due to the devaluation of the Turkish Lira, shrinking GDP, and rising inflation and unemployment levels in the spring of 2019 (*BBC* March 11, 2019).

Many warn against the continuation of the EU's treatment of Turkey as "more like a security partner rather than an EU candidate country."[28] The "resistance to immigration, Islamophobia, and xenophobia" in the EU assure a continuation of this approach.[29] As stated by a prominent scholar of Turkish politics, "Since 2005, it had been the EU (or at least an important part of it) that had turned away from Turkey, rather than the other way around" (Hale 2013, p. 257). Many interviewees note that the EU and Turkey are now "in the game of pretending about the prospects of EU accession"[30] and that "there is no credibility to Turkey's EU accession prospects."[31] Since December 2016, no accession negotiations have been initiated. The EU accession process potentially entered into an "irreversible coma" after the constitutional referendum (Marc Pierini, quoted in Peterson and Miller Llama 2017). A number of EU leaders have called for suspending Turkey's EU accession negotiations (Baczynska 2017), and the European Parliament voted in a non-binding fashion to suspend the accession negotiation talks with Turkey. On June 26, 2018, the European Council declared that "Turkey's accession negotiations have therefore effectively come to a standstill and no further chapters can be considered

---

[27] Interview with a Turkish official, Washington DC, September 30 2016.
[28] Exchange with a German NGO official, Berlin, Germany, December 16, 2016.
[29] Interview with a British journalist via Skype, October 14, 2016.
[30] Exchange with a German journalist, Berlin, Germany, 16 December 2016.
[31] Interview with a British journalist via Skype, October 14, 2016.

for opening or closing and no further work towards the modernization of the EU–Turkey Customs Union is foreseen" (European Council 2018).

However, as noted by a Senior Transatlantic Fellow at the German Marshall Fund, "Nobody [in the EU] is going to break [the EU–Turkey accession talks] off . . . [as] that would push the ball, which is currently on Erdoğan's court, back to the EU's court" (Stelzenmueller 2017). Suspension of accession negotiations is not in the EU's or the West's interests, as it would also put an end to reforms in Turkey and remove a mechanism for the provision of EU feedback (European Stability Initiative [ESI] 2017). The lack of any credible possibility of Turkey's EU membership in light of the recent developments in EU–Turkey relations as well as the deterioration of democracy and the rule of law make Turkey "less permeable to European pressure" (Cornell et al. 2012, p. 11) and less interested in EU membership than it has been in recent decades (Cornell et al. 2012, Pierini 2016b). This leads some to argue that the EU has lost its power of attraction in Turkey.[32]

Repeated threats by Turkish leaders to bring back the death penalty are indicative of Turkey "moving further away from the EU norms" and getting alienated from the idea of EU membership.[33] Many hold the opinion that it is only a matter of time before Turkey revokes its relations with the EU, including the agreement on accepting refugees from Europe. In its dealings with the EU, over time Turkish authorities stopped pretending that the EU accession negotiations are realistic and started questioning their willingness to join the EU. Even if the Turkey–EU relationship is revitalized, "it may not be enough for persuading the public [on the desirability of its EU accession]."[34] Many project that a privileged partnership, rather than full membership, is likely to be in the future of the EU–Turkey relationship. Some recommend the EU to make concessions to Ankara on the renegotiation of the Customs Union Agreement or the visa liberalization process, adding that such "concessions must be linked to red lines, such as the re-introduction of the death penalty and torture" (Seufert 2017, p. 8). Nevertheless, the European Council (2018) has already declared that the modernization of the Customs Union Agreement is out of the question as long as Turkey moves further away from the EU.

[32] Exchange with a Turkish scholar, Berlin, December 16, 2016.
[33] Interview with a British journalist via Skype, October 14, 2016.
[34] Exchange with a Turkish scholar, Berlin, December 16, 2016.

Turkey and the transatlantic actors are moving into a transactional period (Lesser 2017, Albright et al. 2012) "without the flywheel of a long-term trajectory for cooperation," making the relations look "security-heavy and unpredictable" (Lesser 2017). Strategic cooperation between the parties seems to be increasingly unrealistic, given the mutual distrust and grievances between Turkey and the transatlantic allies, intensified security competition, and increasing perception of the West as a threat to Turkish security. Therefore, the third scenario seems to be the most likely one, as Turkey seems to be more interested in breaking its boundaries against the West.

CONCLUSION

This book differentiates between different degrees of intra-alliance opposition and identifies which tools are used in which process of intra-alliance conflict/opposition. It demonstrates the progression of Turkey's motivations within the Western alliance over time and argues that Turkey has been initially experimenting with different foreign policy tools in an attempt to increase the space of what is acceptable in interactions within the transatlantic community. Through these foreign policy tools, Turkey has been initially seeking to maintain a more equitable relationship with the West, to accomplish the resolution of the Cyprus problem in line with its key interests, and to consolidate its power and sphere of influence in the Middle East and the Western Balkans. It was employing lower-intensity intra-alliance opposition tools while still emphasizing its willingness to pursue the goals of joining the Union and proving its value for the transatlantic alliance. Therefore, Turkish foreign policy behavior between 2010 and 2014 is best categorized as boundary testing.

As the prospects of its EU membership became dim, and its relationship with the United States and other NATO allies deteriorated due to irreconcilable national interests with regard to the Middle East and an emerging crisis of trust, Turkey seems to have adopted an increasingly aggressive and confrontational foreign policy vis-à-vis the West. From 2014 to 2016, Turkey's goals changed as the country aspired to level the playing field against the West. Therefore, it engaged in boundary challenging against the West during that time period. The goal was to signal that the country had other options beyond the Western alliance while still keeping the existing lines of communication with the alliance open. Using boundary challenging, Turkey made contingency plans to enhance its future leverage against the West as a result of its increasing apprehension that its long-desired Western status will not be realized. During this process, Turkey was still willing to operate within the boundaries of its alliance with the West. It used the refugee deal with the EU to extract some perquisites from the West and simultaneously considered alternative energy projects like TANAP and TurkStream and contributed to the operations against the IS after an initial ambivalence.

Nevertheless, especially since the failed coup attempt of 2016, Turkish intra-alliance opposition behavior has increasingly turned into boundary breaking. Since July 2016, it has become evident that Turkey seeks to acquire an independent voice against the EU, the USA, and NATO, i.e. independence outside the alliance. Thus far, Turkey has not engaged in direct military confrontation against the West. If Turkey decides to abolish the death penalty or engages in hot conflict with one of its EU neighbors, such as the Republic of Cyprus or Greece, or with the USA, then it would be considered to be engaging in hard balancing against the West.

The three factors outlined in this chapter provoke unease and reinforce ambitions on the part of Turkey to provide a hedge against the West and to give impetus to the development of a more confrontational course in its foreign policy. This chapter concludes that international/regional, issue-specific, and domestic factors serve as important explanatory factors behind Turkey's increasing boundary-breaking behavior. If the domestic political and economic developments – such as the increasing crackdown on the opposition, the approved changes in the April 2017 constitutional referendum, the transition to a presidential system, the economic recession, trade/sanctions wars, and the suspension of Turkey from the F-35 JSF program – are any harbinger of the developments to come, the tensions between Turkey and the West can only be expected to escalate in the near future to an irreversible point.

The future of Turkey's relations with the West depends on a variety of conditions, such as the issues that are at stake, the irreconcilability of the positions of the parties on such issues, and the perceived value of the existing relationship for each party. Turkey and the West still need each other. Turkey is still a NATO member, and an ally of the USA and the EU, even though it is often characterized as "a difficult and sometimes problematic ally."[35] The EU is still Turkey's top import and export partner, and Turkey is the EU's fifth-largest import and fourth-largest export partner (European Commission 2019b). Turkey and the West need each other in order to deal with the common security challenges in the Middle East, the

---

[35] Interview with a British journalist via Skype, October 14, 2016.

Balkans, and Eastern Europe. The high level of interdependence and the common security concerns between Turkey and the West may provide incentives for avoiding hard-balancing behavior. The challenge for the West is that of engaging Turkey in a mutually beneficial way, through a mix of policy tools that can encourage it to abandon its boundary-breaking foreign policy behavior in its search for a new place in the changing international and regional orders.

Bibliography

Abramowitz, Morton, and Eric Edelman (Eds.). 2015. "Turkey: An Increasingly Undependable Ally." Bipartisan Policy Center, April. Available at: https://bipar tisanpolicy.org/wp-content/uploads/2015/04/BPC-Turkey-Alliance.pdf (accessed April 5, 2019).

Abramowitz, Morton, and Eric Edelman (Eds.). 2016. "Beyond the Myth of Partnership: Rethinking US Policy toward Turkey." Bipartisan Policy Center, December. Available at: https://cdn.bipartisanpolicy.org/wp-content/uploads/2016/12/BPC-Turkey-Partnership-Myth.pdf (accessed April 5, 2019).

Acheson, Dean. 1969. *Present at the Creation: My Years in the State Department.* New York: W. W. Norton & Company.

Ackerman, Elliot. 2017. "Turkey Is a Dictatorship Masquerading as a NATO Democracy." *Foreign Policy*, March 29. Available at: http://foreignpolicy.com/2017/03/29/the-dictatorship-in-natos-clubhouse-erdogan-kurds-turkey/?utm_s ource=Sailthru&utm_medium=email&utm_campaign=New%20Campaign& utm_term=%2AEditors%20Picks (accessed April 5, 2019).

Afanasieva, Dasha, and Alexander Dziadosz. 2014. "Kurdish Convoy Heads to Syria to Take on Islamic State." Reuters, October 29. Available at: www.reu ters.com/article/us-mideast-crisis-peshmerga-idUSKBN0II09X20141029 (accessed April 5, 2019).

Al Jazeera. 2017. "NATO Countries Could Have Been More Frank." Video Interview with Turkish Defense Minister Fikri Işık, March 25. Available at: www.aljazeera .com/programmes/talktojazeera/2017/03/fikri-isik-nato-countries-frank-17032312 2127878.html (accessed April 5, 2019).

Albert, Eleanor. 2015. "The Shanghai Cooperation Organization." Council on Foreign Relations, October 14. Available at: www.cfr.org/china/shanghai-coop eration-organization/p10883 (accessed April 5, 2019).

Albright, Madeleine. 1998. Press Conference by the US Secretary of State, NATO Headquarters, Brussels, December 8. Available at: www.nato.int/docu/speech/1998/s981208x.htm (accessed April 5, 2019).

Albright, Madeleine K., Stephen J. Hadley, and Steven A. Cook. 2012. *US–Turkey Relations: A New Partnership*. New York: Council on Foreign Relations.

Alic, Anes. 2010. "Vying for Influence in the Balkans." Radio Free Europe, June 2.

Alırıza, Bülent, and Samuel J. Brannen. 2013. "Turkey Looks to China on Air and Missile Defense?" Center for Strategic and International Studies, October 8. Available at: www.csis.org/analysis/turkey-looks-china-air-and-missile-defense (accessed April 5, 2019).

Almukhtar, Sarah, and Tim Wallace. 2015. "Why Turkey Is Fighting the Kurds Who Are Fighting ISIS." *New York Times*, August 12.

Altunışık, Meliha Benli. 2013. "The Middle East in Turkey–USA Relations: Managing the Alliance." *Journal of Balkan and Near Eastern Studies* 15(2): 157–173.

Alves, Ana C. 2014. "Building Soft Power: China's Positive Economic Statecraft in Africa – Historical Comparisons." Paper presented at the International Conference China and Africa, Media, Communications and Public Diplomacy, September 10–11, Beijing, China. Available at: www.cmi.no/file/2910-.pdf (accessed April 5, 2019).

Anadolu Agency. 2012. "Turkey–Albania Trade Volume Not Satisfactory." April 6. Available at: www.aa.com.tr/en/economy/43978–turkey-albania-trad e-volume-not-satisfactory (accessed April 5, 2019).

Anadolu Agency. 2013. "Balkan Turks to Support Erdogan upon Gezi Park in Gostivar." June 14. Available at: http://aa.com.tr/en/turkey/balkan-turks-to-s upport-erdogan-upon-gezi-park-in-gostivar/238534 (accessed April 5, 2019).

Anderson, Linda. 2017. "Work with Turkey, Don't Overwhelm It." *US News and World Report*, March 9.

Annen, Neils. 2016. Conference Remarks, Conference on Turkey, Middle East Institute. Washington, DC, September 30.

Aras, Bülent. 2017. "Turkish Foreign Policy after July 15." *Istanbul Policy Center*, February. Available at: http://ipc.sabanciuniv.edu/wp-content/uploads/2017/02/Turkish-Foreign-Policy-After-July-15_Bulent-Aras.pdf (accessed April 5, 2019).

Arin, Kubilay. 2014. "The New Turkey: A Rival to the West in the Near East." *E-International Relations*. Available at: www.e-ir.info/2014/06/05/the-new-turkey-a-rival-to-the-west-in-the-near-east/ (accessed April 5, 2019).

Art, Robert J. 2005. "Correspondence: Striking the Balance." *International Security* 30(3): 177–196.

Athanassopoulou, Ekavi. 1994. "Turkey and the Balkans: The View from Athens." *The International Spectator* 29(4): 55–64.

Aydın, Mustafa, and Sinem A. Açıkmeşe. 2007. "Europeanization through EU Conditionality: Understanding the New Era in Turkish Foreign Policy." *Journal of Southern Europe and the Balkans* 9(3): 263–274.

Aydın-Düzgit, Senem, and Fuat E. Keyman. 2014. "Democracy Support in Turkey's Foreign Policy." Carnegie Endowment for International Peace. Available at: http://carnegieendowment.org/2014/03/25/democracy-support-i n-turkey-s-foreign-policy-pub-55096 (accessed April 5, 2019).

Baczynska, Gabriela. 2017. "EU Ankara Negotiator Calls for Suspension of Turkey Accession Talks." *Reuters*, April 26. Available at: www.reuters.com/ article/us-turkey-eu-piri-idUSKBN17S0Q7 (accessed April 5, 2019).

Bağcı, Hüseyin. 2001. "Türkiye ve AGSK: Beklentiler, Endişeler [Turkey and the European Security and Defense Identity: Expectations, Concerns]." In İdris Bal (Ed.), 21. *Yüzyılın Eşiğinde Türk Dış Politikası [Turkish Foreign Policy at the Turn of the 21st Century]*. Istanbul: Alfa, pp. 593–615.

Bakeer, Ali. 2018. "Impending Sanctions on Iran Will Make Turkey's Energy Imports More Expensive and Contribute to the Devaluation of the Lira." *Carnegie Endowment for International Peace*, June 20. Available at: http://car negieendowment.org/sada/76644 (accessed April 5, 2019).

Baldwin, David A. 1985. *Economic Statecraft*. Princeton: Princeton University Press.

Barysch, Katinka. 2007. "Turkey's Role in European Energy Security." *Centre for European Reform Essays*. December. Available at: www.cer.org.uk/sites/defa ult/files/publications/attachments/pdf/2011/essay_turkey_energy_12dec07-138 1.pdf (accessed April 5, 2019).

Barysch, Katinka. 2010. "Turkey and the EU: Can Stalemate Be Avoided?" Centre for European Reform, Policy Brief, December.

Barysch, Katinka. 2011. "Why the EU and Turkey Need to Coordinate Their Foreign Policies." Carnegie Endowment for International Peace. August 31. Available at: https://carnegieendowment.org/2011/08/31/why-eu-and-turkey-n eed-to-coordinate-their-foreign-policies-pub-45452 (accessed April 5, 2019).

Batalla-Adam, Laura. 2012. "Turkey's Foreign Policy in the AKP Era: Has There Been an Axis Shift?" *Turkish Policy Quarterly* 11(3): 139–148.

BBC. 2016. "Turkey's Erdogan Criticises EU over Syria Refugee Deal." July 26. Available at: www.bbc.com/news/world-europe-36892393 (accessed April 5, 2019).

BBC. 2019. "Turkey's Economy Slides into Recession." March 11. Available at: www.bbc.com/news/business-47522338 (accessed April 5, 2019).

Bechev, Dimitar. 2012. "Turkey in the Balkans: Taking a Broader View." *Insight Turkey* 14(1): 131–146.

Bechev, Dimitar. 2017. "Southeast Europe." In Gerald Stang (Ed.), *Securing the Energy Union: Five Pillars and Five Regions*. Paris: EU Institute for Security Studies, pp. 11–16.

Beesley, Arthur. 2017. "Brussels Pressed to Rethink Turkey Ties." *Financial Times*, April 24.

Bekdil, Burak E. 2017. "Turkey Aims to Produce Long-Range Missiles." *DefenseNews*, February 6. Available at: www.defensenews.com/articles/tur key-aims-to-produce-long-range-missiles (accessed April 5, 2019).

Bernd, Riegert. 2016. "NATO and Turkey: Allies, Not Friends." *Deutsche Welle*, August 2. Available at: www.dw.com/en/nato-and-turkey-allies-not-friends/a- 19444991 (accessed April 5, 2019).

Bershidsky, Leonid. 2017. "Turkey's Troubled NATO Status." *Bloomberg*, March 14. Available at: www.bloomberg.com/view/articles/2017-03-14/tur key-s-nato-status-grows-more-troubled (accessed April 5, 2019).

Bertrand, Natasha. 2016. "NATO's Second Largest Military Power Is Threatening a Dramatic Pivot to Russia and China." *Business Insider*, November 22. Available at: www.businessinsider.com/turkey-russia-china-sha nghai-cooperation-organization-2016-11 (accessed April 5, 2019).

Bilgesam. 2014. "Balkanlar ve Turkiye" [Balkans and Turkey], Report No. 64, December, Istanbul.

Bilgin, Pınar. 2003. "The Peculiarity of Turkey's Position in EU/NATO Military/ Security Cooperation: A Rejoinder to Missiroli." *Security Dialogue* 34(3): 345–349.

Bislimi, Faton. 2011. "EU Foreign Policy towards Balkans: An Opportunity or a Challenge." In Cüneyt Yenigün and Ferdinand Gjana (Eds.), *Balkans: Foreign Affairs, Politics, and Socio-Cultures*. Tirana: Epoka University Publications, pp. 597–617.

Bonsey, Noah. 2017. "What's at Stake in the Syrian Peace Talks in Astana?" *International Crisis Group*, January 24. Available at: www.crisisgroup.org/mi ddle-east-north-africa/eastern-mediterranean/syria/what-stake-syrian-peace-tal ks-astana (accessed April 5, 2019).

Bozkır, Volkan. 2016. Conference Remarks, Conference on Turkey, Middle East Institute. Washington DC, September 30.

Bölükbaşı, Süha. 1988. *The Superpowers and the Third World: Turkish-American Relations and Cyprus*. London: University Press of America.

Börzel, Tanja A. 2002. "Member State Responses to Europeanization." *JCMS: Journal of Common Market Studies* 40(2): 193–214.

Börzel, Tanja A., and Thomas Risse. 2007. "Europeanization: The Domestic Impact of European Union Politics." In Knud Erik Jørgensen, Mark Pollack, and Ben Rosamond (Eds.), *The Handbook of European Union Politics*. Thousand Oaks, CA: Sage, pp. 483–504.

Bremmer, Ian. 2017a. "Donald Trump's New World Order Puts Nation over Globe." *Time*, January 12. Available at: http://time.com/4632670/donald-tru mp-new-world-order/ (accessed April 5, 2019).

Bremmer, Ian. 2017b. "The Wave to Come." *Time*, May 11. Available at: http:// time.com/4775441/the-wave-to-come/ (accessed April 5, 2019).

Brljavać, Bedrudin. 2011. "Turkey Entering the European Union through the Balkan Doors: In the Style of a Great Power?" *Romanian Journal of European Affairs* 48(3): 521–531.

Brooks, Stephen G., and William C. Wohlforth. 2005. "Hard Times for Soft Balancing." *International Security* 30(1): 72–108.

Bugajski, Janusz, and Heather A. Conley. 2011. "A New Transatlantic Approach for the Western Balkans: Time for a Change in Serbia, Kosova, and Bosnia-Herzegovina." *Center for Strategic and International Studies*, November. Available at: http://csis.org/files/publication/111110_Bugajski_TransatlanticA pproach_web.pdf (accessed April 5, 2019).

Bump, Philip. 2017. "Was Erdogan Personally Involved in His Bodyguards' Attacks on Protesters in DC?" *The Washington Post*, May 16. Available at: www.washingtonpost.com/news/politics/wp/2017/05/19/was-erdogan-person ally-involved-in-his-bodyguards-attacks-on-protesters-in-d-c/?utm_ term=.33b9d0a9f2c5 (accessed April 5, 2019).

Burwell, Frances G. 2008. "Rebuilding US–Turkey Relations in a Transatlantic Context." In Frances G. Burwell (Ed.), *The Evolution of US–Turkish Relations in a Transatlantic Context*. Carlisle, PA: Strategic Studies Institute, pp. 1–28.

Büyük, Hamdi Fırat. 2016. "Turkey's 'Soft Power' Risks Backfiring in Balkan." *BalkanInsight*, February 26. Available at: www.balkaninsight.com/en/article/turkey-s-soft-power-risks-backfiring-in-balkans-02-25-2016 (accessed April 5, 2019).

Cain, Phil. 2010. "The Limits of Turkey's Balkans Diplomacy." *World Politics Review*, November 10.

Cantir, Christian, and Ryan Kennedy. 2015. "Balancing on the Shoulders of Giants: Moldova's Foreign Policy toward Russia and the European Union." *Foreign Policy Analysis* 11(4): 397–416.

Capie, David. 2004. "Between a Hegemon and a Hard Place: The 'War on Terror' and Southeast Asian–US Relations." *Pacific Review* 17(2): 223–248.

Capoccia, Giovanni, and Daniel R. Kelemen. 2007. "The Study of Critical Junctures: Theory, Narrative, and Counterfactuals in Historical Institutionalism." *World Politics* 59(3): 341–369.

Catalinac, Amy L. 2010. "Why New Zealand Took Itself out of ANZUS: Observing 'Opposition for Autonomy' in Asymmetric Alliances." *Foreign Policy Analysis* 6(4): 317–338.

Checkel, Jeffrey T. 2008. "Process Tracing." In Audie Klotz and Deepa Prakash (Eds.), *Qualitative Methods in International Relations*. London: Palgrave Macmillan, pp. 114–127.

Chulkovskaya, Yekaterina. 2017. "Will Turkey Leave NATO?" *Al-Monitor*, January 9. Available at: www.al-monitor.com/pulse/originals/2017/01/russia-turkey-erdogan-putin-membership-shanghai-sco-eu.html (accessed April 5, 2019).

Chulov, Martin, Constanze Letsch, and Fazel Hawramy. 2014. "Turkey to Allow Kurdish Peshmerga across Its Territory to Fight in Kobani." *The Guardian*, October 20.

Chung, Jaewook. 2016. "Capability Change, Economic Dependence and Alliance Termination." *The Korean Journal of International Studies* 14(2): 209–240.

Cockburn, Patrick. 2014. "ISIS in Kobani: Turkey's Act of Abandonment May Mark an 'Irrevocable Breach' with Kurds across the Region." *The Independent*, October 7.

Cook, Steven A. 2018. "We Wanted Turkey to Be a Partner: It Was Never Going to Work." *The Washington Post*, August 17. Available at: www.washingtonpost.com/outlook/turkey-is-an-overrated-american-ally/2018/08/17/652ce464-a18a-11e8-93e3-24d1703d2a7a_story.html?utm_term=.e698dobbc25e (accessed April 5, 2019).

Cornell, Svante, Gerald Knaus, and Manfred Scheich. 2012. "Dealing with a Rising Power: Turkey's Transformation and Its Implications for the EU." *Centre for European Studies*, Brussels. Available at: www.martenscentre.eu/sites/default/files/publication-files/livret-ces-turkey.pdf (accessed April 5, 2019).

Council of Europe. 2017. "110th Plenary – Turkey – Proposed Constitutional Amendments 'Dangerous Step Backwards' for Democracy." Venice Commission,

March 10. Available at: www.venice.coe.int/webforms/events/?id=2369 (accessed April 5, 2019).

Cunningham, Erin. 2018. "US Pastor Andrew Brunson Leaves Turkey after Being Detained for Two Years." *The Washington Post*, October 12. Available at: www .washingtonpost.com/world/middle_east/turkish-court-orders-release-of-us-pas tor-andrew-brunson/2018/10/12/a793df78-ccbf-11e8-ad0a-0e01efba3cc1_s tory.html?utm_term=.3ccede2fb628 (accessed April 5, 2019).

Cupolo, Diego. 2018. "Turkey's Dangerous Game of 'Hostage Diplomacy.'" *The Atlantic*, May 6. Available at: www.theatlantic.com/international/archive/2018/ 05/turkey-andrew-brunson-erdogan-coup-gulen-kurds/559748/ (accessed April 5, 2019).

Çağaptay, Soner. 2015. "Is the US–Turkey Relationship Crumbling?" *The Washington Institute*, PolicyWatch 2367, February 5. Available at: www.was hingtoninstitute.org/policy-analysis/view/is-the-u.s.-turkey-relationship-crum bling (accessed April 5, 2019).

Çakır, Mustafa. 2014. "An Economic Analysis of the Relationship between Turkey and the Balkan Countries." *Adam Akademi Sosyal Bilimler Dergisi* 4 (2): 77–86.

Çandar, Cengiz. 2016. "Is the EU Really Ready to Commit to Turkey?" *Al-Monitor*, March 13. Available at: www.al-monitor.com/pulse/originals/2016/ 03/turkey-european-union-refugee-deal-tango-partners.html (accessed April 5, 2019).

Çavuşoğlu, Mevlüt. 2018. "America Has Chosen the Wrong Partner." *New York Times*, January 18. Available at: www.nytimes.com/2018/01/28/opinion/us-tur key-syria-allies.html (accessed April 5, 2019).

Çayhan, Esra. 2003. "Towards a European Security and Defense Policy: With or without Turkey?" *Turkish Studies* 4(1): 35–54.

Çeviköz, Ünal. 2016. "Could Turkey Become a New Energy Trade Hub in South East Europe?" *Turkish Policy Quarterly* 15(3): 67–76.

Dağı, İhsan. 2014. Speech Transcript, "Turkey: An Emerging Power in a Changing Middle East" Conference, Council on Foreign Relations, Istanbul, June 18. Available at: www.cfr.org/projects/world/turkey-an-emerging-power-in-a-changing-middle-east/pr1685 (accessed April 5, 2019).

Daily Sabah. 2016. "Turkey to Chair 2017 Energy Club of Shanghai Cooperation Organization." November 23. Available at: www.dailysabah.com/energy/201 6/11/23/turkey-to-chair-2017-energy-club-of-shanghai-cooperation-organiza tion (accessed April 5, 2019).

Daily Sabah. 2017. "We May Cancel Turkey-EU Refugee Deal, Foreign Minister Çavuşoğlu Says." March 15. Available at: www.dailysabah.com/diplomacy/201 7/03/15/we-may-cancel-turkey-eu-refugee-deal-foreign-minister-cavusoglu-says (accessed April 5, 2019).

Daily Sabah. 2018. "TANAP, TAP Pipelines Interconnect at Turkey–Greece Border." November 21. Available at: www.dailysabah.com/energy/2018/11/2 2/tanap-tap-pipelines-interconnect-at-turkey-greece-border (accessed April 5, 2019).

Daily Sabah. 2019. "Turkey, EU Look to Further Harness Growing Economic Cooperation." February 28. Available at: www.dailysabah.com/economy/201

9/02/28/turkey-eu-look-to-further-harness-growing-economic-cooperation (accessed April 5, 2019).

Dalay, Galip. 2017. "Turkey's Unpalatable Choices in Syria." *German Marshall Fund of the United States*, March 7. Available at: www.gmfus.org/publications/turkeys-unpalatable-choices-syria (accessed April 5, 2019).

Danforth, Nick. 2014. "The Empire Strikes Back." *Foreign Policy*, March 27.

Danopoulos, Constantine. 1997. "Turkey and the Balkans: Searching for Stability." In Constantine P. Danopoulos and Kostas G. Messas (Eds.), *Crises in the Balkans: Views from the Participants*. Oxford: Westview Press, pp. 211–224.

Davutoğlu, Ahmet. 1994. "The Clash of Interests: An Explanation of the World (Dis)Order." *Intellectual Discourse* 2(2): 107–130.

Davutoğlu, Ahmet. 2001. *Stratejik Derinlik* [Strategic Depth]. Istanbul: Küre Publishers.

Davutoğlu, Ahmet. 2008. "Turkey's Foreign Policy Vision: An Assessment of 2007." *Insight Turkey* 10(1): 77–96.

Davutoğlu, Ahmet. 2009. Address delivered at the opening ceremony of the Ottoman Legacy and Balkan Muslim Communities Today Conference, Conference Proceedings, Sarajevo, October 16, pp. 13–19. Available at: http://cns.ba/wp-content/uploads/2014/03/osmansko-naslijede-i-muslimanske-zajednice-Balkana-danas-zbornik-radova.pdf (accessed April 5, 2019).

Davutoğlu, Ahmet. 2010. "Turkish Foreign Policy and the EU in 2010." *Turkish Policy Quarterly* 8(3): 11–17.

De Luce, Dan, and Paul McLeary. 2017. "Trump to Tell Turkey: We Are Going to Take Raqqa with the Kurds." *Foreign Policy*, May 5.

Demirtaş, Birgül. 2015. "Turkish Foreign Policy towards the Balkans: A Europeanized Foreign Policy in a De-Europeanized National Context?" *Journal of Balkan and Near Eastern Studies* 17(2): 123–140.

Dempsey, Judy. 2014. "Europe's Energy Strategy and South Stream's Demise." *Carnegie Europe*, December 4. Available at: http://carnegieeurope.eu/strategiceurope/?fa=57386 (accessed April 5, 2019).

Dempsey, Judy. 2015. "Judy Asks: Is the EU Selling out to Turkey?" *Carnegie Europe*, December 2. Available at: http://carnegieeurope.eu/strategiceurope/?fa=62155 (accessed April 5, 2019).

Deutsche Welle. 2017. "German Military Leaves Turkey's Incirlik Airbase." September 28. Available at: www.dw.com/en/german-military-leaves-turkeys-incirlik-airbase/a-40717584 (accessed April 5, 2019).

Deutsche Welle. 2019. "European Parliament Votes to Suspend Turkey's EU Membership Bid." March 13. Available at: www.dw.com/en/european-parliament-votes-to-suspend-turkeys-eu-membership-bid/a-47902275 (accessed April 5, 2019).

DeYoung, Karen. 2019. "US Suspends Turkey's Participation in F-35 Fighter Program over Ankara's Purchase of Russian System." *Washington Post*, April 1. Available at: www.washingtonpost.com/world/national-security/us-suspends-turkeys-participation-in-f-35-fighter-program-over-ankaras-purchase-of-russian-system/2019/04/01/c38a16be-54b6-11e9-8ef3-fbd41a2ce4d5_story.html?utm_term=.e7d5d08a9337 (accessed April 1, 2019).

Dimitriadi, Angeliki. 2016. "Deals without Borders: EU's Foreign Policy on Migration." *European Council on Foreign Relations Policy Brief*, April 4. Available at: www.ecfr.eu/page/-/ECFR-165-DEALS_WITHOUT_BORDERS.pdf (accessed April 5, 2019).

Dombey, Daniel. 2010. "Obama Warns Turkey on Iran and Israel." *Financial Times*, August 15.

Duke, Simon. 2008. "The Future of EU–NATO Relations: A Case of Mutual Irrelevance through Competition." *Journal of European Integration* 3(1): 27–43.

Dursun-Özkanca, Oya. 2008. "Turkey and the EU: Implications of Membership Scenarios on Transatlantic Security Relations." In Sven Biscop and Johan Lembke (Eds.), *EU Enlargement and the Transatlantic Alliance: A Security Relationship in Flux*. London: Lynne Rienner, pp. 119–136.

Dursun-Özkanca, Oya. 2010. "Turkey's Neo-Ottomanism in the Balkans." *Prishtina Insight*, September 3.

Dursun-Özkanca, Oya. 2016. "Turkey and the European Union: Strategic Partners or Competitors in the Western Balkans?" *Journal of Regional Security* 11(1): 33–54.

Dursun-Özkanca, Oya. 2017. "Turkish Soft Balancing against the EU? An Analysis of the Prospects for Improved Transatlantic Security Relations." *Foreign Policy Analysis* 13(4): 894–912.

Ekinci, Didem. 2013. "Balkan Energy Networks and Turkey: Pitfalls and Opportunities within the European Context." In Muhidin Mulalić, Hasan Korkut, and Elif Nuroğlu (Eds.), *Turkish-Balkans Relations: The Future Prospects of Cultural, Political and Economic Transformations and Relations*. Istanbul: Tasam Yayinlari.

Ekinci, Mehmet Uğur. 2014. "A Golden Age of Relations: Turkey and the Western Balkans During the AK Party Period." *Insight Turkey* 16(1): 103–125.

Emmott, Robin. 2016. "Exclusive: Turkey Purges NATO Military Envoys after Failed Coup." *Reuters*, October 12. Available at: www.reuters.com/article/us-turkey-nato-exclusive-idUSKCN12C16Q (accessed April 5, 2019).

Energy Community. 2015. "Energy Governance in Turkey." October. Available at: www.energy-community.org/portal/page/portal/ENC_HOME/DOCS/3894261/25824B882CF017E0E053C92FA8C0EE59.PDF (accessed April 5, 2019).

Eralp, Atila. 2009. "Temporality, Cyprus Problem and Turkey–EU Relationship." *EDAM Discussion Paper Series* 2, July.

Eralp, Doğa Ulaş. 2010. "Turkey and Bosnia-Herzegovina: A Future Reflecting on the Past." *SETA Policy Brief* 46, August.

Erbach, Gregor. 2015. "Energy Union: New Impetus for Coordination and Integration of Energy Policies in the EU." *European Parliamentary Research Service Briefing*, PE 551.310, March 5. Available at: www.europarl.europa.eu/RegData/etudes/BRIE/2015/551310/EPRS_BRI(2015)551310_EN.pdf (accessed April 5, 2019).

Erdemir, Aykan. 2017. Conference Remarks, "What Is the Future of EU–Turkey Relations" Conference. Wilson Center, Washington DC, April 24.

Erdemir, Aykan, and Eric S. Edelman. 2018. "Erdogan's Hostage Diplomacy." *Foundation for Defense of Democracies*, May 31. Available at: www.fdd.org/an

alysis/2018/05/31/erdogans-hostage-diplomacy-western-nationals-in-turkish-pris ons/ (accessed April 5, 2019).

Erdemir, Aykan, and Merve Tahiroğlu. 2018. "Trump Waives Iran Sanctions for Turkey." *Foreign Policy*, November 12. Available at: https://foreignpolicy.com/ 2018/11/12/trump-waives-iran-sanctions-for-turkey/ (accessed April 5, 2019).

Erdoğan, Emre. 2017. "Presidential Referendum: A Pivotal Moment in Turkey's Prolonged Election Cycle." *German Marshall Fund of the United States*, April 13. Available at: www.gmfus.org/publications/presidential-referendum-pivotal-moment-turkeys-prolonged-election-cycle (accessed April 5, 2019).

Erdoğan, Recep Tayyip. 2018. "Erdogan: How Turkey Sees the Crisis with the U.S." *New York Times*, August 10. Available at: www.nytimes.com/2018/08/ 10/opinion/turkey-erdogan-trump-crisis-sanctions.html (accessed April 5, 2019).

Erkuş, Sevil. 2019. "Turkey Sticks to S-400 Deal Despite Pressure." *Hürriyet Daily News*, February 21. Available at: www.hurriyetdailynews.com/turkey-s ticks-to-s-400-deal-despite-us-pressure-141375 (accessed April 5, 2019).

Eroğlu, Zehra. 2005. "Turkish Foreign Policy towards the Balkans in the Post-Cold War Era." Unpublished Master's Thesis, Middle Eastern Technical University, April.

European Stability Initiative. 2017. *The Chapter Illusion: For Honesty and Clarity in EU–Turkey Relations*. May 15, Berlin. Available at: www.esiweb.org/pdf/E SI%20-%20The%20Turkey%20chapter%20illusion%20-%2015%20May% 202017.pdf (accessed April 5, 2019).

EurActiv.com. 2009. "NATO 'Alarmed' by Lack of Cooperation with EU." September 18.

EurActiv.com. 2016. "Erdogan to Meet Putin for a 'New Beginning.'" August 8. Available at: www.euractiv.com/section/global-europe/news/erdogan-to-meet-putin-for-a-new-beginning/ (accessed April 5, 2019).

Euronews. 2015. "Interview with Didier Billion about Turkey's Future in Europe." October 26. Available at: www.euronews.com/2015/10/26/inter view-with-didier-billion-irisabout-turkey-s-future-in-europe (accessed April 5, 2019).

European Commission. 2009. *Turkey Progress Report 2009*, Brussels, October 14. Available at: http://ec.europa.eu/enlargement/pdf/key_docu ments/2009/tr_rapport_2009_en.pdf (accessed April 5, 2019).

European Commission. 2012a. "Proposal for a Council Decision concerning the Conclusion of the Agreement between the European Union and the Republic of Turkey on the Readmission of Persons Residing without Authorisation." COM (2012) 239 Final, Brussels, June 22. Available at: http://eur-lex.europa.eu/Lex UriServ/LexUriServ.do?uri=COM:2012:0239:FIN:EN:PDF (accessed April 5, 2019).

European Commission. 2012b. "Positive EU–Turkey Agenda Launched in Ankara." Memo/12/359, Brussels, May 17. Available at: http://europa.eu/rapi d/press-release_MEMO-12-359_en.htm (accessed April 5, 2019).

European Commission. 2015a. "Press Release: EU–Turkey Joint Action Plan." Brussels, October 15. Available at: http://europa.eu/rapid/press-release_MEM O-15-5860_en.htm (accessed April 5, 2019).

European Commission. 2015b. "Meeting of Heads of State or Government with Turkey: EU–Turkey Statement." Brussels, November 29. Available at: http://europa.eu/rapid/press-release_STATEMENT-15–6194_en.htm (accessed April 5, 2019).

European Commission. 2015c. "Energy Union: Secure, Sustainable, Competitive, Affordable Energy for Every European." Press Release, Brussels, February 25. Available at: http://europa.eu/rapid/press-release_IP-15–4497_en.htm (accessed April 5, 2019).

European Commission. 2016a. "Impact Assessment: Recommendation for a Council Decision Authorising the Opening of Negotiations with Turkey on an Agreement on the Extension of the Scope of the Bilateral Preferential Trade Relationship and on the Modernisation of the Customs Union." SWD (2016) 475 Final, Brussels, December 21. Available at: http://ec.europa.eu/smart-regulation/impact/ia_carried_out/docs/ia_2016/swd_2016_0475_en.pdf (accessed April 5, 2019).

European Commission. 2016b. "EU and Turkey Strengthen Energy Ties." January 28. Available at: http://ec.europa.eu/energy/en/news/eu-and-turkey-strengthen-energy-ties (accessed April 5, 2019).

European Commission. 2017a. "Fifth Report on the Progress Made in the Implementation of the EU–Turkey Statement." Report from the Commission to the European Parliament, the European Council and the Council. COM (2017) 204 Final. Brussels, March 2. Available at: https://ec.europa.eu/home-affairs/sites/homeaffairs/files/what-we-do/policies/european-agenda-migration/20170302_fifth_report_on_the_progress_made_in_the_implementation_of_the_eu-turkey_statement_en.pdf (accessed April 5, 2019).

European Commission. 2017b. "Connecting Europe Facility." *Innovation and Networks Executive Agency.* Available at: https://ec.europa.eu/inea/en/connecting-europe-facility (accessed April 5, 2019).

European Commission. 2017c. "Joint Statement by High Representative/Vice-President Federica Mogherini and Commissioner Johannes Hahn on the Venice Commission's Opinion on the Amendments to the Constitution of Turkey and Recent Events." Brussels, March 13. Available at: http://europa.eu/rapid/press-release_STATEMENT-17–588_en.htm (accessed April 5, 2019).

European Commission. 2018a. "A Credible Enlargement Perspective for and Enhanced EU Engagement with the Western Balkans." Strasbourg, February 6. Available at: https://ec.europa.eu/commission/sites/beta-political/files/communication-credible-enlargement-perspective-western-balkans_en.pdf (accessed April 5, 2019).

European Commission. 2018b. "Progress Report on the Implementation of the European Agenda on Migration." Communication from the Commission to the European Parliament, the European Council and the Council. COM (2018) 250 Final. Brussels, March 14. Available at: https://ec.europa.eu/neighbourhood-enlargement/sites/near/files/com_2018_250_f1_communication_from_commission_to_inst_en_v10_p1_969116.pdf (accessed April 5, 2019).

European Commission. 2019a. "Turkey: European Civil Protection and Humanitarian Aid Operations." Brussels, March 11. Available at: https://ec.europa.eu/echo/where/europe/turkey_en (accessed April 5, 2019).

European Commission. 2019b. "Trade: Turkey." Brussels, February 15. Available at: http://ec.europa.eu/trade/policy/countries-and-regions/countries/t urkey/ (accessed April 5, 2019).

European Council. 2000. *Presidency Conclusions*, Annex VI: ESDP, Paragraph 3, Nice, December 7–9. Available at: www.consilium.europa.eu/ueDocs/cms_Da ta/docs/pressData/en/ec/00400-r1.%20ann.eno.htm (accessed April 5, 2019).

European Council. 2002a. *Presidency Conclusions*, Annex II: ESDP: Implementation of the Nice Provisions on the Involvement of the Non-EU European Allies, Brussels, October 24–25.

European Council. 2002b. *Presidency Conclusions*, Annex II, Paragraph 3, Copenhagen, December 12–13.

European Council, 2004a. *Presidency Conclusions*, Brussels, June 17–18.

European Council, 2004b. *Joint Action on the Establishment of the European Defence Agency*, 2004/551/CFSP, Brussels, July 12.

European Council. 2009. *PMG Recommendations on Concrete Measures to Improve EU–NATO Cooperation*, 17344/09, Annex, Brussels, December 8.

European Council. 2015. "Meeting of Heads of State or Government with Turkey – EU–Turkey Statement." Brussels, November 29. Available at: www .consilium.europa.eu/en/press/press-releases/2015/11/29-eu-turkey-meeting-st atement/ (accessed April 5, 2019).

European Council. 2016. "EU–Turkey Statement." Press Release 144/16, Brussels, March 18. Available at: www.consilium.europa.eu/press-releases-pdf/2016/3/40 802210113_en.pdf (accessed April 5, 2019).

European Council. 2018. "Council Decisions on Enlargement and Stabilisation and Association Process." Annex 10555/18, Brussels, June 26. Available at: www.consilium.europa.eu/media/35863/st10555-en18.pdf (accessed April 5, 2019).

European Council. 2019. "Press Statement Following the 54th Meeting of the Association Council Between the European Union and Turkey," Brussels, March 15. Available at: www.consilium.europa.eu/en/press/press-releases/201 9/03/15/press-statement-following-the-54th-meeting-of-the-association-coun cil-between-the-european-union-and-turkey-brussels-15-march-2019/ (accessed April 5, 2019).

European External Action Service. 2016. *EU–NATO Cooperation*. Available at: https://eeas.europa.eu/sites/eeas/files/eu_nato_factsheet-final.pdf (accessed April 5, 2019).

European Parliament. 2016. "Visa Liberalisation for Turkey: EU Criteria Must Be Met, Say MEPs." Justice and Home Affairs Press Release. Brussels, May 10. Available at: www.europarl.europa.eu/news/en/news-room/20160509IP R26368/visa-liberalisation-for-turkey-eu-criteria-must-be-met-say-meps (accessed April 5, 2019).

European Parliament. 2019. "European Parliament Resolution of 13 March 2019 on the 2018 Commission Report on Turkey." Strasbourg, March 13. Available at: www.europarl.europa.eu/sides/getDoc.do?type=TA&reference=P8-TA-20 19–0200&format=XML&language=EN (accessed April 5, 2019).

F-35.com. 2019. "Turkey: Building on Decades of Partnership." Available at: www.f35.com/global/participation/turkey (accessed April 5, 2019).

Fearon, James D. 1994. "Signaling versus the Balance of Power and Interests: An Empirical Test of a Crisis Bargaining Model." *Journal of Conflict Resolution* 38 (2): 236–269.

Fearon, James D. 1995. "Rationalist Explanations for War." *International Organization* 49(3): 379–414.

Fearon, James D. 1997. "Signaling Foreign Policy Interests: Tying Hands versus Sinking Costs." *The Journal of Conflict Resolution* 41(1): 68–90.

Ferguson, Chaka. 2012. "The Strategic Use of Soft Balancing: The Normative Dimensions of the Chinese-Russian 'Strategic Partnership.'" *The Journal of Strategic Studies* 35(2): 197–222.

Fischer, Severin. 2016. "Turkey and the Energy Transit Question." *Carnegie Europe.* August 23. Available at: http://carnegieeurope.eu/strategiceurope/643 82 (accessed April 5, 2019).

Flemes, Daniel, and Wehner, Leslie. 2015. "Drivers of Strategic Contestation: The Case of South America." *International Politics* 52(2): 162–177.

Fortmann, Michel, T. V. Paul, and James J. Wirtz. 2004. "Conclusions: Balance of Power at the Turn of the New Century." In T. V. Paul, James J. Wirtz, and Michel Fortmann (Eds.), *Balance of Power: Theory and Practice in the 21st Century.* Stanford, CA: Stanford University Press, pp. 360–374.

France24.com. 2018. "Syria: The Astana Peace Process." September 5. Available at: www.france24.com/en/20180905-syria-astana-peace-process (accessed April 5, 2019).

Friedman, Max P., and Tom Long. 2015. "Soft Balancing in the Americas: Latin American Opposition to US Intervention, 1989–1936." *International Security* 40(1): 120–156.

Gall, Carlotta. 2018. "US and Turkey Agrees on Kurds' Withdrawal from Syrian Town." *New York Times*, June 4. Available at: www.nytimes.com/2018/06/04/world/middleeast/turkey-syria-kurds-manbij.html (accessed April 5, 2019).

Galves DeRolle, Patricia. 2015. "What Does It Mean to Be an Emerging Power?" *Modern Diplomacy*, May 3. Available at: https://moderndiplomacy.eu/2015/05/03/what-does-it-mean-to-be-an-emerging-power/ (accessed April 5, 2019).

Garamone, Jim. 2018. "President Signs Fiscal 2019 Defense Authorization Act at Fort Drum Ceremony." *US Department of Defense News*, August 13. Available at: https://dod.defense.gov/News/Article/Article/1601016/president-signs-fiscal-2019-defense-authorization-act-at-fort-drum-ceremony/ (accessed April 5, 2019).

Gauthier-Villars, David. 2018. "Turkey's Erdogan Says He'll Defy US Sanctions on Iran." *Wall Street Journal*, November 6. Available at: www.wsj.com/articles/tur keys-erdogan-says-hell-defy-u-s-sanctions-on-iran-1541538429 (accessed April 5, 2019).

George, Alexander L., and Andrew Bennett. 2005. *Case Studies and Theory Development in Social Sciences.* Boston: MIT Press.

Gibson, Tom. 2019. "CPJ Joins Call for Turkey to Release Jailed Journalists." The Committee to Protect Journalists, February 14. Available at: https://cpj .org/blog/2019/02/eu-turkey-release-jailed-journalists.php (accessed April 5, 2019).

Gotev, Georgi. 2016. "Gazprom Revives 'Poseidon' Adriatic Link." *EurActiv. com*, February 26. Available at: www.euractiv.com/section/energy/news/gaz prom-revives-poseidon-adriatic-link/ (accessed April 5, 2019).

Göl, Ayla. 2013. *Turkey Facing East: Islam, Modernity, and Foreign Policy.* Manchester: Manchester University Press.

Greenhill, Kelly M. 2011. *Weapons of Mass Migration: Forced Displacement, Coercion, and Foreign Policy.* Ithaca, NY: Cornell University Press.

Grieco, Joseph M. 1988. "Anarchy and the Limits of Cooperation: A Realist Critique of the Newest Liberal Institutionalism." *International Organization* 42(3): 485–507.

Gurbanov, Ilgar. 2015. "Repercussions of Turkish Stream for the Southern Gas Corridor: Russia's New Gas Strategy." *Naturalgaseurope.com*, April 16. Available at: www.naturalgaseurope.com/analysis-turkish-streamsouthern-ga s-corridor-russia-gas-strategy-23199 (accessed April 5, 2019).

Gümrükçü, Tuvan, and Ece Toksabay. 2017. "Turkey, Russia Signed Deal on Supply of S-400 Missiles." *Reuters*, December 29. Available at: www.reuters .com/article/us-russia-turkey-missiles/turkey-russia-sign-deal-on-supply-of-s-4 00-missiles-idUSKBN1EN0T5 (accessed April 5, 2019).

Güney, Aylin. 2008. "Anti-Americanism in Turkey: Past and Present." *Middle Eastern Studies* 44(3): 471–487.

Hakura, Fadi. 2018a. "The West Cannot Afford Losing Turkey to Russia and Iran." *CNN.com*, August 14. Available at: www.cnn.com/2018/08/14/opi nions/west-losing-turkey-opinion-intl/index.html (accessed April 5, 2019).

Hakura, Fadi. 2018b. "EU–Turkey Customs Union: Prospects for Modernization and Lessons for Brexit." *Chatham House*, December. Available at: www.cha thamhouse.org/sites/default/files/publications/research/2018–12-12-eu-turkey-customs-union-hakura.pdf (accessed April 5, 2019).

Hale, William. 2013. *Turkish Foreign Policy since 1774.* 3rd Edition. New York: Routledge.

Han, Ahmet K., and Behlül Özkan. 2017. "Turkey's Euphrates Shield: Mission Creep?" *German Marshall Fund of the United States*, March 13. Available at: www.gmfus.org/publications/turkeys-euphrates-shield-mission-creep (accessed April 5, 2019).

Harris, Gardiner. 2017. "Turkish Attempt to Close Gap with the West Seems to Widen It." *New York Times*, March 13. Available at: www.nytimes.com/2017/03/13/world/europe/turkey-news-media-relations.html (accessed April 5, 2019).

Harvey, Benjamin. 2018. "Erdogan Warns U.S. Troops in Syria to Keep Away from Kurd Forces." *Bloomberg*, February 13. Available at: www.bloomberg .com/news/articles/2018–02-13/erdogan-warns-u-s-troops-in-syria-to-keep-aw ay-from-kurd-forces (accessed April 5, 2019).

Harvey, William S. 2011. "Strategies for Conducting Elite Interviews." *Qualitative Research* 11(4): 431–441.

Hatipoğlu, Emre, and Glenn Palmer. 2016. "Conceptualizing Change in Turkish Foreign Policy: The Promise of the 'Two-Good Theory.'" *Cambridge Review of International Affairs* 29(1): 231–250.

He, Kai. 2008. "Institutional Balancing and International Relations Theory: Economic Interdependence and Balance of Power Strategies in Southeast Asia." *European Journal of International Relations* 14(3): 489–518.

He, Kai. 2015. "Contested Regional Orders and Institutional Balancing in the Asia Pacific." *International Politics* 52(2): 208–222.

He, Kai, and Huiyun Feng. 2008. "If Not Soft Balancing, Then What?: Reconsidering Soft Balancing and US Policy towards China." *Security Studies* 17(2): 363–395.

Hintz, Lisel. 2016. "'Take It Outside!' National Identity Contestation in the Foreign Policy Arena." *European Journal of International Relations* 12(2): 335–361.

Hintz, Lisel. 2018. *Identity Politics Inside Out: National Identity Contestation and Foreign Policy in Turkey*. Oxford: Oxford University Press.

Hoffman, Max, Michael Werz, and John Halpin. 2018. "Turkey's 'New Nationalism' Amid Shifting Politics." *Center for American Progress*, February 11. Available at: www.americanprogress.org/issues/security/reports/2018/02/11/446164/turkeys-new-nationalism-amid-shifting-politics/ (accessed April 5, 2019).

Hofmann, Stephanie. 2009. "Overlapping Institutions in the Realm of International Security: The Case of NATO and ESDP." *Perspectives on Politics* 7(1): 45–52.

Holsti, Ole R., Terrence P. Hopmann, and John D. Sulivan. 1973. *Unity and Disintegration in International Alliances*. New York: Wiley.

Horowitz, Shale, and Michael D. Tyburski. 2012. "Reacting to Russia: Foreign Relations of the Former Soviet Bloc." In Kristen P. Williams, Steven E. Lobell, and Neal G. Jesse (Eds.), *Beyond Great Powers and Hegemons: Why Secondary States Support, Follow, or Challenge*. Stanford: Stanford University Press, pp. 161–176.

Hufnagel, Saskia. 2013. *Policing Cooperation across Borders: Comparative Perspectives on Law Enforcement within the EU and Australia*. Farnham: Ashgate Publishers.

Human Rights Watch. 2016. "EU/Turkey: Mass, Fast-Track Returns Threaten Rights." March 8. Available at: www.hrw.org/news/2016/03/08/eu/turkey-mass-fast-track-returns-threaten-rights (accessed April 5, 2019).

Human Rights Watch. 2017. "Turkey: Events of 2016." Available at: www.hrw.org/world-report/2017/country-chapters/turkey (accessed April 5, 2019).

Hürriyet Daily News. 2009. "Rasmussen Urges Turkey to Allow Pact between EU, NATO." August 28. Available at: www.hurriyetdailynews.com/n.php?n=rasmussen-urges-turkey-to-allow-pact-between-eu-and-nato-2009-08-28 (accessed April 5, 2019).

Hürriyet Daily News. 2016. "New PM Signals Shift in Foreign Policy: More Friends than Enemies." May 25. Available at: www.hurriyetdailynews.com/new-pm-signals-shift-in-foreign-policy-more-friends-than-enemies.aspx?pageID=238&nID=99616&NewsCatID=338 (accessed April 5, 2019).

Hürriyet. 2018. "Hükümetten F-35 Açıklaması [The F-35 Announcement from the Government]." June 14. Available at: www.hurriyet.com.tr/gundem/hukumetten-f-35-aciklamasi-40867533 (accessed April 5, 2019).

Ikenberry, G. John. 1998. "Institutions, Strategic Restraint, and the Persistence of American Postwar Order." *International Security* 23(3): 43–78.

Ikenberry, G. John. 2001. *After Victory: Institutions, Strategic Restraint, and the Rebuilding of Order after Major Wars.* Princeton, NJ: Princeton University Press.

International Crisis Group. 2017. "Fighting ISIS: The Road to and beyond Raqqa." *Crisis Group Middle East Briefing No 53*, April 28. Available at: https://d2071a ndvipowj.cloudfront.net/b053-fighting-isis-the-road-to-and-beyond-raqqa.pdf (accessed April 5, 2019).

International Crisis Group. 2019. "Turkey's PKK Conflict: A Visual Explainer." March 6. Available at: www.crisisgroup.org/content/turkeys-pkk-conflict-visu al-explainer (accessed April 5, 2019).

İdiz, Semih. 2016. "Turkish–US Ties Face Fresh Turbulence over Iraq, Syria." *Al-Monitor*, January 12. Available at: www.al-monitor.com/pulse/originals/2016/ 01/turkey-usa-relations-iraq-syrian-kurds-potential-flashpoints.html (accessed April 5, 2019).

İnalcık, Halil. 1993. "The Turks and the Balkans." *Turkish Review of Balkan Studies* 651(1): 9–42.

Jeffrey, James. 2016. Conference Remarks, Conference on Turkey, Middle East Institute. Washington DC, September 30.

Jeffrey, James. 2017. "Trump's Plan to Arm Kurds Lays Bare the Strategic Vacuum in Syria." *Foreign Policy*, May 9. Available at: https://foreignpolicy.c om/2017/05/09/trumps-plan-to-arm-kurds-lays-bare-the-strategic-vacuum-in-syria/?utm_source=Sailthru&utm_medium=email&utm_campaign=FP&utm_ term=Flashpoints (accessed April 5, 2019).

Jenkins, Gareth, H. 2016. Conference Remarks, Conference on Turkey, Middle East Institute. Washington DC, September 30.

Jennings, Gareth. 2014. "Turkey Frustrated at European Reluctance for Deeper Defence Co-Operation." *IHS Jane's 360*, December 2. Available at: www.janes .com/article/46591/turkey-frustrated-at-european-reluctance-for-deeper-defen ce-co-operation (accessed April 5, 2019).

Jesse, Neal G., Steven E. Lobell, Galia Press-Barnathan, and Kristen P. Williams. 2012. "The Leader Can't Lead when the Followers Won't Follow: The Limitations of Hegemony." In: Kristen P. Williams, Steven E. Lobell, and Neal G. Jesse (Eds.), *Beyond Great Powers and Hegemons: Why Secondary States Support, Follow, or Challenge.* Stanford: Stanford University Press, pp. 1–32.

Joffe, Josef. 2002. "Defying History and Theory: The United States as the Last Remaining Superpower." In G. John Ikenberry (Ed.), *America Unrivaled: The Future of Balance of Power.* Ithaca, NY: Cornell University Press.

Jones, Dorian. 2019. "US-Turkish Tensions Rise Amid Warnings of a Rupture." *Voice of America News*, April 4. Available at: www.voanews.com/a/us-turkish-t ensions-rise-amid-warnings-of-a-rupture/4862300.html (accessed April 5, 2019).

Judah, Tim. 2010. "Bring the Balkans Back into the Heart of Europe." *Financial Times*, July 27.

Kabalan, Marwan. 2019. "Can the Astana Process Survive the US Withdrawal from Syria?" *Al Jazeera.com*, February 16. Available at: www.aljazeera.com/

indepth/opinion/astana-process-survive-withdrawal-syria-190215144132776. html (accessed April 5, 2019).

Karakullukçu, Memduh. 2014. Speech Transcript, Turkey: An Emerging Power in a Changing Middle East Conference, *Council on Foreign Relations*, Istanbul, June 18. Available at: www.cfr.org/projects/world/turkey-an-emerging-power-in-a-changing-middle-east/pr1685 (accessed April 5, 2019).

Karam, Joyce. 2019. "US Pentagon Warns Turkey of 'Grave Consequences' Over Russian Missiles." *The National*, March 9. Available at: www.thenational.ae/world/the-americas/us-pentagon-warns-turkey-of-grave-consequences-over-ru ssian-missiles-1.834733 (accessed April 5, 2019).

Karan, Ceyda. 2019. "'*S-400'den Vazgeçmek Ulusal Savunma Sistemini Kurmak İsteyen Turkiye'yi Zarara Uğratır*' [Giving Up on S-400 will Damage Turkey's Aspirations to Establish Its Own National Defense System]." *Sputnik*, February 26. Available at: https://tr.sputniknews.com/ceyda_karan_eksen/201 902251037884632-turkiye-vazgecmek-ulusal-savunma-sistem-zarar/ (accessed April 5, 2019).

Karpat, Kemal H. 1996. "The Ottoman Rule in Europe from the Perspective of 1994." In Vojtech Mastny and R. Craig Nation (Eds.), *Turkey between East and West: New Challenges for a Rising Regional Power*. Boulder, CO: Westview Press, pp. 1–44.

Kasapoğlu, Can. 2017a. "Operation Euphrates Shield: Progress and Scope." *Al Jazeera*, February 3. Available at: www.aljazeera.com/indepth/opinion/2017/02/operation-euphrates-shield-progress-scope-170201133525121.html (accessed April 5, 2019).

Kasapoğlu, Can. 2017b. "Why Turkey Might Buy Russia's S-400 Defense System." *Al Jazeera*, March 24. Available at: www.aljazeera.com/indepth/opinion/2017/03/turkey-buy-russia-s400-missile-defence-system-170323131 5375 09.html (accessed April 5, 2019).

Kasapoğlu, Can, Doruk Ergün, and Sinan Ülgen. 2017. "Operation Euphrates Shield: Lessons Learned." *EDAM Foreign Policy and Security Studies Series* 3, April. Available at: http://edam.org.tr/en/File?id=3208 (accessed April 5, 2019).

Kaya, Ayhan. 2013. "Yunus Emre Cultural Centers: The AKP's Neo-Ottomanism and Islamism." *Perspectives* 5(13): 56–60.

Kelley, Judith. 2005. "Strategic Non-Cooperation as Soft Balancing: Why Iraq Was Not Just about Iraq." *International Politics* 42(2): 153–173.

Keohane, Daniel. 2006. "Unblocking EU–NATO Co-operation." *Centre for European Reform Bulletin*, June/July, Issue 48.

Ker-Lindsay, James. 2007. "The Policies of Greece and Cyprus towards Turkey's EU Accession." *Turkish Studies* 8(1): 71–83.

Khong, Yuen Koong. 2004. "Coping with Strategic Uncertainty: The Role of Institutions and Soft Balancing in Southeast Asia's Post-Cold War Strategy." In Jae-Jung Suh, Peter J. Katzenstein and Allen Carlson (Eds.), *Rethinking Security in East Asia: Identity, Power and Efficiency*. Stanford, CA: Stanford University Press.

Kınıklıoğlu, Suat. 2014. Speech Transcript, Turkey: An Emerging Power in a Changing Middle East Conference, Council on Foreign Relations, Istanbul,

June 18. Available at: www.cfr.org/projects/world/turkey-an-emerging-power-in-a-changing-middle-east/pr1685 (accessed April 5, 2019).

Kim, Tongfi. 2016. *The Supply Side of Security: A Market Theory of Military Alliances*. Stanford: Stanford University Press.

Kiper, Çınar. 2013. "Sultan Erdogan: Turkey's Rebranding into the New, Old Ottoman Empire." *The Atlantic*. Available at: http://theatlantic.com/interna tional/archive/2013/04/sultan-edrogan-turkeys-rebranding-into-the-new-old-ottoman-empire/274724/ (accessed April 5, 2019).

Kirişçi, Kemal. 2009. "The Transformation of Turkish Foreign Policy: The Rise of the Trading State." *New Perspectives on Turkey* 40(1): 29–57.

Kirişci, Kemal. 2014. "Will the Readmission Agreement Bring the EU and Turkey Together or Pull Them Apart?" *Brookings*, February 4. Available at: www.br ookings.edu/opinions/will-the-readmission-agreement-bring-the-eu-and-tur key-together-or-pull-them-apart/ (accessed April 5, 2019).

Kirişci, Kemal. 2016. "Is Turkish Foreign Policy Becoming Pragmatic Again?" *Brookings Institute*, July 11. Available at: www.brookings.edu/blog/order-fro m-chaos/2016/07/11/is-turkish-foreign-policy-becoming-pragmatic-again/ (accessed April 5, 2019).

Kirişçi, Kemal. 2018. *Turkey and the West: Fault Lines in a Troubled Alliance*. Washington DC: Brookings Institute Press.

Kohen, Sami. 2010. "Balkan Açılımı" [The Balkan Opening]. *Milliyet*, April 27.

Koops, Joachim A. 2011. *The European Union as an Integrative Power? Assessing the EU's "Effective Multilateralism" towards NATO and the United Nations*. Brussels: Brussels University Press.

Kopač, Janez, and Mehmet Ekinci. 2015. "Turkey as a Member of the Energy Community." *Daily Sabah*, February 17. Available at: www.dailysabah.com/opi nion/2015/02/17/turkey-as-a-member-of-the-energy-community (accessed April 5, 2019).

Köksal, Nil. 2017. "Why Trump Will Likely Leave Erdogan Empty-Handed." CBC News, May 15. Available at: www.cbc.ca/news/world/trump-erdogan-tu rkey-united-states-white-house-washington-1.4111829 (accessed April 5, 2019).

Kramer, Heinz. 2000. *A Changing Turkey: The Challenge to Europe and the United States*. Washington DC: Brookings Institution Press.

Kucera, Joshua. 2015. "Turkey Finally Abandons Controversial Chinese Missile Deal." *Eurasianet.org*, November 15. Available at: www.eurasianet.org/node/ 76106 (accessed April 5, 2019).

Kupchan, Charles. 1988. "NATO and the Persian Gulf: Examining Intra-alliance Behavior." *International Organization* 42(2): 317–346.

Kupchan, Charles. 2011. "The False Promise of Unipolarity: Constraints on the Exercise of American Power." *Cambridge Review of International Affairs* 24 (2): 165–173.

Kurizaki, Shuhei. 2007. "Efficient Secrecy: Public versus Private Threats in Crisis Diplomacy." *American Political Science Review* 101(3): 543–558.

Kut, Şule. 1999. "Turkey in the Post-Communist Balkans: Between Activism and Self- Restraint." *Turkish Review of Balkan Studies* 4: 39–45.

Kütük, Dilek. 2015. "Deepening Relations between the Balkans and Turkey: Economic Growth and Patterns of Development." *Journal of Turkish Weekly*, May 6. Available at: www.turkishweekly.net/2015/05/06/news/deepening-rela tions-between-the-balkans-and-turkey-economic-growth-and-patterns-of-deve lopment/ (accessed April 5, 2019).

Lake, Eli. 2018. "Turkey's Exemption from US Sanctions against Iran Is Yet Another Sign that Tensions Are Easing." *Bloomberg.com*, November 5. Available at: www.bloomberg.com/opinion/articles/2018-11-05/u-s-sanctions-on-iran-why-is-turkey-exempt (accessed April 5, 2019).

Larrabee, F. Stephen. 2011. "The 'New Turkey' and American-Turkish Relations." *Insight Turkey* 13(1): 1–9.

Larrabee, F. Stephen. 2016. "The Turkish-Russian Rapprochement: How Real? How Durable?" *The National Interest*, November 21. Available at: http://natio nalinterest.org/blog/the-buzz/the-turkish-russian-rapprochement-how-real-ho w-durable-18468 (accessed April 5, 2019).

Larrabee, F. Stephen, and Ian O. Lesser. 2003. *Turkish Foreign Policy in an Age of Uncertainty*. Santa Monica, CA: RAND Corporation.

Lavenex, Sandra, and Emek M. Uçarer. 2004. "The External Dimension of Europeanization: The Case of Immigration Policies." *Cooperation and Conflict* 39(4): 417–443.

Lee, Matthew. 2019. "US Targets 'Vast Network' for Evading Sanctions." *APNews.com*, March 26. Available at: www.apnews.com/3c2e71ce056447599 bd3f685170d8297 (accessed April 5, 2019).

Leeds, Brett Ashley, and Burcu Savun. 2007. "Terminating Alliances: Why Do States Abrogate Agreements?" *Journal of Politics* 69(4): 1118–1132.

Lesser, Ian. 2017. "Turkey and the West: A Relationship Unmoored?" *German Marshall Fund of the United States*, May 15. Available at: www.gmfus.org/blog/ 2017/05/15/turkey-and-west-relationship-unmoored (accessed April 5, 2019).

Lesser, Ian, and Bruno Lete. 2017. "Reducing Risks in Turkey's Neighborhood." *German Marshall Fund of the United States*, March 10. Available at: www.gmf us.org/blog/2017/03/10/reducing-risks-turkeys-neighborhood (accessed April 5, 2019).

Lew, Jacob J., and Richard Nephew. 2018. "The Use and Misuse of Economic Statecraft." *Foreign Affairs*, November/December. Available at: www.foreign affairs.com/articles/world/2018–10-15/use-and-misuse-economic-statecraft (accessed April 5, 2019).

Levy, Jack S. 1989. "Diversionary Theory of War: A Critique." In Manus I. Midlarsky (Ed.), *Handbook of War Studies*. Boston: Unwin-Hyman, pp. 259–288.

Levy, Jack S. 2004. "What Do Great Powers Balance against and When?" In T. V. Paul, James J. Wirtz, and Michel Fortmann (Eds.), *Balance of Power: Theory and Practice in the 21st Century*. Stanford, CA: Stanford University Press, pp. 29–51.

Lieber, Keir A., and Gerard Alexander. 2005. "Waiting for Balancing: Why the World Is Not Pushing Back." *International Security* 30(1): 109–139.

Lieberman, R. C. 2002. "Ideas, Institutions, and Political Order: Explaining Political Change." *American Political Science Review* 96(4): 697–712.

Lindbäck, Leif. 2009. "Norway's Experiences with EDA." EDA Bulletin 12, June.
Linden, Ronald H., and Yasemin İrepoğlu. 2013. "Turkey and the Balkans: New Forms of Political Community?" *Turkish Studies* 14(2): 229–255.
Loğoğlu, O. Faruk. 2008. "The State of US–Turkey Relations: A Turkish Perspective." In Frances G. Burwell (Ed.), *The Evolution of US–Turkish Relations in a Transatlantic Context*. Carlisle, PA: Strategic Studies Institute, pp. 29–42.
Long, Andrew G., Timothy Nordstrom, and Kyeonghi Baek. 2007. "Allying for Peace: Treaty Obligations and Conflict between Allies." *The Journal of Politics* 69(4): 1103–1117.
Loveluck, Louisa, and Karen DeYoung. 2017. "A Russian-Backed Deal on 'Safe Zones' Leaves US Wary." *The Washington Post*, May 4.
Lustick, Ian. 1996. "History, Historiography, and Political Science: Multiple Historical Records and the Problem of Selection Bias." *American Political Science Review* 90(3): 605–618.
Lynch, Colum. 2010. "Turkey Urges UN Security Council to Condemn Israeli Attack On Aid Flotilla." *The Washington Post*, May 31. Available at: www.washington post.com/wp-dyn/content/article/2010/05/31/AR2010053102860.html (accessed April 5, 2019).
MacFarquhar, Neil. 2010. "UN Approves New Sanctions to Deter Iran." *New York Times*, June 9.
Makovsky, Alan. 2015. "Turkey's Growing Energy Ties with Moscow." *Center for American Progress*, May 6. Available at: https://cdn.americanprogress.org/wp-content/uploads/2015/05/TurkeyEnergy2UPDATED.pdf (accessed April 5, 2019).
Mares, David R. 2016. "Brazil: Revising the Status Quo with Soft Power?" In T. V. Paul (Ed.), *Accommodating Rising Powers: Past, Present, and Future*. Cambridge University Press, pp. 246–267.
Martin, Natalie. 2015. *Security and the Turkey–EU Accession Process: Norms, Reforms and the Cyprus Issue*. Basingstoke: Palgrave Macmillan.
McCalla, Robert B. 1996. "NATO's Persistence after the Cold War." *International Organization* 50(3): 445–475.
McLeary, Paul. 2017. "Turkey Threatens US Forces in Syria, as Putin Presses for Safe Zones." Foreign Policy, May 3.
Mearsheimer, John J. 1983. *Conventional Deterrence*. Ithaca, NY: Cornell University Press.
Mearsheimer, John J. 2001. *The Tragedy of Great Power Politics*. New York: Norton.
Meerts, Paul. 2015. *Diplomatic Negotiation: Essence and Evolution*. The Hague: Clingendael.
Mehr News Agency. 2019. "Turkey Criticizes US Sanctions on Iran." March 3. Available at: https://en.mehrnews.com/news/143041/Turkey-criticizes-US-sanctions-on-Iran (accessed April 5, 2019).
Menon, Anand, and Jennifer Welsh. 2011. "Understanding NATO's Sustainability: The Limits of Institutionalist Theory." *Global Governance* 17: 81–94.
Michalopoulos, Sarantis. 2017. "Hungary Warns about Growing Foreign Influence in the Balkans." *EurActiv.com*, April 3. Available at: www.euractiv

.com/section/enlargement/news/hungary-warns-about-growing-foreign-influ
ence-in-the-balkans/?nl_ref=34679074 (accessed April 5, 2019).

Miller, Ross A. 1999. "Regime Type, Strategic Interaction, and the
Diversionary Use of Force." *Journal of Conflict Resolution* 43(3):
388–402.

Miskimmon, Alister, Ben O'Loughlin, and Laura Roselle. 2013. *Strategic
Narratives: Communication Power and the New World Order.* New York:
Routledge.

Missiroli, Antonio. 2002. "EU–NATO Cooperation in Crisis Management: No
Turkish Delight for ESDP." *Security Dialogue* 33(1): 9–26.

Mitrović, Marija. 2014. *Turkish Foreign Policy towards the Balkans: The
Influence of Traditional Determinants on Davutoğlu's Conception of Turkey-
Balkan Relations.* German Turkish Master's Program in Social Sciences
Working Paper Series No. 10, Humboldt University.

Mitrović Bošković, Marija, Dušan Reljić, and Alida Vraăć. 2015. "Elsewhere in
the Neighborhood: Reaching out to the Western Balkans." In B. Senem Çevik
and Philip Seib (Eds.), *Turkey's Public Diplomacy.* Basingstoke: Palgrave
Macmillan, pp. 99–120.

Mogherini, Federica. 2016. Remarks by High Representative/Vice-President
Federica Mogherini on EU–Turkey Relations at the Plenary Session of the
European Parliament, November 22. Available at: https://eeas.europa.eu/head
quarters/headquarters-homepage/15566/remarks-high-representativevice-presi
dent-federica-mogherini-eu-turkey-relations-plenary_en (accessed April 5,
2019).

Morgan, T. Clifford. 1990. "Issue Linkages in International Crisis Bargaining."
American Journal of Political Science 34(2): 311–333.

Morrow, James D. 1991. "Alliances and Asymmetry: An Alternative to the
Capability Aggregation Model of Alliances." *American Journal of Political
Science* 35(4): 904–933.

Muhasilović, Selin Çalık. 2016. "Turkey Shield against Religious Extremism in
Balkans, Its Presence Spreads Moderation." *Daily Sabah*, January 25. Available
at: www.dailysabah.com/politics/2016/01/26/turkey-shield-against-religious-
extremism-in-balkans-its-presence-spreads-moderation (accessed April 5,
2019).

Murinson, Alexander. 2012. "Turkish Foreign Policy in the Twenty-First Century."
Mideast Security and Policy Studies No. 97, The Begin-Sadat Center for Strategic
Studies, Bar-Ilan University, September. Available at: http://besacenter.org/mid
east-security-and-policy-studies/turkish-foreign-policy-in-the-twenty-first-cen
tury-3-2/ (accessed April 5, 2019).

Müftüler-Baç, Meltem. 2008. "The European Union's Accession Negotiations
with Turkey from a Foreign Policy Perspective." *Journal of European
Integration* 30(1): 63–78.

Nas, Çiğdem, and Özer, Yonca (Eds.). 2016. *Turkey and the European Union:
Processes of Europeanisation.* London: Routledge.

NATO. 1999. An Alliance for the 21st Century, Washington Summit
Communiqué, Press Release NAC-S(99)64, April 24. Available at: www.nato
.int/docu/pr/1999/p99-064e.htm (accessed April 5, 2019).

NATO. 2002. NATO Prague Summit Declaration by Heads of State and Government, NATO Press Release 2002/127, November 21.

NATO. 2007. "NATO–EU Operational Co-Operation." Parliamentary Assembly, 2007 Annual Session Committee Report, 166 DSCTC 07 E bis, Reykjavik, Iceland.

NATO. 2010a. *NATO–EU: A Strategic Partnership.* Available at www.nato.int/cps/en/natolive/topics_49217.htm (accessed April 5, 2019).

NATO. 2010b. Press Briefing by NATO Secretary General, Anders Fogh Rasmussen and EU High Representative for Foreign Affairs and Security Policy Catherine Ashton, May 25. Available at: www.nato.int/nato_static/assets/audio/audio_2010_05/20100525_100525a-nato-eu-pc.mp3 (accessed April 5, 2019).

NATO. 2016a. "Connected Forces Initiative." June 22. Available at: www.nato.int/cps/en/natohq/topics_98527.htm (accessed April 5, 2019).

NATO. 2016b. "NATO AWACS Increases Assurance Measures to Turkey." March. Available at: www.shape.nato.int/2016/nato-awacs-increases-assurance-measures-to-turkey (accessed April 5, 2019).

NATO. 2017. "Secretary General Welcomes Closer NATO–EU Cooperation." May 18. Available at: www.nato.int/cps/en/natohq/news_143861.htm (accessed April 5, 2019).

NATO. 2018. "Relations with the European Union." February 13. Available at: www.nato.int/cps/ua/natohq/topics_49217.htm (accessed April 5, 2019).

Official Journal of the EU. 2006. "Agreement between the European Union and the Republic of Turkey Establishing a Framework for the Participation of the Republic of Turkey in the European Union Crisis Management Operations." L 189/17, Vol. 49, July 12.

Official Journal of the EU. 2010. The Role of NATO in the Security Architecture of the EU, C76, E/69-E/75, March 25. Available at: http://eur-lex.europa.eu/LexUriServ/LexUriServ.do?uri=OJ:C:2010:076E:0069:0075:EN:PDF (accessed April 5, 2019).

Oğuzlu, Tarık. 2007. "Soft Power in Turkish Foreign Policy." *Australian Journal of International Affairs* 61(1): 81–97.

Oran, Baskin (Ed.). 2010. *Turkish Foreign Policy 1919–2006: Facts and Analyses with Documents.* Salt Lake City: University of Utah Press.

Organisation for Economic Co-operation and Development (OECD). 2016. "Aid at a Glance Charts." Available at: www.oecd.org/development/aid-at-a-glance.htm (accessed April 5, 2019).

Oruç, Merve şebnem. 2016. "Will Turkey Join Shanghai Cooperation Organization?" *Daily Sabah*, November 25. Available at: www.dailysabah.com/columns/merve-sebnem-oruc/2016/11/26/will-turkey-join-shanghai-cooperation-organization (accessed April 5, 2019).

Oswald, Franz. 2006. "Soft Balancing between Friends: Transforming Transatlantic Relations." *Journal of Contemporary Central and Eastern Europe* 14(2): 145–160.

Öniş, Ziya. 2003. "Turkey and the Middle East after September 11: The Importance of the EU Dimension." *Turkish Policy Quarterly* 2(4): 83–92.

Öniş, Ziya. 2008. "Turkey–EU Relations: Beyond the Current Stalemate." *Insight Turkey* 10(4): 35–50.
Öniş, Ziya, and Şuhnaz Yılmaz. 2009. "Between Europeanization and Euro-Asianism: Foreign Policy Activism in Turkey during the AKP Era." *Turkish Studies* 10(1): 7–24.
Önsoy, Murat, and şebnem Udum. 2015. "The Role of Turkey in Western Balkan Energy Security." *Asia Europe Journal* 13(2): 175–192.
Özbudun, Ergun. 2014. "AKP at the Crossroads: Erdoğan's Majoritarian Drift." *South European Society and Politics* 19(2): 155–167.
Özcan, Mesut. 2008. *Harmonizing Foreign Policy: Turkey, the EU and the Middle East*, Aldershot: Ashgate.
Özcan, Nihat A. 2017. "Türk-Alman Gerilimi ve Incirlik Konusu [Turkish-German Tensions and the Topic of Incirlik]." *Milliyet*, May 19.
Özkan, Mehmet. 2012. "Turkiye'nin Balkan Politikasi" [Turkey's Balkan Policy]. In Öner Buçukçu (Ed.), *Balkan Savaşlarının 100. Yılında Büyük Göç ve Muhaceret Edebiyatı Sempozyumu* [Great Migration Literature Symposium on the 100th Anniversary of the Balkan Wars]. Sarajevo: TürkiyeYazarlar Birliği, pp. 213–216.
Papayoanou, Paul A. 1997. "Intra-alliance Bargaining and U.S. Bosnia Policy." *The Journal of Conflict Resolution* 41(1): 91–116.
Pape, Robert A. 2005. "Soft Balancing against the United States." *International Security* 30(1): 7–45.
Park, Bill. 2015. "Turkey's Isolated Stance: An Ally No More, or Just the Usual Turbulence?" *International Affairs* 91(3): 581–600.
Paul, T. V. 1994. *Asymmetric Conflicts: War Initiation by Weaker Powers*, New York: Cambridge University Press.
Paul, T. V. 2004. "Introduction: The Enduring Axioms of Balance of Power Theory and Their Contemporary Relevance." In T. V. Paul, James J. Wirtz, and Michel Fortmann (Eds.), *Balance of Power: Theory and Practice in the 21st Century*. Stanford: Stanford University Press, pp. 1–25.
Paul, T. V. 2005. "Soft Balancing in the Age of US Primacy." *International Security* 30(1): 46–71.
Paul, T. V. 2016. "The Accommodation of Rising Powers in World Politics." In T. V. Paul (Ed.), *Accommodating Rising Powers: Past, Present, and Future*. Cambridge University Press, pp. 3–32.
Paul, T. V., James J. Wirtz, and Michel Fortmann (Eds.). 2004. *Balance of Power: Theory and Practice in the 21st Century*. Stanford: Stanford University Press.
PBS NewsHour. 2018. "Turkey Doesn't Have to Choose between U.S. and Russia, Foreign Minister Says." June 4. Available at: www.youtube.com/watch?v=W c1e91iDiRw (accessed April 5, 2019).
Pearson, W. Robert. 2016. Conference Remarks, Conference on Turkey, Middle East Institute. Washington DC, September 30.
Pearson, W. Robert. 2017. "Strikes on Syria: Game Changer for US–Turkey Relations?" *The Middle East Institute*, April 7. Available at: www.mei.edu/co ntent/article/strikes-syria-game-changer-us-turkey-relations (accessed April 5, 2019).

Peterson, Scott. 2017. "US–Turkey Deal on ISIS Assault? Why That's A Tough Sell for Tillerson." *Christian Science Monitor*, March 29. Available at: www.csmo nitor.com/World/Middle-East/2017/0329/US-Turkey-deal-on-ISIS-assault-Wh y-that-s-a-tough-sell-for-Tillerson (accessed April 5, 2019).

Peterson, Scott, and Sarah Miller Llana. 2017. "Is This the End of Turkey's Flirtation with Europe?" *The Christian Science Monitor*, March 15. Available at: www.csmonitor.com/World/Middle-East/2017/0315/Is-this-the-end-of-Tur key-s-flirtation-with-Europe (accessed April 5, 2019).

Pieper, Moritz. 2017. "The Transatlantic Dialogue on Iran: The European Subaltern and Hegemonic Constraints in the Implementation of the 2015 Nuclear Agreement with Iran." *European Security* 26(1): 99–119.

Pierini, Marc. 2016a. "Will Turkey and the EU See the Bigger Picture?" *Carnegie Europe*, March 3. Available at: http://carnegieeurope.eu/strategiceurope/?f a=62955&mkt_tok=3RkMMJWWfF9wsRovvK7BZKXonjHpfsX57usqUKS g38431UFwdcjKPmjr1YoETMdoaPyQAgobGp5I5FEIQ7XYTLB2t6oMWA %3D%3D (accessed April 5, 2019).

Pierini, Marc. 2016b. "In Search of an EU Role in the Syrian Conflict." *Carnegie Europe*, August 18. Available at: http://carnegieeurope.eu/2016/08/18/in-searc h-of-eu-role-in-syrian-war/j3q3?mkt_tok=eyJpIjoiWm1Oak5UbGlZMk5sTk RFMCIsInQiOiJKMXFaQUo2SGpxa1lYQit3SmJuTzloMnhpbWhtZFM1 T25lZWtWSnAoZDJxSzlpNFhaVnZ4VlRpemZoSUVKUoFaeXF5dVVncjhY WVhObXcrUGZZKzc4cG9mcGtoSGF3aopyTkFFblhyR1hHSToifQ%3D%3 D (accessed April 5, 2019).

Pierini, Marc. 2016c. "Turkey, Russia, and the European Diplomatic Chessboard." *Carnegie Europe*, October 17. Available at: http://carnegieeu rope.eu/strategiceurope/?fa=64870&mkt_tok=eyJpIjoiTnpabFlqUTFZamRp WVRRNCIsInQiOiI4TmxobnVkRFlXOGRaUXRlVUpiNDlaTXVhSld3 To44akJtdEFRSoxxMEE2Ko8xR3dTMHJjTmUxeG9BeVpYXC9GUnJmNVl cLzlUeG9UbWxZTldcL25KZoNUNE5iT3lnQWxtelJySThWQ3E5SWpLM DoifQ%3D%3D (accessed April 5, 2019).

Pierini, Marc. 2016d. "The Looming EU–Turkey Visa Drama." *Carnegie Europe*, April 28. Available at: http://carnegieeurope.eu/strategiceurope/63485 (accessed April 5, 2019).

Pierini, Marc. 2017. "Turkey's Domestically Driven Foreign Policy." *Carnegie Endowment for Peace*, February 27. Available at: http://carnegieeurope.eu/stra tegiceurope/68109?mkt_tok=eyJpIjoiTUROaE9XRTVNRFZpWXpVMiIsInQ iOiJ2UkFRWEtRKzJOMVNwMFJPdlhiZm9oZGFIRm5XeHNZWE15c1pD RmZNMoozYWxlcFFOMjNpbnYxY3ZKUoxidjQyVXQrakwoN3JoK3Rz N1FIMEE1QzZvQkNkQVNQcmdva1RadidwUlloa3hEYjcwR2kxcEJobm1 XZndpdHExNWlFdiJ9 (accessed April 5, 2019).

Pierson, Paul. 2000. "Increasing Returns, Path Dependence, and the Study of Politics." *American Political Science Review* 94(2): 251–267.

Pitel, Laura, and Arthur Beesley. 2016. "Erdogan Threatens to Let 3 Million Refugees into Europe." *Financial Times*, November 25. Available at: www .ft.com/content/c5197e60-b2fc-11e6-9c37-5787335499a0 (accessed April 5, 2019).

Poast, Paul. 2013. "Issue Linkage and International Cooperation: An Empirical Investigation." *Conflict Management and Peace Science* 30(3): 286–303.

Populari. 2014. A Political Romance: Relations between Turkey and Bosnia and Herzegovina, May. Available at: http://populari.org/files/docs/411.pdf (accessed April 5, 2019).

PressTV. 2017. "Turkey–Russia Talks on S-400 Missiles Progressing." February 22. Available at: www.presstv.ir/Detail/2017/02/22/511713/turkey-russia-s-400-missiles (accessed April 5, 2019).

Putnam, Robert D. 1988. "Diplomacy and Domestic Politics: The Logic of Two-Level Games." *International Organization* 42(3): 427–460.

Ramsay, Kristopher W. 2011. "Cheap Talk Diplomacy, Voluntary Negotiations, and Variable Bargaining Power." *International Studies Quarterly* 55(4): 1003–1023.

Rasmussen, Anders Fogh. 2013. Monthly Press Conference by NATO Secretary General, Brussels, May 6.

Rašidagić, Ešref Kenan. 2013. "A Critical Analysis of Turkish Foreign Policy towards the Western Balkans." In Muhidin Mulalić, Hasan Korkut, and Elif Nuroğlu (Eds.), *Turkish-Balkans Relations: The Future Prospects of Cultural, Political and Economic Transformations and Relations*. Istanbul: Tasam Yayinlari, pp. 179–196.

Regional Cooperation Council (RCC). 2017. "Regional Cooperation Council: An Overview." Available at: www.rcc.int/pages/2/overview (accessed April 5, 2019).

Reid, David. 2018. "Erdogan Says Turkey Will Boycott US Electronic Goods, Including Apple's iPhone." *CNBC.com*, August 14. Available at: www.cnbc.com/2018/08/14/erdogan-says-turkey-will-boycott-us-electronic-goods-including-apple.html (accessed April 5, 2019).

Reuters. 2016. "Fed Up with EU, Erdogan Says Turkey Could Join Shanghai Bloc." November 20. Available at: www.reuters.com/article/us-turkey-europe-erdogan-idUSKBN13F0CY (accessed April 5, 2019).

Reuters. 2017. "Turkey Says All Deals with the EU in Jeopardy if No Visa Liberalization." March 11. Available at: www.reuters.com/article/us-turkey-eu-visa-idUSKBN16I081 (accessed April 5, 2019).

Reuters. 2018. "Turkey's Erdogan Says Will Ask EU for Rest of 3 Billion Euro Aid for Refugees." March 19. Available at: www.reuters.com/article/us-eu-turkey/turkeys-erdogan-says-will-ask-eu-for-rest-of-3-billion-euro-aid-for-refugees-id USKBN1GV1V8 (accessed April 5, 2019).

Ripsman, Norrin M., Jeffrey W. Taliaferro, and Steven E. Lobell. 2016. *Neoclassical Realist Theory of International Politics*. New York: Oxford University Press.

RT. 2015. "Russia Halts Turkish Stream Project over Downed Jet." December 2. Available at: www.rt.com/business/324230-gazprom-turkish-stream-cancellation/ (accessed April 5, 2019).

RT. 2018. "'Who Will Heat Us during Winter?': Turkey Rejects US Plan to Torpedo Iran's Oil Exports." July 25. Available at: www.rt.com/news/434225-turkey-iran-us-oil/ (accessed April 5, 2019).

Robins, Philip. 2003. *Suits and Uniforms: Turkish Foreign Policy since the Cold War*. London: Hurst and Co.

Robinson, Linda. 2017. "To Take Raqqa the US Must Work with Its Partner in Its Fight against ISIS." *RAND*, March 13. Available at: www.rand.org/blog/2017/03/to-take-raqqa-the-us-must-work-with-its-partner-in.html (accessed April 5, 2019).

Roblin, Sebastien. 2018. "America's Big Fear: Turkey Mixing F-35s and Russia's S-400 Air Defense System." *The National Interest*, July 7. Available at: https://nationalinterest.org/blog/buzz/americas-big-fear-tur key-mixing-f-35s-and-russias-s-400-air-defense-system-25152 (accessed April 5, 2019).

Rose, Gideon. 1998. "Neoclassical Realism and Theories of Foreign Policy." *World Politics* 51(1): 144–172.

Rubin, Michael. 2018. "It's Time for Turkey and NATO to Go Their Separate Ways." *The Washington Post*, August 16. Available at: www.washington post.com/news/democracy-post/wp/2018/08/16/its-time-for-turkey-and-nat o-to-go-their-separate-ways/?utm_term=.e1a78b72b60f (accessed April 5, 2019).

Rüma, İnan S. 2011. "Turkish Foreign Policy towards the Balkans: New Activism, Neo-Ottomanism or/So What?" *Turkish Policy Quarterly* 9(4): 133–140.

Sakkas, John, and Nataliya Zhukova. 2013. "The Soviet Union, Turkey and the Cyprus Problem, 1967–1974." *Les Cahiers Irice* 10(1): 123–135. doi:10.3917/lci.010.0123.

Saltzman, Ilai Z. 2012a. "Soft Balancing as Foreign Policy: Assessing American Strategy toward Japan in the Interwar Period." *Foreign Policy Analysis* 8(2): 131–150.

Saltzman, Ilai Z. 2012b. *Securitizing Balance of Power Theory: A Polymorphic Reconceptualization*. New York: Lexington Books.

Sayarı, Sabri. 2000. "Turkish Foreign Policy in the Post-Cold War Era: The Challenges of Multi-regionalism." *Journal of International Affairs* 54(1): 169–182.

Schaefer, Mark E., and John G. Poffenbarger. 2014. *The Formation of the BRICS and Its Implication for the United States: Emerging Together*. New York: Palgrave Macmillan.

Schelling, Thomas. 1960. *The Strategy of Conflict*. Cambridge, MA: Harvard University Press.

Schimmelfennig, Frank, and Ulrich Sedelmeier. 2005. *The Europeanization of Central and Eastern Europe*. Ithaca, NY: Cornell University Press.

Schmitt, Eric. 2014. "US Airdrops Weapons and Supplies to Kurds Fighting in Kobani." *New York Times*, October 20.

Schweller, Randall. 2003. "The Progressiveness of Neoclassical Realism." In Colin Elman and Miriam Fendius Elman (Eds.), *Progress in International Relations Theory*. Cambridge: MIT Press, pp. 311–347.

Sechser, Todd S. 2011. "Militarized Compellent Threats, 1918–2001." *Conflict Management and Peace Science* 28(4): 377–401.

Sechser, Todd S., and Matthew Fuhrmann. 2013. "Crisis Bargaining and Nuclear Blackmail." *International Organization* 67(1): 173–195.

Selçuk, Orçun. 2012. "Turkish Airlines as a Soft Power Tool in the Context of Turkish Foreign Policy." Unpublished Master of Arts Thesis. Atatürk Institute for Modern Turkish History, Boğaziçi University, June.

Seligman, Lara. 2018. "Trump Blocks Fighter Jet Transfer Amid Deepening US–Turkey Rift." *Foreign Policy*, August 13. Available at: https://foreignpolicy.com/2018/08/13/trump-blocks-fighter-jet-transfer-amid-deepening-us-turkey-rift-f35/ (accessed April 5, 2019).

Serwer, Daniel. 2016. "Stronger Erdogan, Weaker Turkey." *Peacefare.net*, August 5. Available at: www.peacefare.net/2016/08/02/stronger-erdogan-weaker-turkey/ (accessed April 5, 2019).

Serwer, Daniel. 2017. "Outside Influences in the Balkans." *Peacefare.net*, 26 April.

Seufert, Günter. 2017. "Ever Further from the West: Why Ankara Looks to Moscow." *Stiftung Wissenschaft und Politik Comments* 2, February. Available at: www.swp-berlin.org/fileadmin/contents/products/comments/2017C02_srt.pdf (accessed April 5, 2019).

Slantchev, Branislav L. 2005. "Military Coercion in Interstate Crises." American Political Science Review 99(4): 533–547.

Smale, Alison. 2017. "Germany to Withdraw Forces from Incirlik Base in Turkey." *New York Times*, June 7. Available at: www.nytimes.com/2017/06/07/world/europe/germany-turkey-air-base.html (accessed April 5, 2019).

Smith, Hannah L. 2018. "Turkey Rejects Trump's Call for Iran Sanctions." *The Times*, July 25. Available at: www.thetimes.co.uk/article/turkey-rejects-trumps-call-for-iran-sanctions-p90dpc7lo (accessed April 5, 2019).

Snyder, Glenn H. 1984. "The Security Dilemma in Alliance Politics." *World Politics* 36(4): 461–495.

Snyder, Glenn H. 1991. "Alliances, Balance and Stability." *International Organization* 45(1): 121–142.

Snyder, Glenn H. 1997. *Alliance Politics*. Ithaca, NY: Cornell University Press.

Sokollu, Senada. 2013. "Erdogan Loses Support among Balkan Migrants." *Deutsche Welle*, June 20. Available at: www.dw.com/en/erdogan-loses-support-among-balkan-migrants/a-16894828 (accessed April 5, 2019).

Solana, Javier. 2008. "Report on the Implementation of the European Security Strategy: Providing Security in a Changing World." S407/08, Brussels, December 11. Available at: www.consilium.europa.eu/uedocs/cms_data/docs/pressdata/en/reports/104630.pdf.

Somun, Hajrudin. 2011. "Turkish Foreign Policy in the Balkans and 'Neo-Ottomanism': A Personal Account." *Insight Turkey* 13(3): 33–41.

Sönmez, Göktuğ. 2015. "Turkey's Renewed Ambitions on the Eurasian Energy Chessboard." *Research Turkey* 4(3): 24–32, Centre for Policy and Research on Turkey, London. Available at: http://researchturkey.org/?p=8222 (accessed April 5, 2019).

Spasojević, Dušan. 2014. "The Turkish-German Balkan Equation." *LSEE Blog*, July 17. Available at: http://blogs.lse.ac.uk/lsee/2014/07/17/the-turkish-german-balkan-equation/ (accessed April 5, 2019).

Sprenger, Sebastian. 2018. "Turkey Defiant on Purchase of Russian S-400 Anti-Missile Weapon." *DefenseNews.com*, July 11. Available at: www.defensenews

.com/smr/nato-priorities/2018/07/11/turkey-defiant-on-purchase-of-russian-s-400 -anti-missile-weapon/ (accessed April 5, 2019).

Sputnik News. 2018. "Turkey Slams US Demand to Drop S-400 Deal in Exchange for F-35s as 'Blackmail.'" June 14. Available at: https://sputniknews.com/mid dleeast/201806141065408430-turkey-us-f-35-demands/ (accessed April 5, 2019).

Starr, Barbara. 2016. "Turkey's Power Cut Off to Incirlik Air Base a Problem for Pentagon." *CNN.com*, July 19. Available at: www.cnn.com/2016/07/19/poli tics/incirlik-air-base-turkey-failed-coup-power-cutoff/ (accessed April 5, 2019).

Stelzenmueller, Constanze. 2017. Conference Remarks, What Is the Future of EU–Turkey Relations Conference. Wilson Center, Washington DC, April 24.

Stojanović, Dušan. 2011. "Turkey Uses Economic Clout to Gain Balkan Foothold." *The Washington Post*, March 14. Available at: www.washington post.com/wp-dyn/content/article/2011/03/14/AR2011031404398.html (accessed April 5, 2019).

Stratfor. 2015. "The Problems Foreign Powers Find in the Balkans." May 19. Available at: www.stratfor.com/analysis/problems-foreign-powers-find-bal kans (accessed April 5, 2019).

Strauss, Delphine. 2009. "Turkey's Ottoman Mission." *Financial Times*, November 23.

Şenyuva, Özgür, and Ciğdem Üstün. 2015. "A New Episode in EU-Turkish Relations: Why So Much Bitterness?" *German Mashall Fund of the United States*, December 21. Available at: www.gmfus.org/publications/new-episode-eu-turkish-relations-why-so-much-bitterness (accessed April 5, 2019).

Šoštarić, Maja. 2011. "Bosnia, Revisited: Turkey's Gains, Challenges and Future Aspirations." *Balkananalysis.com*, July 12. Available at: www.balkanalysis.co m/turkey/2011/07/12/bosnia-revisited-turkey's-gains-challenges-and-future-as pirations/ (accessed April 5, 2019).

Tanasković, Darko. 2010. "Neoosmanizam: Povratak Turske na Balkan [Neo-Ottomanism: Return of Turkey to the Balkans]", Banja Luka, *Official Gazette*.

Tanasković, Darko. 2013. *Neo-Ottomanism: A Doctrine and Foreign Policy Practice*. Belgrade: Association of Non-Governmental Organisations of Southeast Europe-CIVIS.

Taşpınar, Ömer. 2008. *Turkey's Middle East Policies: Between Neo-Ottomanism and Kemalism*. Washington DC: Carnegie Endowment for International Peace.

TEPAV. 2015. "Strengthening the Connectivity and Business Synergies in the SEE." Sarajevo, June 21. Available at: www.tepav.org.tr/upload/files/haber/14 38241943-0.2___Economic_Diagnostics_of_SEE_6_and_Turkey.pdf (accessed April 5, 2019).

Terzi, Özlem. 2010. *The Influence of the European Union on Turkish Foreign Policy*. London: Routledge.

The Associated Press. 2017. "Will Death Penalty Be the Death Knell for EU–Turkey Talks?" April 18. Available at: www.foxnews.com/world/2017/04/18/ will-death-penalty-be-death-knell-for-eu-turkey-talks.html (accessed April 5, 2019).

The Associated Press. 2018. "Turkey against Severing Economic Ties with Iran Despite US Sanctions." July 25. Available at: www.haaretz.com/middle-east-n

ews/turkey/turkey-against-severing-economic-ties-with-iran-despite-us-sanc
tions-1.6314188 (accessed April 5, 2019).

The Economist. 2016. "Turkey and the EU: Refugees and Terror." March 26.
Available at: www.economist.com/news/europe/21695236-europe-approves-c
ritical-deal-send-asylum-seekers-back-turkey-just-terrorism-reaches (accessed
April 5, 2019).

The Economist. 2019. "Turkey Leads the World in Jailed Journalists."
January 16. Available at: https://www.economist.com/graphic-detail/2019/01/
16/turkey-leads-the-world-in-jailed-journalists (accessed April 5, 2019).

The Market Mogul. 2016. "The EU and the Turkish Stream." March 11.
Available at: http://themarketmogul.com/the-eu-and-the-turkish-stream/
(accessed April 5, 2019).

The Telegraph. 2017. "A Year on from EU–Turkey Deal, Refugees and Migrants
in Limbo Commit Suicide and Suffer from Trauma." March 14. Available at:
www.telegraph.co.uk/news/2017/03/14/year-eu-turkey-deal-refugees-migrant
s-limbo-commit-suicide-suffer/ (accessed April 5, 2019).

Thelen, Kathleen. 1999. "Historical Institutionalism in Comparative Politics."
Annual Review of Political Science 2(1): 369–404.

TimeTurk.com. 2015. "Güneydoğu Avrupa Ülkeleri İş Birliği Süreci
Parlamenter Asamblesi Toplantısı [SEECP Parliamentary Assembly
Meeting]." February 9. Available at: www.timeturk.com/tr/2015/02/08/gune
ydogu-avrupa-ulkeleri-is-birligi-sureci-parlamenter-asam.html (accessed
April 5, 2019).

Tisdall, Simon. 2018. "Turkey's Ever-Closer Ties with Russia Leave US Lacking
Key Ally in Syria." *The Guardian*, April 11. Available at: www.theguardian.c
om/world/2018/apr/11/turkey-ever-closer-ties-with-russia-leave-us-lacking-ke
y-ally-on-syria (accessed April 5, 2019).

Tocci, Natalie. 2010. "The Baffling Short-Sightedness in the EU–Turkey–Cyprus
Triangle." *Istituto Affari Internazionali*, Document IAI 1021, October.

Tocci, Natalie, and Mark Houben. 2001. "Accommodating Turkey in ESDP."
CEPS Policy Brief No. 5, May.

Todorova, Maria. 1996. "The Ottoman Legacy in the Balkans." In L. Carol
Brown (Ed.), *Imperial Legacy. The Ottoman Imprint on the Balkans and the
Middle East.* New York: Columbia University Press, pp. 45–77.

Tol, Gönül, and Robert W. Pearson. 2016. "Turkey–US Relations and the Next
US Administration." *Middle East Institute Policy Focus* 25, October. Available
at: www.mei.edu/sites/default/files/publications/PF25_TolPearson_USTurkey_
web.pdf (accessed April 5, 2019).

Tolay, Juliette. 2014. "The EU and Turkey's Asylum Policies in Light of the Syrian
Crisis." *Global Turkey in Europe*, Policy Brief 10. Available at: http://pubblica
zioni.iai.it/pdf/GTE/GTE_PB_10.pdf (accessed April 5, 2019).

Trager, Robert F. 2010. "Diplomatic Calculus in Anarchy: How Communication
Matters." *American Political Science Review* 104(2): 347–368.

TRT World. 2019. "Turkish Defence Minister Hosts US Special Envoy to Discuss
Manbij Road Map." March 5. Available at: www.trtworld.com/turkey/turkish-
defence-minister-hosts-us-special-envoy-to-discuss-manbij-road-map-24688
(accessed April 5, 2019).

Tsakonas, Panayotis. 2008. "From 'Perverse' to 'Promising' Institutionalism? NATO, EU and the Greek-Turkish Conflict." In Dimitris Bourantonis, Kostas Ifantis, and Panayotis Tsakonas (Eds.), *Multilateralism and Security Institutions in an Era of Globalization*. Oxford: Routledge, pp. 233–251.

Tsebelis, George. 2002. *Veto Players: How Political Institutions Work*. Princeton, NJ: Princeton University Press.

Turak, Natasha. 2018. "Turkish Lira Recovers Sharply against the Dollar after Record Nosedive." *CNBC.com*, August 14. Available at: www.cnbc.com/2018/08/14/turkish-lira-recovers-sharply-against-the-dollar-after-record-nosedive.html (accessed April 5, 2019).

Turan, Ilter. 2017. "Turkey's Constitutional Debate: Presidentialism Alla Turca or Parliamentary Government." *German Marshall Fund of the US*, April 10. Available at: www.gmfus.org/publications/turkeys-constitutional-debate-presi dentialism-alla-turca-or-parliamentary-government (accessed April 5, 2019).

Turkish International Cooperation and Development Agency (TİKA). 2017. Turkish Development Assistance Report 2014. Available at: www.tika.gov.tr/upload/2016/INGILIZCE%20SITE%20ESERLER/KALKINMA%20RAPOR LARI/DA%20Report%202014.pdf (accessed April 5, 2019).

Turkish Ministry of Foreign Affairs. 2017. "Turkey and the Shanghai Cooperation Organization Dialogue Partnership Memorandum Was Signed in Almaty." Available at: www.mfa.gov.tr/turkey-and-the-shanghai-cooperation-organization-dialogue-partnership-memorandum-was-signed-in-almaty.en.mf a (accessed April 5, 2019).

Turkish Ministry of Foreign Affairs. 2019a. "Turkey–EU Relations." Available at: www.mfa.gov.tr/relations-between-turkey-and-the-european-union.en.mfa (accessed April 5, 2019).

Turkish Ministry of Foreign Affairs. 2019b. "Turkey's International Security Initiatives and Contributions to NATO and EU Operations." Available at: www .mfa.gov.tr/iv_-european-security-and-defence-identity_policy-_esdi_p_.en.mfa (accessed April 5, 2019).

Turkish Ministry of Foreign Affairs. 2019c. "III. The European Union Common Security and Defence Policy (CSDP) and NATO-EU Strategic Cooperation." Available at: www.mfa.gov.tr/iii_-turkey_s-views-on-current-nato-issues.en.mfa (accessed April 5, 2019).

Turkish Ministry of Foreign Affairs. 2019d. "Turkish Energy Profile and Strategy." Available at: www.mfa.gov.tr/turkeys-energy-strategy.en.mfa (accessed April 5, 2019).

Turkish Ministry of Foreign Affairs. 2019e. "Press Release Regarding Turkey 2018 Human Rights Report of the US Department of State." No. 55, March 14. Available at: www.mfa.gov.tr/no_55_-abd-insan-haklari-raporu-h k.en.mfa (accessed April 5, 2019).

Turkish Statistical Institute (TurkStat). 2017. "Foreign Trade Statitstics". Available at: www.turkstat.gov.tr/PreTablo.do?alt_id=1046 (accessed April 5, 2019).

Turkish Review. 2012. "Economic Performance, Domestic Terrorism and Military Solutions," October 1. Available at: www.turkishreview.org/depart

ments/economic-performance-domestic-terrorism-and-military-solu
tions_540603 (accessed April 5, 2019).

Tusk, Donald. 2016. Remarks after the Signature of the EU–NATO Declaration, July 8. Available at: www.consilium.europa.eu/en/press/press-releases/2016/o7/08-tusk-remarks-eu-nato-joint-declaration/ (accessed April 5, 2019).

Türbedar, Erhan. 2011. "Turkey's New Activism in the Western Balkans: Ambitions and Obstacles." *Insight Turkey* 13(3): 139–158.

Türbedar, Erhan. 2012. "Türk Dış Politikası Balkanlar'da Nasıl Algılanıyor? [How Is the Turkish Foreign Policy Perceived in the Balkans?]" *Türkiye Ekonomi Politikaları Araştırma Vakfı*, No. 201225, April. Available at: www.tepav.org.tr/upload/files/1335363622–9.Turk_Dis_Politikasi_Balkanlar___da_Nasil_Algi laniyor.pdf (accessed April 5, 2019).

Türkeş, Mustafa, ş. İnan Rüma, and Sait Akşit. 2012. "Kriz Sarmalında Bosna-Hersek: 'Devlet Krizi' [Cycles of Crises in Bosnia-Herzegovina: the 'State Crisis']." *Boğaziçi Üniversitesi-TÜSİAD Dış Politika Forumu Araştırma Raporu* DPF 2012-RR 02.

Uğur, Mehmet. 2010. "Open-Ended Membership Prospect and Commitment Credibility: Explaining the Deadlock in EU–Turkey Accession Negotiations." *Journal of Common Market Studies* 48(4): 967–991.

United States. 2014. *National Defense Authorization Act for Fiscal Year 2015*. 113/291 (December 19, 2014). Washington: US Government Publishing Office.

United States. 2017. *Countering America's Adversaries through Sanctions Act*. 115/44 (August 2, 2017). Washington: US Government Publishing Office.

United States. 2018. *National Defense Authorization Act for Fiscal Year 2019*. 115/232 (August 13, 2018). Washington: US Government Publishing Office.

United States Department of Defense. 2018. "Status of the US Relationship with the Republic of Turkey: Unclassified Executive Summary." *FY19 NDAA Sec 1282 Report*, November 26. Available at: https://fas.org/man/eprint/dod-tur key.pdf (accessed April 5, 2019).

United States Department of State. 2017. "US Relations with Turkey." Available at: www.state.gov/r/pa/ei/bgn/3432.htm (accessed April 5, 2019).

United States General Accounting Office. 1982. "The Defense and Economic Cooperation Agreement – US Interests and Turkish Needs." ID-82–31, May 7.

Ülgen, Sinan. 2008. "The Evolving EU, NATO and Turkey Relationship: Implications for Transatlantic Security." *EDAM Discussion Paper Series* 2, April.

Ülgen, Sinan. 2014. Speech Transcript, Turkey: An Emerging Power in a Changing Middle East Conference, Council on Foreign Relations, Istanbul, June 18. Available at: www.cfr.org/projects/world/turkey-an-emerging-power-in-a-cha nging-middle-east/pr1685 (accessed April 5, 2019).

Ülgen, Sinan. 2016. "Turkey Power Shift Upends EU Refugee Deal." *Politico*, May 5. Available at: www.politico.eu/article/turkey-power-shift-hurts-eu-refu gee-deal-migration-ahmet-davutoglu-recep-tayyip-erdogan/ (accessed April 5, 2019).

Ünal, Ali. 2017a. "Turkey Likely to Close S-400 Missile Deal with Russia." *Daily Sabah*, February 22. Available at: www.dailysabah.com/defense/2017/02/22/ turkey-likely-to-close-s-400-missile-deal-with-russia (accessed April 5, 2019).

Ünal, Ali. 2017b. "Turkey to Buy 2 Batteries of S-400 Systems from Russia." *Daily Sabah*, March 23. Available at: www.dailysabah.com/politics/2017/03/ 24/turkey-to-buy-2-batteries-of-s-400-systems-from-russia (accessed April 5, 2019).

Ünlühisarcikli, Özgür. 2018. "Polarization Paves the Way for Populism and Majoritarianism in Turkey," *The German Marshall Fund of the United States*, March 21. Available at: www.gmfus.org/blog/2018/03/21/polariza tion-paves-way-populism-and-majoritarianism-turkey?utm_source=emai l&utm_medium=email&utm_campaign=%23metoo%20underscores%20hu man%20rights%20abuses%20at%20core%20of%20liberal%20democracies (accessed April 5, 2019).

Ünver, Akın. 2014a. "Pax Erdogana: Is This the End of an Era?" *Al Jazeera*, October 27. Available at: www.aljazeera.com/indepth/opinion/2014/10/pax-erd ogana-this-end-an-era-2014102751353514897.html (accessed April 5, 2019).

Ünver, Akın. 2014b. Speech Transcript, Turkey: An Emerging Power in a Changing Middle East Conference, *Council on Foreign Relations*, Istanbul, June 18. Available at: www.cfr.org/projects/world/turkey-an-emerging-power-in-a-changing-middle-east/pr1685 (accessed April 5, 2019).

Van Eekelen, Willem F. 2005. "The Parliamentary Dimension of Defense Procurement Requirements, Production, Cooperation and Acquisition." *Geneva Centre for the Democratic Control of Armed Forces Occasional Paper* No. 5, March.

Vejvoda, Ivan. 2016. "The Balkans: No War in Sight." Commentary, *The German Marshall Fund of the United States*. February 17. Available at: www.gmfus.org/ commentary/balkans-no-war-sight#sthash.ohgBMFGj.dpuf (accessed April 5, 2019).

Vicini, Caroline. 2016. Conference Remarks, Middle East Institute Conference on Turkey, Washington DC, September 30.

Vogel, Toby, and Constant Brand. 2010. "NATO Chief Urges EU to Give Turkey Security Role." *European Dialogue*, September 29. Available at: www.eurodia logue.eu/osce/NATO-Chief-Urges-EU-To-Give-Turkey-Security-Role (accessed April 5, 2019).

Voskopoulos, George. 2013. "Turkey and the Balkan Subordinate Security System: From the Cold War to the Post-Cold War Era." In Muhidin Mulalić, Hasan Korkut, and Elif Nuroğlu (Eds.), *Turkish-Balkans Relations: The Future Prospects of Cultural, Political and Economic Transformations and Relations*. Istanbul: Tasam Yayinlari, pp. 235–256.

Vračić, Alida. 2016. "Turkey's Role in the Western Balkans." Stiftung Wissenschaft und Politik, RP 11, December, Berlin.

Walker, William, and Paul Gummett. 1989. "Britain and the European Armaments Market." *International Affairs* 65(3): 419–442.

Wallander, Celeste A. 2000. "Institutional Assets and Adaptability: NATO after the Cold War." *International Organization* 54(4): 705–735.

Walsh, Alistair. 2017. "Turkey Will Not Beg for German Troops to Stay at Incirlik Base." *Deutsche Welle*, May 18. Available at: www.dw.com/en/turkey-will-no t-beg-for-german-troops-to-stay-at-incirlik-base/a-38887076 (accessed April 5, 2019).

Walt, Stephen M. 1987. *The Origins of Alliances.* Ithaca, NY: Cornell University Press.

Walt, Stephen M. 1997. "Why Alliances Endure or Collapse." *Survival* 39(1): 156–179.

Walt, Stephen M. 2006. *Taming American Power: The Global Response to US Primacy.* New York: W. W. Norton & Company.

Walt, Stephen M. 2009. "Alliances in a Unipolar World." *World Politics* 61(1): 86–120.

Walt, Stephen M. 2013. "On Iran, Try Backscratching, Not Blackmail." *Foreign Policy,* February 22. Available at: http://foreignpolicy.com/2013/02/22/on-iran-try-backscratching-not-blackmail/ (accessed April 5, 2019).

Wang, Lina. 2016. "Will Turkey Join the Shanghai Cooperation Organization Instead of the EU?" *The Diplomat,* November 24. Available at: http://thediplo mat.com/2016/11/will-turkey-join-the-shanghai-cooperation-organization-inst ead-of-the-eu/ (accessed April 5, 2019).

Weiser, Benjamin. 2017. "Erdogan Helped Turks Evade Iran Sanctions, Reza Zarrab Says," *New York Times,* November 30. Available at: www.nytimes .com/2017/11/30/world/europe/erdogan-turkey-iran-sanctions.html (accessed April 5, 2019).

Wemer, David. 2018. "NATO Ministers Preach Unity, but Divisions Persist." *Atlantic Council,* July 11. Available at: www.atlanticcouncil.org/blogs/new-at lanticist/framing-the-debate-nato-engages (accessed April 5, 2019).

Whitaker, Beth Elise. 2010. "Soft Balancing among Weak States? Evidence from Africa." *International Affairs* 86(5): 1109–1127.

Wikileaks. 2010. "What Lies Beneath Ankara's New Foreign Policy." January 20. Available at: https://wikileaks.org/plusd/cables/10ANKARA87_a.html (accessed April 5, 2019).

Wirtz, James J. 2004. "The Balance of Power Paradox." In T. V. Paul, James J. Wirtz, and Michel Fortmann (Eds.), *Balance of Power: Theory and Practice in the 21st Century.* Stanford, CA: Stanford University Press, pp. 127–149.

World Bulletin. 2013. "Erdoğan Expresses Willingness to Improve Ties with Surinam." March 8. Available at: www.worldbulletin.net/?aType=haber&Art icleID=104400 (accessed April 5, 2019).

Yavuz, Ercan. 2011. "Defense Giants Compete in Turkish Tender for Long-Range Missiles." *Today's Zaman,* January 2.

Yavuz, M. Hakan. 2001. "Değişen Türk Kimliği ve Dış Politika: Neo-Osmanlılığın Yükselişi" [Changing Turkish Identity and Foreign Policy: The Rise of Neo-Ottomanism]. In Saban H. Çalış, İhsan D. Dağı, and Ramazan Gözen (Eds.), *Türkiye'nin Dış Politika Gündemi: Kimlik, Demokrasi, Güvenlik [Turkish Foreign Policy Agenda: Identity, Democracy, and Security].* Ankara: Liberte Yayınları.

Yenigün, Cüneyt. 2011. "Turkey's Balkan Policy: Resurrection of Turkey in the Balkans." In Cüneyt Yenigün and Ferdinand Gjana (Eds.), *Balkans: Foreign Affairs, Politics, and Socio-Cultures.* Tirana: Epoka University Publications, pp. 531–550.

Yeşiltaş, Murat, and Ali Balcı. 2013. "Dictionary of Turkish Foreign Policy in the AK Party Era: A Conceptual Map." *Sam Papers* 7: 1–37.

Yılmaz, Buğra. 2014. *The Readmission Agreement between the EU and Turkey: Compatible with the Right to Seek Asylum?* Masters Thesis in International Public Law, Uppsala University, Department of Law. Available at: https://www.diva-portal.org/smash/get/diva2:722210/FULLT EXT01.pdf (Accessed 5 April 2019).

Yılmaz, Hakan. 2011. "Euroscepticism in Turkey: Parties, Elites, and Public Opinion." *South European Society and Politics* 16(1): 185–208.

Yinanç, Barçin. 2018. "How Will Turkey Trade with Iran with Sanctions Back and Halkbank on Target?" *Hürriyet Daily News*, July 10. Available at: www .hurriyetdailynews.com/opinion/barcin-yinanc/how-will-turkey-trade-with-ira n-with-sanctions-back-and-halkbank-on-target-134372 (accessed April 5, 2019).

Yohannes, Athina Tesfa. 2011. "Easing Back in: The Balkan's Re-Introduction to Turkey." BILGESAM (*Wise Man Center for Strategic Studies*), Istanbul, April 4. Available at: www.bilgesam.org/en/incele/1875/-easing-back-in–the-balkans–re-introduction-to-turkey/#.VwVnX8eodSU (accessed April 5, 2019).

Young, Alex. 2016. "Turkey Banks on the Balkans." *BNE Intellinews*, January 5. Available at: www.intellinews.com/comment-turkey-banks-on-the-balkans-87924/ (accessed April 5, 2019).

Zaman, Amberin. 2017. "Kurds Call on US to Set Up No-Fly Zone After Turkish Attacks." *Al Monitor*, April 25. Available at: www.al-monitor.com/pulse/origi nals/2017/04/turkey-strike-kurds-sinjar-syria.html (accessed April 5, 2019).

Zanotti, Jim. 2011. "Turkey–US Defense Cooperation: Prospects and Challenges." Congressional Research Service Report 7–5700 R41761, April 8.

Zanotti, Jim, and Clayton Thomas. 2017. "Turkey: Background and US Relations in Brief." Congressional Research Service Report 7–5700 R44000, March 21.

Zarakol, Ayse. 2011. *After Defeat: How the East Learned to Live with the West.* Cambridge: Cambridge University Press.

Zarakol, Ayse (Ed.). 2017. *Hierarchies in World Politics.* Cambridge: Cambridge University Press.

Zierler, David. 2014. "Foreign Relations of the United States, 1977–1980, Volume XXI" *Office of the Historian.* US Department of State. Available at: https://hist ory.state.gov/historicaldocuments/frus1977-80v21/preface (accessed April 5, 2019).

Index

Acheson, Dean, 66
active diplomacy, as statecraft tool, 32, 33, 35
  in Western Balkans, 42–6
    as Neo-Ottomanism, 45–6, 57–8
    as Office Development Assistance donor, 45
    Ottoman Empire nostalgia as influence on, 43–6
    pragmatic Neo-Ottomanism, 17, 48, 61
    Serbian relations improved by, 43–6
activism, in Turkey's foreign policy, 23
Additional Protocol. *See* Ankara Protocol
Akar, Hulusi, 133–4
Albania, 69
Albright, Madeleine, 67
alternative alliances, 25, 34–5, 36, 114–16, 124
Ankara Document, 67–8
Ankara Protocol (Additional Protocol) (2004), 5
  Cyprus under, 72–3, 74
Annen, Neils, 86
anti-Westernism, in Turkey's foreign policy, 1–2, 13–14
al-Assad, Bashar, 126
Astana peace process, 139–40

balancing or balance of power of theory
  external balancing, 27
  hard balancing, soft balancing and, 44, 27, 164–5

internal balancing, 27
Berlin-Plus arrangements, 65, 68–9, 75
Billion, Didier, 93
blackmail, as statecraft tool, 20, 35, 36, 92–6, 136–8
Bosnia and Herzegovina, Membership Action Plan for, 44, 56
Bozkır, Volkan, 12–13
Bremmer, Ian, 115
Brunson, Andrew, 13, 110
Bulgaria, 69

CAATSA. *See* Countering America's Adversaries Through Sanctions Act
Canikli, Nurettin, 122
Carter, Ashton, 135, 143
CEF. *See* Connecting Europe Facility
CFI. *See* Connected Forces Initiative
cheap talk diplomacy, 31–2, 33–4, 35, 54, 59, 73, 82
China, missile defense systems from, 117–18
Common Security and Defence Policy (CSDP), 56–7, 70–1, 78–9, 81–2
compellent threats, 19, 20, 31–2, 34, 36, 92–6, 113, 114–16, 124, 132–4
Connected Forces Initiative (CFI), 120
Connecting Europe Facility (CEF), 99
Constructivism, in Turkey's foreign policy, 23–4
Cook, Steven, 96, 138
cooperative balancing, with Russia, 34, 124
  in intra-alliance opposition, 138–41

207

cooperative balancing, with Russia (cont.)
  in S-400 missile defense system purchase,
    116–21
  in Turkish Stream project, 103–7
costly signaling, 20, 33–4, 36, 113, 121–3,
    124, 134–5
Countering America's Adversaries Through
    Sanctions Act (CAATSA), US, 121
coups, military
  failed, ix, 1–2, 6–7, 12–13, 93–4, 105–6,
    142, 145, 159, 160, 161, 172
  political elites during, 60
  in Turkey, 1–2
Croatia, 69
CSDP. *See* Common Security and Defence
    Policy
Customs Union Agreement, 4, 5, 8, 72–3, 81
  EU-Turkey Refugee Deal and, 89–91
  Turkey's energy policies under, 99
Cyprus
  under Ankara Protocol, 72–3, 74
  Energy Community and, 100–1
  in ESDP, Turkey veto of, 63–6
  in NATO, veto of application, 63, 64–6,
    76–7, 78–9
  Turkey and, military intervention by,
    10

Çağlayan, Zafer, 109–10
Çavuşoğlu, Mevlüt, 2, 95, 133–4, 137–8.
  See also S-400 missile defense
    systems
Çelik, Ömer, 96
Çevik, İlnur, 133

Davutoğlu, Ahmet, 3, 42
Defence and Economic Cooperation
    Agreement, 10
defense issues. *See* S-400 missile defense
    systems
Democratic Union Party (PYD), 127–32
diversionary theory, 29–30

economic statecraft, in energy policies, 35
  in international sanctions against Iran,
    108–11
  Turkish Stream project, 107–8
ECT. *See* Energy Community Treaty
EDA. *See* European Defence Agency
EEC. *See* European Economic Community
Energy Community, 99, 101–2

Cyprus and, 100–1
Energy Community Treaty (ECT), Turkey's
    membership in, 98–103
  through issue-linkage bargaining, 100–3,
    111
  strategic noncooperation in, 99–100
energy policies, Turkey and
  Connecting Europe Facility and, 99
  under Customs Union Agreement, 99
  economic statecraft in
    in international sanctions against Iran,
      108–11
    Turkish Stream project influenced by,
      107–8
  ECT and, Turkey's refusal of full
      membership in, 98–103
    through issue-linkage bargaining,
      100–3, 111
    strategic noncooperation in, 99–100
  Energy Community and, 99, 101–2
    Cyprus and, 100–1
  Energy Union and, 103
  international sanctions against Iran as
      influence on, 108–11
    economic statecraft strategies, 108–11
    exemptions from, 110–11
  Turkish Stream project, 103–8
    economic feasibility of, 107–8
    economic statecraft as influence on,
      107–8
    with Russia, cooperative balancing in,
      103–7
    Trans-Adriatic Pipeline and, 104
    Trans-Anatolian Pipeline and, 104
Energy Union, 103
entangling diplomacy, 20, 31–2, 33, 35,
    72–7, 82, 154–5
Erdemir, Aykan, 115
Erdoğan, Recep Tayyip, 2, 7–8, 13. *See also*
    energy policies; intra-alliance
    opposition; S-400 missile defense
    systems; Turkey, foreign policy of
  foreign policy in Western Balkans
      influenced by, 59–60
  Gülen extradition demands by, 13
  Putin and, 105–6
  response to US economic
      sanctions, 166
  on SCO membership, 114–15
Estonia, 69
EU. *See* European Union

EULEX. *See* European Union Rule of Law Mission in Kosovo
European Council, 8, 169–0
European Court of Human Rights, 88
European Defence Agency (EDA), 69–70, 81
European Economic Community (EEC), 4
European Parliament, 7–8
European Security and Defence Policy (ESDP)
  Cyprus involvement in, Turkey veto of, 63–6
  EDA and, 69–70
  Joint Declaration on, 68–9
  non-EU states' participation in, 67–8
  Turkey and
    entangling diplomacy strategy, 72–7
    soft balancing by, 70–1
    strategic noncooperation in, 66–72
    veto of Cyprus involvement, 63–6
European Union (EU). *See also* Energy Community Treaty; energy policies; EU-Turkey Refugee Deal; intra-alliance opposition; Turkey, foreign policy of
  accession process into, EU-Turkey Refugee Deal, 91–2
  Customs Union Agreement, 4, 5
  EU-Turkey Joint Action Plan, 6–7, 84
  FTAs with, 86
  Instrument for Pre-Accession Funding, 50
  NATO and, 65–80
    Berlin-Plus Agreement between, 65, 68–9, 75
    strategic noncooperation with, 66–72
  Turkey and, relationship with, 1–2
  in EEC, 4
  EU-Turkey Joint Action Plan, 6–7
  historical perspective on, 4–9
  in WEU, 4
  Turkey's relationship with, 1–2
  in Western Balkans, Turkey's foreign policy and, 50–60
  competitive elements of, 52–3
  decline of EU participation in, 52
  Islam as influence on, Muslim favoritism and, 53, 54–5
  membership in EU as factor for, 55–6
  Stabilisation and Association Process, 50–1

European Union Rule of Law Mission in Kosovo (EULEX), 56–7
Europeanization, of foreign policies, in Turkey, 23
  "golden age" of, 23
Euroskepticism, among Turkish elites, 6
EU-Turkey Joint Action Plan, 6–7, 84
EU-Turkey Refugee Deal
  compellent threats and blackmail, 92–6
  Customs Union Agreement and, 89–91
  EU accession process and, 91–2
  under European Court of Human Rights jurisprudence, 88
  EU-Turkey Statement in, 85
  issue-linkage bargaining strategy in, 85–92
    FTAs and, 86, 90–1
  overview of, 83–5, 96–7
  Readmission Agreement in, 86–8
  Syrian refugees under, 84
  visa liberalization process under, 86–9
    Roadmap Towards a Visa Free Regime as influence on, 87–8
external balancing, 27

foreign direct investment (FDI), in Western Balkans, 49
foreign policy. *See* Turkey, foreign policy of
framework of intra-alliance opposition. *See* intra-alliance opposition
Free Trade Agreements (FTAs), 86

Gezi Park protests, 59–60
Gül, Abdullah, 43, 44
Gülen, Fethullah, 12–13, 160

Hahn, Johannes, 7–8
Hook, Brian, 110
hostage diplomacy, 13, 34–5, 36

Independent European Programme Group (IEPG), 66–7
Instrument for Pre-Accession (IPA) Funding, 50
inter-institutional balancing, 33, 36, 77–80, 82, 154–5
internal balancing, 27
international relations (IR)
  intra-alliance opposition in, 25–30
  diversionary theory in, 29–30
  neoliberalism in, 25, 29

international relations (IR) (cont.)
  neorealism theory, 25–9. *See also* soft
    balancing theory
  regional powers and, foreign policy
    motivations of, 3
International Security Assistance Force
  (ISAF), 64
intra-alliance opposition, within Turkey's
    foreign policy, 24–37, 145–6,
    171–3. *See also* Middle East
  framework of, 30–7
    boundary breaking in, 36, 150, 167
    boundary challenging in, 35–6
    boundary testing in, 35
    processes of, 35–7
  IR theory and, 25–30
    diversionary theory in, 29–30
    neoliberalism in, 25, 29
    neorealism theory, 25–9. *See also* soft
      balancing theory
  NATO and, 141–5
  Russia and, through cooperative
    balancing, 138–41
    during Astana peace process, 139–40
    in Syria, 138–41
  statecraft tools in, 31–5, 148. *See also*
    statecraft tools
    active diplomacy, 32, 33
    alternative and countervailing
      alliances, 34–5
    blackmail, 35, 92–6, 136–8
    issue-linkage bargaining, 32–3
    strategic noncooperation, 33–4
IPA Funding. *See* Instrument for
  Pre-Accession Funding
IR. *See* international relations
Iran, international sanctions against, 108–11
  Turkey's response to
    economic statecraft strategies in,
      108–11
    exemptions as part of, 110–11
IS. *See* Islamic State
ISAF. *See* International Security Assistance
  Force
Islam
  Muslim favoritism and, 53, 54–5
  Turkey's foreign policy influenced by, 24
  in Western Balkans, international foreign
    policy influenced by, 53, 54–5
Islamic State (IS), 127–41
Israel, Turkey and, 11

issue-linkage bargaining, as statecraft tool,
    32–3, 82, 154–5
  for ECT membership, 100–3, 111
  in EU-Turkey Refugee Deal, 85–92
  in NATO, 77–80
Istanbul Declaration, 44
Işık, Fikri, 95–6, 128
Ivashov, Leonid, 116

İncirlik Air Base, 19–20, 120, 136–8, 145–6,
    150, 162. *See also* territorial/asset
    denial

JCPOA. *See* Joint Comprehensive Plan of
  Action
Jeffrey, James, 133–4
Joint Comprehensive Plan of Action
  (JCPOA), 108–9
Joint Strike Fighter (JSF) Program, 3

Kalın, Ibrahim, 119–20
Katainen, Jyrki, 89
Kerry, John, 129
KFOR. *See* Kosovo Force
Khashoggi, Jamal, 110–11
Kissinger, Henry, 10
Kofman, Michael, 115
Koplow, Michael, 115
Kosovo Force (KFOR), 56–7
Kurdistan Workers' Party (PKK),
    127–32
Kurds, peace process for, 129–32
Kurtulmuş, Numan, 7

Latvia, 69
Lesser, Ian, 86
Lithuania, 69
Loğoğlu, Faruk, 9

MAP. *See* Membership Action Plan
Mavi Marmara incident, 11
McCain, John, 136
Membership Action Plan (MAP), 44, 56
Merkel, Angela, 51
Middle East, intra-alliance opposition
    tools and, 132–41. *See also specific
    countries*
  asset denial in, 136–8
  blackmail power in, 136–8
  compellent threats in, 132–4
  costly signaling strategies, 134–5

territorial denial in, 136–8
US role in, 132–8

National Defense Authorization Act
(NDAA), US, 118, 122
NATO. *See* North Atlantic Treaty
Organization
NDAA. *See* National Defense Authorization
Act
neoliberalism theory, 25, 29
Neo-Ottomanism, 45–6, 57–8
neorealism theory, 25–9. *See also* soft
balancing theory
Alliance Security Dilemma in, 25–6
External Threat hypothesis in, 25
failures of, 29
9/11. *See* September 11 terrorist attacks
North Atlantic Treaty Organization (NATO)
Connected Forces Initiative, 120
EU and, 65–80
Berlin-Plus Agreement between, 65,
68–9, 75
strategic noncooperation with, 66–72
IEPG in, 66–7
intra-alliance opposition and, 141–5
ISAF and, 64
Kosovo Force, 56–7
non-EU states' participation in, 67–8, 69
S-400 missile defense system purchases
and, responses to, 118–21
Turkey in, 1, 2, 65–80. *See also* Turkey,
foreign policy of
entangling diplomacy by, 72–7
inter-institutional balancing by,
77–80
issue-linkage bargaining by, 77–80
strategic noncooperation of, 66–72
US relationship with, 9–14
veto of Cyprus application to, 63, 64–6,
76–7, 78–9
US-Turkey relations in, 9–14
Western Balkans and, foreign policy
issues in, 56–7
WEU and, 67–8

Official Development Assistance (ODA),
41, 45
OIC. *See* Organization of the Islamic
Conference
Oktay, Fuat, 125
Orbán, Viktor, 57

Organization for Security and Cooperation
in Europe (OSCE), Turkey in, 1
Organization of the Islamic Conference
(OIC), 38
OSCE. *See* Organization for Security and
Cooperation in Europe
Ottoman Empire
nostalgia for, 43–6
Western Balkans during, 40

Özal, Turgut, 10

Partnership for Peace (PfP), 63
Peace Implementation Council (PIC), 38
peacekeeping forces
Kosovo Force, 56–7
in Western Balkans, 38
Pence, Mike, 125
PfP. *See* Partnership for Peace
PIC. *See* Peace Implementation Council
Piri, Kati, 96
PKK. *See* Kurdistan Workers' Party
Plenković, Andrej, 57
power symmetries, in soft balancing theory,
27–8
Putin, Vladimir, 104–6. *See also* Russia;
S-400 missile defense systems
PYD. *See* Democratic Union Party

RCC. *See* Regional Cooperation Council
Readmission Agreement, in EU-Turkey
Refugee Deal, 86–8
Realpolitik, as foreign policy strategy, 61
refugees. *See also* EU-Turkey Refugee Deal
Syrian, 84
Regional Cooperation Council (RCC), 47
Roadmap Towards a Visa Free Regime,
87–8
Romania, 69
Russia
cooperative balancing with, 124
in intra-alliance opposition, 138–41
in S-400 missile defense system
purchase, 116–21
in Turkish Stream project, 103–7
intra-alliance opposition and, through
cooperative balancing, 138–41
during Astana peace process, 139–40
in Syria, 138–41
political relations with Turkey, conflicts
in, 105–6

Russia (cont.)
  S-400 missile defense system purchase
      from, 116–23
    Chinese missile defense systems and,
        117–18
    cooperative balancing strategies in,
        116–21
    NATO response to, 118–21
    as political signaling, 121–3
    US response to, 118, 121–3, 124–5
  SCO and, 105–6
    compellent threats and, 114–16
    origins of, 114
    Turkey as full member of, 113–15

S-400 missile defense systems, purchase of,
    116–23
  Chinese missile defense systems and,
      117–18
  cooperative balancing strategies in,
      116–21
  NATO response to, 118–21
  as political signaling, 121–3
  US response to, 118, 121–3, 124–5
SAP. *See* Stabilisation and Association
    Process
SCO. *See* Shanghai Cooperation
    Organization
SECI. *See* Southeast European Cooperative
    Initiative
security and defense issues. *See* S-400 missile
    defense systems
SEECP. *See* South-East European
    Cooperation Process
September 11 terrorist attacks, in US, 1,
    10–11
Shanghai Cooperation Organization (SCO),
    105–6
  compellent threats and, 114–16
  origins of, 114
  Turkey as full member of, 113–14
  Erdoğan's influence on, 114–15
Shanghai Five organization, 114
Slovakia, 69
Slovenia, 69
soft balancing theory, 26–9
  definition of, 27
  ESDP involvement and, 70–1
  hard balancing and, 27, 28–9, 164–5
    external balancing, 27
    internal balancing, 27

in power symmetries, 27–8
  state behavior in, 28
soft power, in foreign policy, 39–42
  direction of, towards specific populations,
      41–2
  through economic growth, 40–1
  NATO and, 56–7
  through Office Development Assistance, 41
  Turkish Cooperation and Development
      Agency and, 41
South East Europe Initiative, 38
South-East European Cooperation Process
    (SEECP), 38, 47
Southeast European Cooperative Initiative
    (SECI), 38
Srebrenica Massacre, 43
Stabilisation and Association Process (SAP),
    50–1
statecraft tools. *See also* Turkey, foreign
    policy of
  boundary breaking as part of, 150, 167
  in soft balancing theory, 28
Strategic Depth (Davutoğlu), 42
strategic noncooperation, as statecraft tool,
    33–4, 36, 82, 154–5
  for ECT membership, 99–100
  in NATO, 66–72
strategic pragmatism, in Turkey's foreign
    policy, 3
Syria
  intra-alliance opposition in, through
      cooperative balancing with Russia,
      138–41
  Turkey and, 12–13
  US foreign policy in, incompatibility with
      Turkey, 127

Tadić, Boris, 44–5
territorial/asset denial, 20, 34, 36, 136–8
terrorism. *See* September 11 terrorist attacks
Tocci, Nathalie, 6
Townsend, Stephen, 132
Trans-Adriatic Pipeline, 104
Trans-Anatolian Pipeline, 104
transit country, Turkey as, 106–7
Truman Doctrine, 9
Trump, Donald, 12, 108–9, 110, 121, 122,
    133–4, 142, 147, 152, 164, 166
Turkey
  Ankara Protocol (2004), 5, 72–3, 74
  CSDP and, 56–7, 70–1, 78–9, 81–2

Customs Union Agreement and, 4, 5
Cyprus and, military intervention in, 10
Democratic Union Party in, 127–32
ESDP and
    entangling diplomacy as strategy, 72–7
    soft balancing strategy, 70–1
    strategic noncooperation strategy, 66–72
    veto of Cyprus involvement, 63–6
EU and, relationship with, 1–2
    in EEC, 4
    EU-Turkey Joint Action Plan, 6–7
    historical perspective on, 4–9
    in WEU, 4
European Parliament and, 7–8
Euroskepticism among elites in, 6
EU-Turkey Joint Action Plan, 6–7, 84
Gezi Park protests, 59–60
as hard power emerging state, 165
historical perspective on, 4–14
    EU relations in, 4–9
Israel and, 11
Mavi Marmara incident and, 11
Membership Action Plan and, for Bosnia
    and Herzegovina, 44, 56
military coups in, 1–2
in NATO, 1, 2, 65–80
    entangling diplomacy by, 72–7
    inter-institutional balancing by,
        77–80
    issue-linkage bargaining by, 77–80
    strategic noncooperation of, 66–72
    US and, 9–14
    veto of Cyprus application to, 63, 64–6,
        76–7, 78–9
in OSCE, 1
PKK in, 127–32
political relations with Russia, conflicts
    in, 105–6
in SCO, as full member, 113–14
    Erdoğan's influence on, 114–15
September 11 terrorist attacks
    condemned by, 1, 10–11
suspension from JSF Program, 3
Syria and, 12–13
terrorist organizations in, 127–32
as transit country, 106–7
US and. *See also* intra-alliance opposition;
    Turkey, foreign
    policy of
    under Defence and Economic
        Cooperation Agreement, 10

economic sanctions by, 166
historical relationship between, 9–11
NATO and, 9–14
September 11 terrorist attacks in,
    response to, 1, 10–11
under Truman Doctrine, 9
Turkey, foreign policy of, 151–61. *See also*
    intra-alliance opposition; soft
    balancing theory; Western Balkans
activism in, 23
anti-Western elements in, 1–2, 13–14
Constructivism as influence on, 23–4
domestic factors in, 157–61
Europeanization of, 23
"golden age" of, 23
future of, 161–71
    through continuation of status quo,
        163–4
    decline of relations with the West,
        164–71
    improvement of relations with the
        West, 164
international systemic factors in, 151–3
irreconcilable interests in, 153–7
Islam as influence on, 24
methodological approach to, 14–16
Realpolitik influences on, 61
regional sub-systemic factors in, 151–3
strategic pragmatism in, 3
terrorist organizations in, 128
trust issues as factor in, 153–7
US and, incompatible interests between,
    126–32
    over Islamic State, 127–32
    over Kurdish peace process, 129–32
    over Syria, 127
Turkish Cooperation and Development
    Agency, 41
Turkish Stream project, 103–8
    economic feasibility of, 107–8
    economic statecraft as influence on,
        107–8
    with Russia, cooperative balancing in,
        103–7
    Trans-Adriatic Pipeline and, 104
    Trans-Anatolian Pipeline and, 104
Tusk, Donald, 65, 103

United States (US)
    Countering America's Adversaries
        Through Sanctions Act, 121

United States (US) (cont.)
  involvement in political coups, in Turkey,
    1–2
  Joint Comprehensive Plan of Action and,
    withdrawal from, 108–9
  National Defense Authorization Act, 118,
    122
  S-400 missile defense system purchase
    and, 118, 121–3, 124–5
  in Syria, foreign policy for, 127
  Turkey and. *See also* intra-alliance
    opposition; Turkey, foreign policy of
  under Defence and Economic
    Cooperation Agreement, 10
  economic sanctions against, 166
  historical relationship between, 9–11
  NATO and, 9–14
  September 11 terrorist attacks and,
    official condemnation of, 1, 10–11
  under Truman Doctrine, 9

Vicini, Caroline, 88
visa liberalization process, under EU-
  Turkey Refugee Deal, 86–9

Western Balkans, foreign policy in
  through active diplomacy, 42–6
  as Neo-Ottomanism, 45–6, 57–8
  as Official Development Assistance
    donor, 45
  Ottoman Empire nostalgia as influence
    on, 43–6
  Serbian relations improved by, 43–6
  through economic growth
    through FDI, 49
    as soft power, 40–1
    as statecraft, 46–50
    trade integration as part of, 49–50
  Erdoğan as influence on, 59–60
  EU cooperation in, 50–60
    decline of, 52

Islam as influence on, Muslim
  favoritism and, 53, 54–5
Stabilisation and Association Process,
  50–1
Turkey in competition with, 52–3
EU membership as factor in,
  55–6
international skepticism over, 57–8
through Office Development Assistance,
  41, 45
through Organization of the Islamic
  Conference, 38
Ottoman Empire and, 40
  nostalgia for, 43–6
overview of, 60–2
through Peace Implementation Council,
  38
peacekeeping forces in, 38
regional dynamics in, 152–3
through regional ownership, 46–50
  Regional Cooperation Council,
    47
soft power in, 39–42
  direction of, towards specific
    populations, 41–2
  through economic growth, 40–1
  NATO and, 56–7
  through Official Development
    Assistance, 41
  Turkish Cooperation and Development
    Agency and, 41
  through South-East European
    Cooperation Process, 38, 47
  through Southeast European Cooperative
    Initiative, 38
Western European Union (WEU), 4

Yıldırım, Binali, 115

Zarrab, Reza, 109
Zhirinovsky, Vladimir, 116